KU-191-599

Rebels Daughters

Rebels Daughters

BY

E. S. (SOLLY) SACHS

General Secretary

Garment Workers' Union

of South Africa

1928-1952

WITH A PREFACE BY

Father Trevor Huddleston

C.R.

MACGIBBON & KEE

First Published 1957

All Rights Reserved

MacGibbon & Kee

Printed in Great Britain by
Robert Cunningham & Sons Ltd.
Alva

Acknowledgements

I OWE A LASTING DEBT of gratitude to Professor Max Gluckman, head of the Department of Social Anthropology, Manchester University. A distinguished South African himself and the author of many brilliant works on the social structure of the African people, his advice and guidance have been of invaluable assistance to me.

To his wife Mary Gluckman, who has lived in South Africa for many years, I am deeply grateful for reading the manuscript and for numerous suggestions she offered.

The frank criticism of Professor W. Arthur Lewis, Dean of the Faculty of Economics and Social Studies; H. A. L. Turner, Lecturer in Industrial Relations; Mr A. E. Musson, Lecturer in History; all three of the University of Manchester, is deeply appreciated.

I would also like to express my warm and sincere appreciation to Isoldemaria Behr, not only for reading and checking the manuscript, but also for placing her knowledge and her ideas at my disposal at all times. She gave her services with a zeal and devotion which I shall always treasure. My warm thanks are due to Miss Sheila Pollock for typing this manuscript.

The views expressed in the book are entirely my own responsibility.

I express the hope that my effort will justify the objects of Lord Simon of Wythenshawe's endowment and the honour Manchester University has shown me by awarding me a Simon Senior Research Fellowship.

E. S. SACHS

Manchester University
Manchester
England

June 1956

Contents

Preface

A GREAT NUMBER OF BOOKS, both fiction and fact, about South Africa have appeared in recent years. It might be felt indeed that rather too much had been written about that fascinating, vital yet unhappy country.

I do not think this to be true: and that for several reasons. In the first place it is of the utmost importance that, before passing judgment, people should be informed, and informed as fully as possible, of all the forces which go to create such a situation. This is far from having been achieved.

Secondly, it is the white South African who alone can speak from his own inner experience and conviction of the different tensions and struggles in a multi-racial society as they affect him. And not so many white South Africans are able or willing to do this. Mr Sachs is one of the few.

But—most important of all—there are very many spheres of life in modern South Africa which have not found a writer and which indeed have never been penetrated by those capable of writing. It is of one such sphere—the Trade Union—that this book tells. Nothing could be more important.

It is so easily and glibly assumed that 'resistance' to 'apartheid' and to white domination could easily be manifested by the non-European people if they made effective use of their organised labour force. Trade Unionism in Europe is so familiar that it is taken for granted as the power that it is.

This book tells, from within, something of the really heroic efforts needed to create and sustain organisation of such a Trade Union in South Africa: and it tells too of the consequences to those whose work it has been.

I am very proud to have been asked to write this Preface. Mr Sachs by his courageous and most lonely stand against an oppressive Government has paid the penalty of exile from his own country. No man could pay a heavier price than that—as I well know.

I pray that this book may be widely read and appreciated, and that it may—as I am sure it will—stiffen the determination of all decent people to end the horror of racial pride and arrogance before it destroys South Africa.

TREVOR HUDDLESTON C.R.

Introduction

THE STORY OF THE GARMENT WORKERS' UNION of South Africa epitomises the history of South Africa itself during the last thirty years, the period of its Industrial Revolution.

Every major national problem—racial conflict, poor whiteism, mass poverty—played a prominent part in the life and activities of the union. The epic story of the hundred thousand women and thirty thousand men who built the clothing industry, the third largest in the country, reflects the aspirations, passions and violent conflicts of the people as a whole, their economic progress and political backwardness, their nobility and savagery, their love of freedom and acceptance of tyranny.

Most white South Africans bitterly resent the opinions about their country held by people abroad and complain that strangers do not know and cannot understand the difficulties of their multi-racial society. All honest and clear-thinking South Africans will admit with sorrow that their land is tormented by race hatred and that, since May 1948 when the Nationalist Government came to power, this hatred has been intensified to a frightening extent. Other countries have had racial problems, and many still have them today. In the United States race discrimination features prominently in national affairs, and Europe is not altogether free from it. Even in Asia, which has suffered from racial oppression and discrimination for so long, inter-racial strife is still common despite the immense progress the Asian people have made in recent years. All over the world millions are still subjected to indignities, persecution and oppression solely because of their racial origin or the colour of their skin. But, while in other countries racial antagonism is only a small part of the national life, it is no exaggeration to say that in South Africa it is *the* national life and forms the basis of the economic, social, political and cultural structure of the country.

The tremendous economic and industrial progress which the country has made in recent years has so far received scant attention. Abroad, South Africa is known mainly as the land of racial oppression, and within the country, the people are too preoccupied with problems of colour to observe radical social changes.

In the last few decades, hundreds of thousands of Whites and several million non-Whites have been uprooted from the land and have moved into the cities to become workers in mining, industry, commerce, transportation and other spheres. Manufacturing industries have expanded tremendously and the national income has increased about six times. At least one-third of the white people have had their incomes raised from under £50 to over £500 a year, and about a million non-Europeans from a few pounds to more than £150 a year. But this revolution has roused little interest, and most white South Africans still get more emotional satisfaction from watching a black man being kicked off the pavement than from the rise of a large modern factory.

Industrial development has brought much prosperity but has not produced peace. Fear stalks the land and everyone is anxious about the future. Will the Nationalist Government be removed from power? Will South Africa ever relax or abandon its policy of racial oppression? Or will there be a struggle between Black and White which can only mean disaster for both sides? The successive waves of oppression sweeping the country and the sterile, cowardly policy pursued by the United Party—the major opposition party—have created a spirit of despondency among the opponents of the Nationalists. They believe that the Nationalists will remain in power indefinitely, and that a clash between Europeans and non-Europeans is inevitable. The story of the Garment Workers' Union holds out some hope and inspires a measure of confidence in the future. In the little world of the garment workers one sees clearly new forces and new ideas emerging in the country.

South Africans who want to see racial harmony and co-operation in their land will be able to study the methods used by the union to counteract the pernicious propaganda of race hatred. These methods were not always successful or beyond criticism: no doubt very much more could have been achieved, but at least they prove that it is possible to change people imbued with violent race prejudice into courageous fighters for freedom and tolerance.

The clothing industry was not of sufficient economic importance, nor were the workers strong enough, to effect a radical change in South African policy, and in the country's way of life. But the battles fought by the union against reaction and tyranny show how much can be achieved by determination and courage, and serve to indicate the methods that must be followed in the future if South Africa is to become a true democracy.

I want to see South Africa a great nation, admired and respected, not hated by all civilised people. I have therefore decided not to follow the usual pattern of Trade Union histories but to address this book specifically to the workers of South Africa since they can play a decisive rôle in eradicating race hatred and oppression and in building a country which will provide happiness, prosperity and security for everyone. These people are not interested in an academic treatise; they are bored by numerous statistical tables and are more likely to respond emotionally than intellectually to what I write. At the same time, I hope that by writing as a South African for South Africans I will be able to give people abroad a clearer idea of the country's problems.

Yes, I write with passion and emotion.

For twenty-five years I watched at close range the progress of South Africa's Industrial Revolution. I saw thousands of modern factories arise in the cities, on the bare veld of the Witwatersrand, around Cape Town, Durban, Port Elizabeth, and remoter parts. I saw the great change in the lives of the ordinary people with whom I came into daily contact. Poverty, squalor and misery were their former lot; now they enjoy fairly decent standards. But this is only the beginning, and I visualise a great future for the country. I also saw at close quarters the dreadful tragedy of race hatred, the sorrow and suffering of the hated, the degradation of those responsible for promoting it. When I reflect the glorious opportunities South Africa has of building a great industrial civilisation and see the road to inevitable ruin which the country is now following; when I think how happily the people could all live and work together, as I know from my own experience is possible, and find instead men's hearts filled with hatred and fear, I cannot remain calm and dispassionate.

A great fighter for freedom in America[1] wrote:

> I am aware that many object to the severity of my language, but is there not cause for severity? I will be as harsh as Truth, and as uncompromising as Justice. On this subject I do not wish to think, or speak, or write, with moderation. No! No! Tell a

[1] William Lloyd Garrison, *The Liberator*, 1st January 1831

> man whose house is on fire to give a moderate alarm: tell him to moderately rescue his wife from the hands of the ravisher; tell the mother to gradually extricate her babe from the fire into which it has fallen—but urge me not to use moderation in a cause like the present. I am in earnest—I will not equivocate—I will not excuse—I will not retreat a single inch—and I will be heard. The apathy of the people is enough to make every statue leap from its pedestal and hasten the resurrection of the dead.

South Africans are an emotional and passionate people; how could they be otherwise with a hundred and fifty years of tragic conflicts behind them? But whereas the pedlars of race hatred have succeeded in exciting the base passions and emotions of the Whites and more especially of the Afrikaners, I know that in the hearts of the Boer men and women there is a warm humanity and a deep love for freedom; for they themselves have suffered oppression and poverty. The task of all who love liberty is to rouse the finer feelings of the Afrikaners, many of whom are in the forefront of the struggle for a free, tolerant South Africa. Nevertheless the story, though written with feeling, is based on solid fact.

I am writing in the calm, friendly atmosphere of Manchester University, which awarded me a Simon Senior Research Fellowship for 1954-6; but I played a leading rôle in the events I am describing. History must be written objectively we are told. Invariably, each historian decides for himself the meaning of objectivity. I decided however not to allow modesty to distort the history of the union and have projected myself somewhat liberally in the second part of the book. The fault is not mine; it lies elsewhere.

In the middle of the thirties, when the Nationalists had adopted Nazi philosophy, they began to employ Nazi techniques in dealing with their opponents. In their desperate attempt to disrupt and capture the Mine Workers' Union and the Garment Workers' Union, both of which had a predominantly Afrikaner membership, they built up 'bogy men' upon whom they concentrated their fire. Charlie Harris, Secretary of the Mine Workers' Union, and I, as Secretary of the Garment Workers' Union, were selected as the main scapegoats. In the Nationalist press, in parliament, from the pulpits of the Dutch Reformed Churches, even at meetings of the

Afrikaans Cultural Societies, we were vilified and slandered. In June 1939 Harris was shot dead by a young Nationalist fanatic. I escaped assassination, but suffered much physical violence at the hands of the Nationalists. By 1947 the Nationalists had succeeded in capturing the Mine Workers' Union; but our union proved an entirely different proposition. With the loyal support of the members, many of whom were Nationalists, I hit back and instituted twelve Supreme Court actions for defamation against Nationalist publications and Ministers of the Dutch Reformed Churches. I succeeded in obtaining substantial damages in each case, and my defamers had to pay over £20,000 in legal costs. Some actions were settled out of court, but those that went to trial roused tremendous interest throughout the country. I received warm support not only from the workers, but from all democratically minded people, and the successive victories which I scored over the Nationalists served the interests of our union, of the Trade Union movement, and of democracy generally. These court actions played a major rôle in the life and struggles of the union; hence I record them at length. We also instituted many actions against Ministers of the Government who exceeded or abused their powers and there too each victory for the union or myself in the courts had great political significance.

The thousands of young garment workers who have entered the industry and found greatly improved conditions will learn, by reading this story, how they were obtained, and of the great sacrifices made by the pioneers whose energy and courage built the union. The older garment workers and all other workers of South Africa will realise that the Nationalists are their bitter enemy, and that cowardice and defeatism will bring disaster. Courage, determination and sacrifice will be necessary to replace the present philosophy of inhumanity by a spirit of human feeling and tolerance, which alone can save South Africa.

CHAPTER ONE

The South African Trade Union Movement—Historical Background

Guns and Gallows

IN OUTWARD APPEARANCE South Africa is a calm, peaceful land, spacious and sunny; its peoples—Black, White and Coloured, are fundamentally warm-hearted and friendly. The African in his kraal, even in his squalid 'Shanty Town', and in the cities where he is treated as an outcast, is courteous and kind and will share his last crumb with a passing stranger. The hospitality of the Afrikaners is famous and they will readily extend it to strangers, even to Englishmen (Rooineks). I have often found a warm welcome in the homes of even the poorest Afrikaners who lived in the slums of Johannesburg. People who stayed in South Africa during the war remember with deep appreciation the hospitality they received.

Yet South Africa is also a land of violence and of fierce race hatred, with a history marked by a succession of bitter conflicts. Most Afrikaners hate the British, and the British have no love for the Afrikaners. Both hate the Africans, the Coloured and the Indians and, although the degree of their hatred for non-Europeans may vary, few are completely free from it. Strange as it may seem, the non-Europeans show little animosity towards Europeans. They only hate their oppression and degradation. Africans do not want 'to drive the white people into the sea'; they only want freedom.

The discovery of diamonds around Kimberley and of gold on the Rand, in the second half of the last century, led to a sudden imposition of a modern capitalist economy upon South Africa, from outside and by outsiders. Everything was foreign: the mine owners were foreigners (uitlanders), the capital came from abroad, and even the workers were imported. The miners from Cornwall, Yorkshire and South Wales, the engineers from Glasgow and Birmingham, and the other British artisans who came to South

Africa, brought with them not only great skill but a militant trade union spirit. They soon began to build trade unions on the British model. The Amalgamated Society of Carpenters and Joiners was formed in 1881 and other trade unions were established later. For nearly forty years the trade union movement of South Africa was British in spirit, tradition and organisation; indeed most unions were branches of 'Home' trade unions. Today only the Amalgamated Engineering Union is a section of the British A.E.U. The others, whilst friendly towards the British labour movement, have become independent. Afrikaners were not attracted to industry until 1907, and the Africans, who were nearly all indentured labourers, deprived of the most elementary rights, denied social and cultural amenities, and herded into compounds, knew nothing about trade union organisation until about 1917. The double scourge of violence and hatred which has marked the entire national life of the country for over a century has also left its imprint on the trade union movement. The frequency with which the Government has resorted to violence in order to crush the workers, European and non-European, is appalling. In few other countries has the gun been employed so freely in labour disputes as in South Africa.

As early as 1884, when the trade union movement was still in its infancy, four European workers on the diamond mines around Kimberley were shot, in the course of a dispute, by company thugs. In the miners' and engineers' strike on the Rand of 1913 twenty-one people were killed and over eighty wounded by bullets of the Imperial troops which had been called out by Smuts to preserve 'law and order'. Labuschagne, an Afrikaner miner on strike who stood in front of the crowd, facing the dragoons, stepped forward when he saw the soldiers taking aim and pulling off his jacket, opened his shirt and shouted 'Shoot, you bastards'. A volley rang out and he fell dead among the other victims. In 1914, during a strike of the railway workers, Smuts declared Martial Law and had nine leaders of the Transvaal Federation of Trades deported without trial. In 1919, seventy-one thousand African miners came out on strike for an increase in wages. Smuts called out the police: six Africans were killed at the City Deep Mine and the rest were driven back to work. A year later in Port Elizabeth, during a demonstration of the Industrial and Commercial Workers' Union—the first trade union of Africans—a score of

Coloured and African workers were shot in cold blood by a gang of Europeans with rifles they had seized in the police station. In 1922 the miners and some thousands of engineering workers came out on strike on the Rand. The trade unions wished to have the dispute settled by arbitration, but Smuts wanted a 'show down'. After a series of police provocations, during which three strikers were shot at a demonstration outside the gaol of Boksburg (a town sixteen miles east of Johannesburg), the incensed workers seized rifles and for a week civil war raged on the Rand. Dozens of white workers and some Africans were killed before the strike was crushed. Afterwards Smuts set up Special Criminal Courts: eighteen men were sentenced to death and scores were sent to prison for terms ranging from two to ten years. Three of those sentenced to death, Taffy Long, a Welshman, and two South Africans, Hull and Lewis, were executed at the Pretoria Central Prison. They went to the gallows courageously, singing the 'Red Flag'. The executions caused such widespread indignation that Smuts commuted the other death sentences to life imprisonment.

The violence continued. In 1931 a young Zulu, Johannes Nkosi, was murdered by the police during a May Day demonstration in Durban. In 1943 several hundred African municipal workers at Pretoria came out on strike. A European soldier jumped into an armoured car and opened machine-gun fire on a peaceful meeting. Fifteen Africans and one European bystander were killed. In 1946 thirty thousand African miners came out on strike for a small increase in wages. The cost of living was rising and their wages were lower than at the end of the last century. Hundreds of police were mobilised against them: a dozen or more Africans were killed and the rest driven back to work at the point of the bayonet. Since the Nationalist Government has been in power, about 300 Africans have been killed by police action, and recently it has become a common sight to see police with rifles and sten guns 'at the ready' at peaceful meetings of Africans. In the last twenty years mob violence has become a common feature of South African life, and organised gangs of Nationalists armed with bicycle chains, knuckledusters and other weapons, regularly break up trade union, Labour Party and United Party meetings.

Such is the tragedy of South Africa. The white workers, British and Afrikaners, have fought for decades and in blood and tears contributed more to the workers' cause than the labour movement of all the English-speaking countries together; they have produced leaders whose ability, devotion and heroism would fill any workers' movement with pride. Yet racial division has pervaded the trade union movement throughout its history and has become accentuated in recent years.

In 1924, Smuts, sensing that his ruthlessness in the 1922 strike had antagonised the people, and striving to regain some of his former popularity, granted an amnesty to all the strikers who were in prison. About fifteen to twenty thousand people assembled inside and outside the Johannesburg Town Hall to welcome the released workers. Six men, of whom four had been sentenced to death and two to long terms of imprisonment, addressed the large gathering. The tone of their speeches could be summed up in the following general terms:

> We have taken up rifles on behalf of the working class of South Africa and against the dictatorship of the Chamber of Mines, and, should the occasion arise, we shall do so again. We are not frightened of Smuts' gallows and prisons. Our comrades Long, Hull and Lewis walked to the gallows singing the 'Red Flag' and that should serve as an inspiration to all the workers. The workers of South Africa have for too long submitted to the oppression of the mining barons. We should take a leaf out of the book of the Russian workers, destroy the capitalist system and set up socialism.

Five out of the six speakers, however, ended with the slogan: 'Long live a *white* South Africa.'

How often have I listened to white workers who were enthusiastic advocates of socialism and even communism, and yet were still filled with bitterness toward the non-Europeans? Of the new generation of trade unionists, the majority of white members are violently opposed to the Nationalists, and would give anything to get them out of power. Yet I doubt whether even 5 per cent are completely free from race prejudice.

Until the First World War the trade union movement showed little concern for African workers, and took no steps to spread trade unionism amongst them. The organised workers were chiefly artisans who were imbued with the idea of the superiority of the British, and the aristocracy of the craftsman, and could not be bothered with the African who was black, unskilled and uneducated. Even the Afrikaner worker was not welcome, for he too was unskilled and belonged to a different national group.

During the war the trade union movement made great progress and the first national trade union centre—the South African Industrial Federation—was set up. The records of the Federation are not available, but from press reports it seems that already at its congress in 1917 there was a stormy debate on the attitude of the trade union movement toward Africans. The leaders of the white miners championed the colour bar, which had been legally introduced in the mines in 1912, and threatened to secede from the Federation if black workers were organised. There were many delegates however who stood for true trade union principles and urged the organisation of Africans. The Federation adopted a more liberal policy towards Coloured and Indian workers, but rendered no assistance to Africans. Individual labour leaders such as W. H. Andrews, Ivon Jones, S. P. Bunting, began to organise Africans into trade unions in 1917. The Federation collapsed after the 1922 Strike, and in 1925 the South African Trades and Labour Council was formed. The Council, which went out of existence in 1953, had no colour bar in its constitution but did not exert itself to organise African workers, although it frequently rendered them moral and organisational assistance.

There are 400,000 members of trade unions in South Africa, of whom about 75 per cent are European. According to the Report of the Industrial Legislation Commission, the racial composition of 199 trade unions registered under the Industrial Conciliation Act was as follows (U.G. 62/1951—Par 1038):

Mixed	63
Open to all races but comprising Europeans only	54
Europeans only	38
Open to all races but comprising non-Europeans only	22
Open to non-Europeans only	14
Composition unknown	8

The existing three national trade union centres reflect three separate trends towards non-European workers.[1] The Co-ordinating Council, consisting of the Mine Workers, Pretoria Steel Workers and several other small unions with a total affiliated membership of about 30,000, is completely under the domination

[1] See Appendix 2, page 232

of the Nationalist Party. This so-called trade union centre supports apartheid and colour bars, and is more concerned with keeping down the non-European worker than with improving the lot of the European. It spurns international brotherhood and workers' solidarity. The second is the recently established South African Congress of Trade Unions which has a membership of about 40,000 almost exclusively non-European. This national centre is based on fundamental trade union principles, fights for trade union unity, and opposes apartheid and all forms of racial discrimination. The third is the South African Trade Union Council which superseded the South African Trades and Labour Council. It includes Coloured and Indian workers but excludes Africans. Numerically it is the strongest, with a membership of 150,000. Although it practises apartheid within its own ranks, it opposes the apartheid policy of the Nationalists and sometimes renders support to African workers.

African workers are not prohibited by law from organising into trade unions, for the Conspiracy Laws have never been applied in South Africa. But under the Native Labour (Settlement of Disputes) Act, 1953, they are denied all rights of collective bargaining. In addition African workers have to contend with countless difficulties arising from the social colour bar, and the innumerable legal restrictions such as pass laws, Urban Areas Act, and so forth. Securing halls and offices is far from easy, and the presence of police and detectives at meetings and the banning of leaders under the Suppression of Communism Act are not conducive to trade union organisation.

Despite all difficulties, trade unionism among Africans is spreading and, when the 250,000 Africans who have had some contact with trade unionism become effectively organised, the division between Black and White in the trade union movement will largely disappear. Principle and morality are at a low level in South Africa, but power commands respect everywhere; and once the African workers have become strong, the European workers will seek their friendship and co-operation.

CHAPTER TWO

The Early History of the Garment Workers

ALTHOUGH I HAD BEEN ACTIVE in the labour movement since the days of my youth, my election to the position of general secretary to the union was purely fortuitous. In 1927 I entered the University of the Witwatersrand to study economics and law, with the hope of one day being called to the Bar. Having no means, I found odd jobs to support myself. On the 31st March 1927 I was appointed part-time secretary to the Witwatersrand Middlemen Tailors' Association, an organisation of about one hundred craftsmen who were in law neither employers nor employees but independent contractors. They had their own workshops but considered themselves workers; indeed many of them boasted of a militant trade union tradition. But, despite these claims, some of them mercilessly exploited those who worked for them, especially the younger women.

As secretary of the M.T.A. I came into close contact with members of the trade union (which was then known as the Witwatersrand Tailors' Association) working in the tailoring industry and learned a great deal about the workers' conditions, and about the trade. I was familiar with labour law, and helped to establish the Industrial Council for the Bespoke Tailoring Industry, under the provisions of the Industrial Conciliation Act. I was also appointed secretary to the Council on a part-time basis. The Council, which consisted of an equal number of representatives of the W.T.A. and the Transvaal Merchant Tailors' Association, duly concluded an agreement for the industry which I, as secretary, had largely to administer and this brought me into still closer contact with the workers. My labour sympathies were well known, and in October 1928, when Dan Colraine the secretary of the W.T.A. resigned, many of the workers begged me to stand as candidate for the vacant position. I agreed, but, as there were three other candidates, I thought there was little chance of my being elected. To my surprise, I received 90 per cent of the votes in a secret ballot; and on the 14th November I walked straight from the University into the offices of the union, with the vague hope of resuming my studies at some later date.

The union was divided into two distinct sections: (*a*) the Bespoke Tailoring Section, and (*b*) the Factory Section. Each had its own committee and there was a Central Executive Committee to manage the affairs of the union as a whole. The union was a party to two Industrial Councils: the Industrial Council for the Bespoke Tailoring Industry, Witwatersrand, and the Industrial Council for the Clothing Industry, Transvaal, each council having jurisdiction over its own section of the industry as well as its separate industrial agreement. The agreement for the Bespoke Tailoring Industry provided much higher wage rates and better conditions of employment.

The membership of the union was about 1,750, of whom just over two-thirds were in the Factory Section. The finances of the union were administered properly and there were up-to-date and accurate financial records. Almost everything else seemed to be in a state of chaos. Not even copies of the industrial agreements, which regulated wages and other conditions of the members, could be found in the office.

The three committees to which I was directly responsible consisted of higher-paid workers in the industry. Eight were from Britain and the rest came from Eastern Europe, except Mr G. Malan who was the only Afrikaner on the committee. The women workers, who constituted about 75 per cent of the total membership, were not represented at all on any of the committees.

The men had a long trade union tradition and many had taken part in trade union struggles in their countries of origin, as well as in South Africa. They belonged to the old school of trade unionists—knowing little and caring less about labour law and economics. The endless, cumbersome provisions of the South African industrial laws and the employers' arguments about payability, production, profits etc., irritated and had little interest for them. Some considered themselves 'militants' and often made revolutionary speeches; but several of these, who later became employers in the industry, proved worse than the traditional capitalist employers.

There were no records of the previous activities of the union, except for a few odd letters and sets of minutes; but from long talks with old tailors, I gathered the following story.

Toward the end of the last century, groups of tailoring workers, all master craftsmen in Johannesburg and Cape Town, began to organise themselves into unions. Small organisations sprang up, carried on sporadic strikes against sweating conditions, and then disappeared. Only after 1913 did the tailoring workers of Johannesburg succeed in establishing a permanent organisation which conducted regular trade union activity, made agreements with their employers, organised strikes, and succeeded in securing higher wages and better conditions. In the early twenties, Frank Glass, a very able organiser, speaker and writer, was elected secretary. In 1927 he resigned and left South Africa. He was succeeded by Dan Colraine, a boilermaker by trade who had been sentenced to two years' imprisonment for 'sedition' in the 1922 strike.

The appalling conditions which prevailed in the clothing industry in the early years are described in the Report of the Select Committee of the Union House of Assembly on the Regulation of Wages (Specified Trades) Bill, May 1917 (S.C. 4—1917). In paragraph four of the Report the Committee found that 'the payment of wages below what may be called the subsistence minimum is common'.

Mr Walter Marshall, the managing director of Hepworth's Limited, one of the leading firms of Cape Town at that time, admitted on page 30 of the Report that apprentices started at 4*s*. or 5*s*. a week and improvers got from 7*s*. 6*d*. to 10*s*. a week. Since there was no legal definition of the terms 'apprentice' and 'improver', the employer could decide, entirely at his discretion, how long a worker remained an apprentice and when he reached the 'higher' status of improver.

Mr Torbin, the proprietor of the Union Clothing Manufacturing Company, in his evidence, told the Committee that:

> The mother or guardian agrees on the question of the first payment and what she is to get after trial. It may be 5*s*. for a start, but if it is a girl who has just left school, say, and is a little more educated, she is not usually allowed to start for less than 7*s*. 6*d*. or 10*s*. and if I do not suit her she is not compelled to remain with me—there are many other factories. (page 52)

He continues:

> As I said, I am in favour of a minimum wage for women workers and the average wages which I pay to the experienced

hands is 17*s.* 6*d.* That is what I consider a fair average but I could not agree to that as a minimum. If the Board has to fix a minimum wage, I should say a reasonable figure for the experienced hands, girls over eighteen, would be 10*s.* (page 55)

He admitted (page 57) that about three-quarters of the employees were earning under 17*s.* 6*d.* a week.

Another witness, Mrs Agnes Cooke, president of the Women's Citizens Club, stated that returns which she received from employers showed that the wages paid to girl learners ranged from 2*s.* 6*d.* to 10*s.* a week, maximum. In some cases, the girls had to give their services free for six months. Often these unpaid workers were then dismissed and other beginners taken on in their places.

Dealing with conditions apart from wages, Mr Middleman, a member of the firm of A. Fraser and Company, Clothiers of Cape Town, stated (page 88):

There is no supervision and arrangements for sanitation leave much to be desired. From my own knowledge I can say that the hours worked in some of these places are terrible. There is no limit whatever. They work Saturday afternoons and Sundays too; if you go through the town you can hear the machines working all over the place, perhaps more in little workshops than in private houses.

The Select Committee recommended that minimum wage legislation be instituted. A law to regulate wages of young workers was introduced in 1920; it proved valueless and was later repealed.

In 1918 the first Factories Act was introduced, purporting to regulate hours of work and hygiene and safety in factories. The Act was badly drafted and little attention was given to enforcing it. Exploitation continued unchecked for many years, until the workers began to organise into trade unions. Thus the Wage Board, in its report for three years ended 28th February 1929, states (paragraph 299):

There was much sweating of employees in this industry at the time of the sitting of the Economic and Wage Commission in 1925. The low wages prevailing in the Cape Peninsula may be seen from the proposal put before that Commission by the Clothing Manufacturers' Association of the Western Province as an improvement of the then prevailing rates, that scale being as follows:

	Per Week
First year	10*s.*
Second year	12*s.* 6*d.*
Third year	15*s.*
Fourth year	17*s.* 6*d.*

Paragraph 307 says: 'The average weekly wages of female employees in the clothing industry in February 1926 are shown in the following table.'

AREA	JUVENILES UNDER 21 *European per week* *s. d.*	JUVENILES UNDER 21 *Coloured per week* *s. d.*	ADULTS *European per week* *£ s. d.*	ADULTS *Coloured per week* *£ s. d.*
Cape Peninsula	13 10	12 4	1 3 10	19 11
Port Elizabeth	19 8	12 11	1 3 4	15 8
Durban	17 6	19 4	1 3 11	1 3 10
Kingwilliamstown	13 4	—	13 6	—

In 1926 the wages of the Transvaal garment workers were governed by an industrial agreement, and are not included in the Wage Board report.

Clothing factories in the Transvaal started during the First World War, but made little progress until 1925, when the Pact Government formed between General Hertzog of the Nationalist Party and Colonel Creswell of the Labour Party granted industries a measure of tariff protection, and encouraged industrial development generally.

In 1928 about two hundred and fifty men and an equal number of women were employed in the Bespoke Section. Of these, about two hundred worked in four large workshops, where conditions were tolerably good and the provisions of the agreement were strictly observed. Another hundred worked in small workshops, which were also well conducted. The rest were employed in about a hundred little workshops, owned by merchant tailors or by middlemen tailors, where the number of employees ranged from one to five. In these workshops, conditions were poor, bad, or terrible.

Middlemen tailors worked for merchant tailors on a contract system, with rates fixed in a log; but the contract rates were not observed by most merchant tailors, and the middlemen in their turn sweated their workers. Contract rates were not legally enforceable. On the other hand, the wages, hours of work and other conditions of employment for workers were governed by agreement under the Industrial Conciliation Act and could be enforced by criminal prosecutions. The wages of £8 a week for a first-class tailor, £6 10*s.* for a second-class tailor, £3 15*s.* for a first-class tailoress and £3 2*s.* 6*d.* for a second-class tailoress, compared favourably with prevailing standards in other industries, but scores of workers received considerably less than the minimum provided in the agreement—some as little as half or one-third. Working hours were also fixed by agreement at forty-eight per week, but many workers, when they left the workshop, had to take work home with them and toil away until late at night, Saturdays and Sundays, often without receiving any extra pay. Here are two examples of the sweating that prevailed.

Some time in 1929, in the course of an investigation, I found a small workshop where the employer kept a mother and two daughters on the premises from Wednesday until Sunday. They worked practically day and night, and even slept in the workshop. On another occasion I found a young woman of nineteen who had been working continuously from seven a.m. until five o'clock the following morning without receiving any extra pay. Some of these workshops kept no wage registers at all; others 'cooked' their registers and made workers sign for wages which they had not received.

Many of the middlemen and merchant tailors also worked very long hours—often until early in the morning—and had to struggle to make ends meet.

The most exploited section consisted of about 200 Indian workers, many of whom were young boys from twelve to fifteen. They were not members of the union and the vast majority knew nothing about trade unionism. As most of them hardly spoke any English, it was difficult to organise them, and still more difficult to enforce the provisions of the agreement protecting them. Every little tailoring shop seemed to be a family concern, where sons, nephews and other relatives were employed. Their wages on the whole were probably a quarter, or less, than the amount to which they were entitled under the agreement. There were very few Coloured and African workers employed in the tailoring industry.

The clothing industry employed less than a hundred white men and over one thousand women, nearly all Afrikaners, who had only recently left the poverty stricken rural areas to find employment in the cities.

CHAPTER THREE

The Poor White Problem

FROM THE MOMENT I assumed office, I came face to face with the 'Poor White' problem, one of the major tragedies of South Africa.

People abroad believe that all Europeans in South Africa live, and have always lived, in comfort and affluence. In South Africa itself, even during the twenties and thirties when the poor white problem was at its worst, half the white population had no idea of the poverty and misery in which the other half lived. A white skin in South Africa is a protection against racial discrimination: it offers no defence against poverty, and for generations large sections of Whites have lived below subsistence level.

The 'Poor White' problem has been investigated by government commissions and other bodies since the nineties of the last century. Its causes and effects have been admirably described by Professor Macmillan in *Complex South Africa* (Faber and Faber, London 1930), and by Professor De Kiewiet in *A History of South Africa, Social and Economic* (Oxford University Press, 1941). The problem has now been largely solved, chiefly through the growth of the manufacturing industries, but the basic factors underlying it still remain, rooted in the social and economic structure of the country, and need some examination. Indeed, the problem may reappear in a more devastating form unless there is a radical change in the country's political, economic and social policy.

The fundamental cause of the problem is to be found in the Master Race philosophy of the Whites; this has produced a national inertia, a parasitism which has had a paralysing effect upon every sphere of economic activity, and has made it difficult for South Africa to adjust itself to modern conditions. Such progress as the country has made has been the result of resisting or ignoring the Master Race philosophy. Even today when the country is passing through a tremendous industrial revolution there is a bitter conflict between the economic forces and the backward political theory of apartheid. The Master Race philosophy, far from proving beneficial to the Whites, has brought disastrous consequences.

After a hundred and fifty years of white domination, nine successful Kaffir Wars, the seizure by Whites of about 90 per cent of the land and the creation of a mass of landless African labourers, the Europeans in South Africa had failed to build an economy which could provide them with even a measure of comfort and security. The poverty into which they drove the non-Europeans, far from resulting in increased prosperity for the Whites, dragged the majority of them down to almost the same level. They were rescued from complete degeneration and ultimate extinction only by forces which completely disregarded their fantastic notions of racial superiority.

According to the Report of the Carnegie Commission on *The Poor White Problem in South Africa* (Stellenbosch University, 1932) it was conservatively estimated that by 1929 out of a total of about 1,000,000 Afrikaners, more than 300,000 were very poor—that is, they lived on a pauper level. An equal number were poor but lived above the pauper level. These figures were obtained prior to the calamitous depression of 1930 which brought about widespread destitution among all sections of the community.

The Report of the Social and Economic Planning Council (U.G. No. 10, 1945) gives figures of the cash incomes of the European farming families (these are mostly Afrikaners) for the year 1941, when the Poor White problem was becoming less acute. It shows that over 45 per cent of the total farming population had cash earnings of less than £100 a year and of these, about half earned under £50.[1]

The 'Poor White' problem is in fact a 'Poor Afrikaner' problem; for the number of non-Afrikaners among Poor Whites has always been insignificant.

For generations the Europeans planned to establish a permanent slave or feudal society where people with white skins would enjoy leisure, comfort, privileges and all the good things of life. Instead, all they succeeded in creating was a community where the majority was reduced to a state of misery and degradation. Yet that belief in white supremacy remained unshaken; the most poverty-stricken Bywoner whose income was only £10 a year considered himself to be a farmer, not a landless peasant, and thought himself a

[1] See Appendix 2

'Master' in relation to the non-European. The white 'Masters', however, were feudal lords in name only, without any of the privileges the feudal lords of Europe enjoyed. Hopelessness and despair filled their lives; and in the course of time they lost not only the possibility of escape but even the energy to extricate themselves from their misery. The imposition of a modern economy by the introduction of extensive mining operations left them untouched at first. The mines were owned by 'uitlanders' and the wealth produced went into the pockets of foreign investors. As landed aristocrats the Afrikaners had no desire to work in the mines, and as they lacked industrial skill, there were no jobs for them. Indeed, the rise of the mining industry led to their further impoverishment. Land which had formerly been plentiful and cheap had now become scarce and dear. The inauguration of a modern capitalist economy raised the standard of living, but not their incomes. Then came the Boer War, and this brought further economic and social ruin. Commissions which were appointed to investigate the Poor White problem issued lengthy reports, and made numerous recommendations but the poor became poorer and their number increased. Ministers of the Dutch Reformed Churches interested themselves in the problem, offered prayers and a little charity; but what else could they do? Politicians unscrupulously exploited the misery of the poor to secure votes. They shed tears, expressed sympathy, and blamed the British and the Africans—later the Jews—for the widespread poverty of the Afrikaners. Ultimately the Poor White problem was accepted with fatalistic resignation, as a scourge sent by Providence. There was not one statesman in South Africa who had the necessary courage and vision to tell the people that the poverty of more than half of the Afrikaner population was not ordained from Heaven but man-made; or that the position could be remedied by land reforms and the introduction of modern methods in place of cheap, inefficient, semi-slave labour. The problem was acute and a great national effort was needed to solve it. The white people needed to be told plainly that in the twentieth century no slave state is possible; that they must abandon their traditional outlook and learn to organise production and to handle machinery and tools; to build and develop industries and help the African people to advance. The fact that a man's skin is white is not going to materially improve the nation's income, productivity or prosperity, whilst the facts prove beyond doubt that a colour bar in industry is a bar to industrial progress.

Nor is the colour of the skin a mark of civilisation. The cultural and intellectual level of the Poor Whites, indeed of all rural Whites, may readily be guessed. Away from the towns, they lived in scattered communities, often shot buck, and read the Bible. They were usually good, respectable husbands and fathers of large families. The children grew up in rustic simplicity and were taught to obey their parents and fear God. They went regularly to church, listened with reverence when the Bible was read—and vegetated. Intellectually, young and old were dead.

The wealthier farmers would not employ their poorer brethren as workers; they preferred the cheap, docile labour of Africans and Coloured. Many of the poor became Bywoners on the farms of big landowners but very few proved a success: the majority could hardly eke out an existence. As unskilled labourers, in the towns, the Poor Whites had to meet the competition of the Africans. After the unsuccessful strike of the white miners on the Rand in 1907, many Afrikaners found employment in the gold mines and their number increased as time passed. But the mines could absorb only a very limited number and the white population increased considerably.

In the twenties, it seemed as if the problem was insoluble and that the majority of the Afrikaners—more than one-third of the total white population—was condemned to eternal poverty. Then relief came. With very little Government help, in the face of bitter opposition from the Chamber of Mines, the manufacturing industries began to develop; slowly and painfully at first, but later with enormous strides. Poor Afrikaners began to leave the rural areas and trek to the towns to work in the newly established factories.

In Australia, Canada and New Zealand, tens of thousands of agricultural workers have found employment at reasonable standards. In South Africa about a million Africans are employed as agricultural labourers at a wage of less than £30 per year and there is no scope for employment of Europeans. Small-scale farming cannot be carried on profitably. The comparatively few Europeans who have been successful as farmers have received vast sums from the Government in bounties and subsidies. With its primitive and inefficient methods of production, agriculture in South Africa has only been saved from bankruptcy as a result of a number of purely fortuitous circumstances such as the enormous rise in prices of wool and farm produce after the Second World War. At the moment the industry is prospering but production per head and per acre is a fraction when compared with countries where modern methods are employed, and should the world be faced with another depression, which is not impossible, South African agriculture will face actual bankruptcy. To reorganise South African farming on a modern basis a revolution is necessary, not only in production methods, but also in the outlook of the farmers and in the entire political and social structure of the country. In the modern capitalist world farming conducted on a feudal basis cannot prosper.

The mining industry cannot give employment to more than about 30,000 Europeans at the most. In addition, the mining of precious metals is highly speculative and no one can foretell what the position of gold will be in ten or twenty years' time. In another generation or two the precious minerals of the country will be exhausted.

The future prosperity of South Africa depends on extensive industrial development, and substantial progress has already been made in this direction. For industry to progress an extensive local market and increased exports of manufactured goods are imperative. The two essentials for success are modern methods of production to enable the country to compete against countries with up-to-date industrial systems, and a rising standard of living for everyone. In addition the fear and insecurity now so prevalent must be replaced by a peaceful atmosphere which will attract investments both at home and from abroad. The policy of apartheid must inevitably instil in the minds of White South Africans the idea that as members of a Master Race, work and efficiency are beneath their dignity. Why worry about becoming a skilled worker when all that really matters is the possession of a white skin? The millions of non-White workers are denied education, vocational training and the opportunities to develop as full citizens, and are deliberately prevented from making the most of their abilities; instead of increasing their productivity and raising their purchasing power, measures are repeatedly introduced to keep their productivity and consumption at a low level. The policy of apartheid has also resulted in the exclusion from industry of vast sums of capital and thousands of skilled artisans from abroad, both of which are urgently needed by South Africa. Master Race parasitism reduced half the Afrikaner population to paupers. In industry, the social forces in their upward or downward trends operate with far greater speed. I therefore venture to prophesy that unless South Africa rids itself completely of its national backwardness, and introduces modern methods in production and progressive ideas in politics, within one generation the majority of the Afrikaners will be driven back to a state of poverty, compared with which the conditions of Poor Whites in the past will seem a paradise. The Poor Whites on the land enjoyed advantages which the Poor Whites in the cities lack. They were free to move about at will in the spacious and beautiful veld. As they had never enjoyed high standards, they did not feel so acutely the low ones which they were ultimately forced to accept. The workers in industry in the big cities, once industrial development is crippled, will have nothing to fall back upon and their misery will increase immeasurably because they have become accustomed to reasonable standards of living. The future everywhere belongs to science, technology and skilled mechanics and woe betide those countries which lag behind.

Fortunately, the rising manufacturing industries were not hindered by a legal colour bar, and the employers were at liberty to employ whomever they liked. There were no lengthy conferences and debates between employers and workers to decide what jobs should be done by whom. These new industries did not follow the backward semi-feudal methods of the farmers or the semi-slave labour pattern of the mines. They started generally with little capital and poor organisation, and exploited their workers—White, African, Coloured and Indian—mercilessly. But the workers soon organised into trade unions, improved efficiency and productivity and fought with a great measure of success for better conditions. Industry prospered, gave employment to several hundred thousand Whites and to many more non-Whites, helped to create ancillary avenues of employment, and substantially solved the Poor White problem. A careful examination of South African economic development will conclusively prove that where Master Race theories, colour bars and apartheid are applied, the white people do not benefit; on the contrary, they suffer. Conversely, where modern methods and ideas are encouraged, and where economic development is not hampered by backward theories about race, there are benefits for all. The colour bar is not a defence of, but an attack upon, the standards of Europeans.

CHAPTER FOUR

From the Poverty of the Platteland to the Slums of the City: Farm Girls turned into Factory Hands

THE POOR WHITE PROBLEM spread to the factories and the slums of Johannesburg and was soon felt in the offices of the union. There was a constant flow into the office of young Afrikaner women, whose ages ranged from fifteen to twenty-five. Over a thousand were already employed in the clothing industry and many of these would take the new arrivals direct to the factory or send them to the union office to find work for them. They all seemed healthy, decent, well-spoken and well-behaved farm girls who had nothing of the Poor White about them, except their poverty. After exchanging a few words with them, I soon learned that these young women had not come to the Rand for adventure and romance but to earn a few shillings for themselves and to help their parents, some of whom remained on the land, while others had come to the city. They were used to being treated as inferiors by the menfolk on the land and this proved of great help to them in adjusting themselves to their new life. They assumed no superior airs as members of a master race or as the daughters of landowners. They were sensible, practical and free from any illusions, desperately anxious to find jobs quickly, to learn their trade and to earn money. There was no moaning or groaning and they bore their endless troubles with patience and good cheer. Their problems were many and seemed insuperable. The depression of 1930 was approaching and employment was not easy to find for the newcomers. Indeed, many of the old hands were already unemployed. Even when they succeeded in securing work and were not cheated out of part of their wages, they received only £1 for a full week's work, and as there was much slackness in the industry, a full week's work was rare. Out of their meagre earnings the girls had to pay for their board and lodging, for tram or bus fares to and from work, for their clothes, and for other essentials; and they had also to send a few shillings home. The vast majority were forced to live in the slums. For newcomers and old hands alike life was one long bitter struggle.

South Africa has always had 'alien' communities who 'did not belong'. The ten million non-Europeans are considered outsiders, even outcasts, by the Whites. Before the Boer War, the British were looked upon as Uitlanders. Now, in 1928, the thousands of poor Afrikaners who were flocking to Johannesburg seemed like intruders. They did not belong to Johannesburg and Johannesburg certainly did not belong to them.

In few other countries is there such a concentration of wealth on the one hand and of poverty on the other as in South Africa, and few cities show such a marked contrast between luxury and squalor as Johannesburg.

Big cities are symbols of civilisation, culture and riches. They invariably accord a warm welcome to visitors with money; to the penniless stranger, they are hostile and terrifying. The surging crowds, the turmoil in the streets, the callous indifference, which a poor stranger meets in a big city like Johannesburg, make the loneliness of the veld seem cheerful and friendly. Johannesburg, the 'City of Gold', the wealthiest city on the African Continent, with its skyscrapers and palatial homes, also has the largest and the worst slums in the world. Almost the entire non-European population numbering half a million, and constituting more than half of the inhabitants, are even today condemned by the property owners, who run the city, to live in filth and squalor in shanty towns. Tens of thousands of Europeans have also been forced to live in slums in this city of affluence and ostentation. North of Johannesburg lay the suburb of Parktown where the mining magnates had their palatial homes. About a mile away to the West of the city lay Vrededorp where some tens of thousands of Europeans, Coloured, Indians and Africans lived in filth and squalor hardly equalled by the worst slums in the world. Between the two was the Braamfontein Cemetery where rich and poor are equal, class distinction being confined to the size of the tombstones. The houses of Vrededorp were small, single-storey dwellings with ugly exteriors and tiny rooms: the roofs leaked and the window-panes were broken. Electric light was a rarity as it was too expensive. These hovels were often shared by several families. I remember visiting the home of a garment worker in 1931, a widow with six children, who lived in a one-roomed house with no windows at all, only a door and a roof of hessian. These were the sort of conditions to which hundreds of women workers, accustomed to the sunshine and spaciousness of the land, would return after their daily toil in the factories.

South African politicians are in the habit of paying lavish compliments to the South African women, whose courage and virtue they consistently extol. Their concern for the welfare of the women is so persistent that they never miss an opportunity of asking with great indignation, no matter what problem is discussed, 'Would you allow your sister (or daughter) to marry a black man?' But these high-minded chivalrous gentlemen, these saviours of white civilisation who show so much concern for the honour of the white women, did not display the slightest interest in the terrible plight of thousands of white 'sisters' and 'daughters' who toiled for a mere pittance, lived in abysmal poverty, and often went hungry. Millions were voted for rich farmers, for police and prisons, but not a penny to help the unemployed, the sick or the starving. There was no social insurance of any kind and when the women became unemployed they starved. When they were ill, they lingered at home, unable to afford the services of a doctor. Not a penny was spent on hostels or other suitable accommodation for young women workers who were trying hard to earn an honest living. Indeed, as will be shown later, the State, the major political parties, and especially the Nationalist Party, adopted throughout a most bitterly hostile attitude towards the workers and their efforts to improve their conditions.

With regret, it must be stated that even the Labour Party failed in its duty. Here was a glorious opportunity for the Labour Party to establish contact with the poor Afrikaners, and make them into good socialists. The Nationalist Party and the United Party had nothing to offer the poor Afrikaners. Had the Labour Party come forward with a constructive policy and programme, subsequent South African history might have taken an entirely different course. The country would have been on the road to progress instead of fascism and disaster. But the leaders of the Labour Party lacked vision, became corrupted with the spoils of office, and left the poor Afrikaners to the Nationalists. Embittered by tragic memories of the past, surrounded by luxury and splendour whilst they themselves lived in slums in dire poverty, the impoverished Afrikaners became an easy prey to the demagogy of the Nationalists, who cunningly exploited their suffering for their own ends. The slums of Johannesburg, instead of becoming Labour strongholds, provided the storm troopers for the Nationalists when their party later came under Nazi influence. The slum dwellers broke up Labour Party and trade union meetings and finally voted the Nationalists into power. The South African labour and trade union movement has paid a terrible price for its past blunders, and has not yet learned its lesson.

This was the situation with which the union was faced when I became secretary. We had to deal not only with the problems common to workers of other countries, but also with special problems peculiar to South Africa. To secure higher standards we had to fight not only against the employers but also against traditional backwardness and dangerous fantasies. The task ahead of us was enormous.

Statistics and quotations from official records cannot present a true picture of the workers who came into the industry, of their struggles and privations, or of their background. Let some of the women speak for themselves. Their stories, taken together, are representative of the stories of tens of thousands of Afrikaner workers, the 'rebels' daughters', who helped to build the union and the industry.

CHAPTER FIVE

A Rebel's Daughter: Hester Cornelius[1]

I WAS BORN and brought up in the Lichtenburg District, Transvaal. Both my father and my grandfather fought in the Boer War and were taken prisoners. My mother, as a little girl, escaped the horrors of the concentration camps. When grandfather returned after the war he found his farmstead completely destroyed and his family living with relatives.

When my father married he became a building worker and mother looked after the small piece of land he had bought.

During the 1914 rebellion my father and grandfather joined General de la Rey, the leader of the rebel commando in the district. It was a very sad morning for us children when they left. We did not even have a chance to say goodbye to them. For months we did not hear from my father and my longing for him was often unbearable. I remember how I used to tiptoe to my mother's bedroom to look through the wardrobe for a jacket which my father had worn. I would hold the jacket in my arms and kiss it and the familiar smell would soothe my terrible longing for him. To feel near him, I used to put his jacket on, with the excuse that it was cold. My mother must have known my secret, for she never made me take it off.

One cold, dark night, while we were at my grandmother's farm, a neighbour knocked on the door and told us that the dead bodies of my father and grandfather had been found on the battlefield. I will never forget that night of tears. I lay in bed, sobbing until early morning. The next day, we returned to our farm and, for hours, I watched the road leading to the town, imagining that my father would soon come cycling back from his work.

Some time later we received letters from my father and grandfather, saying they had been caught and put into jail. At last we heard from my grandfather that my uncle and he were coming back, but no reference was made to my father. I had a feeling that

[1] Translated from the Afrikaans

my father would also come, but wanted to give us a surprise. And though I was glad to see my grandfather and uncle, my eyes wandered constantly over the crowd at the station, searching for my father; but he was not there. On the way back everyone else was happy, but for me there was only sadness. I tried to hide the tears streaming down my face and climbed off the ox wagon, walking alongside it so as to sob undisturbed.

My father came home a few weeks later, without telling us beforehand. By then I had learned to read my first English book. Very proudly, I fetched it and started reading aloud to him. He listened, pleased at first, and then, suddenly his face changed and he said sternly: 'Do not read that rubbish to me. I was put in jail and, while I was away, they drummed English into her.'

I felt very down-hearted. I loved my new book and was very proud that I could read it so fluently. I had waited so long to show my father that I was no longer the baby he had left behind. It was then I began to understand the tragedy of the Afrikaner people. Nevertheless my love for the English language increased and I soon felt it belonged to me as a second language. But I never again read an English book in the presence of my father.

In 1930, at the age of twenty-two, I came to Johannesburg to look for work. I worked for one year as a table hand in a clothing factory and was then dismissed. In 1931 I tried to find another job, without success—there were hundreds of girls looking for jobs. I returned to the farm and became an ardent Nationalist, believing that the South African Party was to blame for our poverty and unemployment. Later I returned to Johannesburg and found work. My sister Johanna and I shared a back room in Vrededorp with the two Vogel sisters. Although I was a fast worker I was paid only 17*s*. 6*d*. a week and there was a lot of slack time in the industry.

The four of us had to share one bed and that meant that two always had to sleep on the floor. We baked our own bread. For breakfast we had mealie meal and coffee with condensed milk. Now and then we treated ourselves to sixpenny-worth of meat. We could not afford tram fares and always walked to work, a distance of about three miles.

Between the four of us we had two Sunday dresses, one pair of stockings and two hats, so that only two at a time could go out at week-ends. As long as we were healthy we did not worry, but

Johanna was the first one to faint at work. The doctor said that she was perfectly healthy, but undernourished. Some months later Anna Vogel's health gave out and the two of us who were still fairly strong had to eat less to help our patients.

Later we decided to give up the room. The two Vogel sisters and Johanna went to board with a railway worker's family where they had to polish the floor of the house and the stoep (veranda) for their food early each morning before going to work. I went to board with a Mr and Mrs Hayton, who were very good people and helped me in every way.

I began to fight for my rights and the rights of my fellow-workers almost immediately I started work in a factory. The girls in the factory would come to me with all their complaints and I would take them up with the employer. As I was a good worker I was confident he would not sack me. Then I heard about the Garment Workers' Union, and one lunch time we went to the union office. Mr Sachs, the secretary of the union, took down all our complaints, and I felt straightaway that we could rely upon the union to help. The more I saw of the union activities the more I realised how necessary it was for the workers to become organised.

At first I could not understand why Mr Sachs, who was a Jew, fought so hard for the Afrikaner daughters. I spoke to many Nationalists about this very good Jew, who was doing so much to help us. They attacked him bitterly and this made me lose faith in the Nationalist Party. In 1934 I was elected as a member of the executive committee of the union and learnt much more about trade unionism and about Mr Sachs. I saw how angry he used to be when employers treated workers badly, and how hard he worked to improve our conditions. I also learnt that Mr Sachs fought not only for garment workers, but for all the workers. It took a Jew to make me understand that poverty could be wiped out in sunny South Africa and that, if the workers were organised and united, they could gain higher wages and a better life.

In 1932 my sister Johanna was arrested in Germiston whilst taking an active part in the general strike in the clothing industry. My parents came for a few days and I took them to my uncle's family, who were disgusted with Johanna. One of them asked my father what he thought of his daughter going to jail. My father smiled and said she was a chip off the old block.

The first strike in which I took a leading part was in 1936, in

Cape Town. The garment workers of Cape Town were even worse exploited than we in the Transvaal. Our union had sent delegates to Cape Town to organise the workers and I was one of them. The workers came out on strike in several factories and I was arrested together with about twenty others. The workers lost the strike and, even today, they are paid much lower wages than the workers in the Transvaal. Over the years I took part in numerous strikes of garment workers on the Rand and in Port Elizabeth. In 1942 I helped the Johannesburg sweet-workers in their strike for higher wages, and was again arrested, together with Anna Scheepers and Dulcie Hartwell.

Over twenty years have passed since I started work in the clothing industry and, during that period, there has been a complete change in our wages, conditions of work and way of life. It was the union with its courageous, able leaders, which set us free from the hell of starvation wages and slum squalor, and no one else. The Nationalists, the so-called friends of the Afrikaner workers, have never helped us. On the contrary, they have always tried to break our union.

CHAPTER SIX

A Daughter of the Free State: Katie Viljoen

Work Like Hell and be Merry

I WAS BORN in 1912 on a farm near Bloemfontein, in the Orange Free State. My parents were at first well-to-do farmers in the Boshoff district and owned a large farm named 'Banksfontein'. We were a large family—seven boys and three girls.

I went to an Afrikaans school in Boshoff and passed Standard VI. There I learnt very little English, as we only had a half-hour lesson in English once a week, which consisted almost entirely of reading. I was quite good at school and would have liked a higher education, but the decline in my father's fortunes made that impossible.

I left school at the age of fifteen and, to help my parents, took employment in Kimberley as a dressmaker at £2 a month. I stayed with relatives who did not charge me for board and lodging, and regularly sent my parents £1 to 30*s*. a month. I worked in Kimberley for about three years, until 1932 without any increase in wages.

In 1932—a year of depression—I came to Johannesburg and obtained a job with a private dressmaker in Bezuidenhout Valley at 30*s*. a week. Unfortunately she closed the workshop after two weeks. I boarded with a Jewish family, Suzman by name, who were extremely good to me and whom I paid £1 a week for board and lodging.

I knew a girl, Lena van Rensburg, also from Boshoff, who had already worked in the clothing industry for some time, and she found me a job in a dressmaking factory at £1 a week. The firm's motto, inscribed in white letters on black cloth, affixed to the entrance, was: 'Work like Hell and Still be Merry.' It employed about forty women and we did, in fact, work like hell, but were not particularly merry. The firm specialised in making very good frocks and wedding gowns. I was so desperate to find a job that I told the employer I could work an electric machine although I had never used one before, nor had I handled high-class garments. It did not take me long to discover my mistake. The first garment I was given to machine was a white satin wedding gown. I put the material in the machine, pressed the treadle right down and the machine started off at a speed which made my head turn and scared me stiff. I forgot to take my foot off the treadle and the machine kept on racing madly. Very soon I heard a shout from the manager, who had his cutting table in the centre of the room and who bawled: 'Viljoen, you . . . , look what you have done to my frock.'

Trembling with fear, I went up to him and he told me my fortune in more unprintable language. I naturally kept quiet, but the tears streamed down my face. He gave me a day frock to machine, and a friendly fellow-worker, who sat next to me, asked me very kindly where I came from and whether I had ever before worked an electric machine. I admitted my ignorance and confessed that I did not know much about the better type of dressmaking, but was terribly anxious to work, as I had to help my parents. Perhaps she too had poor parents to support, for she was most helpful and, when the manager had turned his back, came up to my machine and showed me how to work the monster.

It was my first day's work in Johannesburg and, like thousands of other women workers, I found the city of gold unfriendly and frightening. As I could not afford tram fares on £1 a week I walked home from work with my friend Lena, who, though she lived in an entirely different suburb, acted as my guide. To make sure that I would not lose my way I took a piece of white chalk with me and made various marks on the route from the factory to my lodgings. Next morning I left the house at five-thirty, as I had to walk a distance of about four miles and work started early.

For a month I walked to and from work every day, but then these long journeys became unbearable. The work was really slave-driving. We started at seven a.m. and finished at six p.m. I could not send anything home to my parents, as my total earnings just covered my board and lodging.

At the end of the first month I went to see my friend Lena again, and she found me a job at Awlwear Overall factory. I started as a shirt machinist at £1 10*s*. a week. Most beginners started at 15*s*. a week, but when Lena told the Manager my sad story he agreed to raise the wage. I was very anxious to send some money to my parents, and I needed new shoes and clothes as the old ones were wearing out. I did not know the town, but I went from building to building inquiring about cheap accommodation and at last, after a great deal of walking, found a room to share with another young girl, a sweet-worker, for which we each had to pay 17*s*. 6*d*. a week.

My budget was made up as follows: Rent 17*s*. 6*d*. per week, saving up for new clothes 7*s*. 6*d*. per week, 10*s*. a month sent to my parents. The balance of 2*s*. 6*d*. a week had to be sufficient for food.

Once a week I used to buy a loaf of bread for 6*d*., and a pound of butter at 1*s*. 8*d*. I lived on bread and butter the whole week and still had 2*d*. left over at the end. Deeply religious, I used to pray every night for enough strength to carry on with my work. I was a very healthy girl, strongly built, weighing a hundred and fifty pounds. I kept my health, but in a short space of time my weight dropped to a hundred and seventeen pounds. My parents never knew the hardships I had to endure.

I knew nothing about trade unionism at that time, but after I had worked for a short while, Johanna Cornelius came and appealed to the workers to join the union. When she mentioned that the contribution was 6*d*. a week, I decided not to join. I did not know what the word 'union' meant, but I knew that if I paid 6*d*. to the union, there would not be enough for a loaf of bread.

A month later, Mr Sachs, the general secretary, came to the factory and spoke to the workers about joining the union. I remember him telling us that, although the employers paid us our wages, it was the union that fixed the amount. About a hundred and fifty workers were employed in the factory, of whom more than half were already members of the union, and after this visit more joined. When Mr Sachs left, a girl, Maria Primavesi, who was sitting next to me at the machine, said that I was a coward for not joining the union. I was too proud to admit that I could not afford to contribute 6*d*. a week, so I merely replied that one day she would find out the reason.

After working for three months I received an increase of 5*s*. a week. I immediately went to Maria, told her why I had not joined before and became a member of the union. From that day onward, I took an active interest in the welfare of the workers of the factory where I was employed. I brought all the workers' complaints before the Manager, who rather liked my courage and straightforwardness. This made me popular with the other workers, who regularly came to me with their complaints. I managed to settle many minor disputes over wages with the management and put a stop to petty underpayments altogether. I also succeeded in getting the cloakroom regularly cleaned and washed and in having tea served for all the workers.

My wages increased every three months, in accordance with the agreement which the union had made with the employers' association and, in time, life became more tolerable. When my weekly wages reached £2 10*s*. I could afford to rent a room for myself and to send money regularly to my parents.

In 1938 I was elected a member of the central executive committee of the union. I found the work on the committee very interesting and took an active part in union work. In the same year the 'Reformers', led by a certain D. B. H. Grobbelaar, started their attacks on the union and on Mr Sachs. I understood at once that these people were not interested in the welfare of the workers, but were out to destroy the union, and I despised them intensely. All the workers in my factory felt the same.

In March 1938 the union had arranged a challenge meeting with Grobbelaar at the City Hall, Johannesburg, and all the workers were greatly excited. A few days before the meeting was held I spoke to the workers and told them that we were going to march as a body to the meeting hall. We received information that a gang of Reformers was going to attack us when we left the factory. The Manager received several anonymous telephone calls saying the mob would be waiting for Katie Viljoen, but on the afternoon of the meeting the workers marched out of the factory and nothing happened. Ours was the only factory where the workers—three abreast—marched to the City Hall, singing home-made songs and shouting: 'Down with Grobbelaar and up with Sachs.' When we arrived at the City Hall we gave three cheers for Solly Sachs. The hall was crowded and an overwhelming majority of the workers showed, in no uncertain manner, their bitter hostility towards Grobbelaar and the Reformer disrupters.

Some months later the union sent me to Port Elizabeth to organise the garment workers there. I had no previous organising experience and fully realised that I had a tremendous job of work ahead of me, but I was determined to do my best. There were about eight hundred garment workers in Port Elizabeth and not many were members of the union. Wages and conditions were bad—much lower than in the Transvaal—and most employers were not well disposed towards the union.

Apart from having to battle against the employers for higher wages and better conditions, there was the tragic position, common in South Africa, that the workers were divided amongst themselves. Many of them had come under the influence of the Reformer disrupters.

In 1942 the union decided, after months of negotiations, to call a strike in Port Elizabeth. The union was asking for increased wages, paid holidays and the introduction of the closed shop. The employers agreed to the first two demands but obstinately refused to accept the principle of the closed shop.

When the strike began, Mr Sachs, Hester Cornelius, Dulcie Hartwell and Anna Scheepers came from head office to help. Phillip, my husband, took leave from his work at the Ford Motor Company to give assistance. We divided our forces. Hester and I and a group of pickets went at about six a.m. to Mosenthal's factory, and Anna and Dulcie went to Teikamdas.

When we arrived at Mosenthal's we found a large number of policemen and a 'pick-up' van. Groups of pickets were placed outside the four or five entrances and, at seven-forty-five a.m., when the factory was opened, not a single worker tried to go to his work. At eight o'clock, however, a group of scabs who had gathered in a worker's house near the factory attempted to force their way through. They were organised and led by the Reformers. A fight ensued, and the police, as usual, protected the scabs, most of whom were by no means against the strikers, but had been misled. At about nine o'clock the sergeant in charge of the police came up and very politely asked whether he and his men could have some of the refreshments which we were serving to the pickets. Many of the police had members of their families working in clothing factories and they themselves have always been badly underpaid. A jug of coffee and plates of sandwiches were soon brought out and the entire police force got into the pick-up van, closed the door and enjoyed the refreshments. They were certainly in no hurry to come out to attend to their duties. Indeed, the sympathy of the police and of the public of Port Elizabeth as a whole was entirely on the side of the workers. Later in the day and during the following days, whenever the strikers assembled in a hall in the centre of the city for refreshments and dancing, quite a few policemen in uniform used to come inside to enjoy a snack and a dance.

At the Teikamdas factory things did not go so well. The majority of the workers were non-European and they were terrified of losing their jobs. A large number of scabs brushed the pickets aside and poor Dulcie, who had come to Port Elizabeth to help in a strike, was knocked over the head by several scabs and found herself covered with blood. She was rushed to a doctor, had her head bandaged and went back to the factory on picket duty; during the lunch hour, when we called a mass meeting in the centre of Port Elizabeth, Dulcie, with a huge bandage over her head, addressed the audience, bearing no malice towards the misguided workers and no hatred towards anyone. Her bandaged head attracted as much attention as her ringing voice.

On the third day of the strike the employers agreed to refer the closed shop to arbitration. Mr T. Freestone, an officer of the Department of Labour, was by mutual consent appointed arbitrator.

A satisfactory agreement was reached and, as soon as the closed shop was introduced, there was complete harmony amongst the workers and between the union and the employers.

* * *

My whole family has always been staunchly Nationalist, except for my sister Jacoba and my brother Johannes, who are United Party supporters with very strong Labour sympathies. Whenever I discuss politics and trade unionism with my brothers Koos and Albert, who are both fanatical Nationalists, I can see clearly the tragedy of the workers of South Africa. Like tens of thousands of others they have had their minds poisoned by the propaganda of the Nationalist Party. Both Koos and Albert are decent men of good character, well-behaved, well-spoken, and both of them fully supported our old parents. Both are men of courage and determination and have a tremendous amount of energy and capacity for hard work. As with many other Afrikaners of their generations, the terrible wrongs of the Boer War still rankle in their hearts. They have many English and Jewish friends, but in their hearts they are fanatical followers of Dr Malan. They read only the Nationalist papers, they hate the non-Europeans and firmly believe in apartheid. To them Communism means 'your sister marrying a "kaffir".' They hate the 'Jew-communist', Solly Sachs, and also dislike the other officials of the union, whom they regard as communists. I often argue with them and tell them: 'But look, it is Solly Sachs who has done so much for the garment workers, the majority of whom are Afrikaners. He fought for improvements in their wages and working conditions, organised them and helped them to gain a better living standard.' The reply is that they do not believe it and that the Government has improved the workers' wages and conditions. I tell them that no Government has ever helped the workers, and that Sachs and the other leaders of the union have often had to fight the Government. They remain unconvinced and say: 'We believe what we want to believe and what we do not want to believe we will not believe.'

CHAPTER SEVEN

An Afrikaner Working Mother: Anna Sophia Swanepoel

I WAS BORN ON 2ND APRIL 1893, on Tapfontein Farm, Edenvale district, Orange Free State. My father was a small farmer. My mother was brought up to be a farmer's wife, but my father was not a farmer by inclination and became a mounted policeman at Thaba 'Nchu, on the border of Basutoland. When I was three years old the family went to live in Thaba 'Nchu.

During the Boer War my father joined the Free State forces under the late General Hertzog. My mother was left with four children, two boys and two girls. My eldest brother, John Albert, who was sixteen, went with my father to fight for the Republic. The family was left stranded and my mother had to fend for herself and her children.

There were some well-to-do farmers near Thaba 'Nchu. These men had gone to war and had sent their women and children to the Cape and my mother was called in to take charge during their absence. There were troop movements and some fighting in the district. The soldiers of both sides helped themselves freely to whatever they could lay their hands on. The British troops seized everything they could. On the approach of the British forces we ran away from the farm, as we had been told that these soldiers would mishandle the women.

When the British arrived in Thaba 'Nchu they seized the house where we were living and turned it into a hospital, allowing the family the use of the back portion. There was an enteric epidemic at the time and the hospital portion of the house was crowded with sick men. The British soldiers behaved very decently towards us. They supplied us with food from the army kitchen and later helped to put up a café, where my mother served tea and home-made cakes and thus eked out a living. One of the soldiers, who was seriously ill, was nursed back to health by my mother and afterwards he helped her a great deal, even to the extent of serving in the café. The neighbours were angry with my mother for nursing a 'rooinek', but she replied she had helped him because he was a sick human being.

I remember, on one occasion, my mother baked nine pans of bread—eighteen loaves—in an outside Dutch oven. The British soldiers had just marched into town and, as they passed and saw the freshly-baked bread, they rushed and took away every loaf and paid in cash. We were left without bread, but mother got £3 *7s. 6d.* for the eighteen loaves. She baked some more bread and, while she was away, the soldiers again rushed to the oven and took away the bread, this time without paying. Next morning soldiers again waited for the bread my mother baked, but now she made a business proposition. She would bake bread and sell it. This was accepted.

At first there was no news from my father and brother. Later we heard that both had been caught by the British and sent to Ceylon as prisoners of war.

Things became unpleasant. Neighbours did not like my mother selling bread to the enemy. The first British regiment which had been stationed in the town moved out. Canvan, the British soldier who had served in the café, also had to go and she was left without any help. My mother asked the British officer to send her and her family to the Bloemfontein concentration camp. This he did and we lived there for nine months.

We had to stand in queues for hours to obtain meat, bread, water and other necessities. There were hundreds, perhaps thousands, of women, children and very old men. Some had come voluntarily to the camp, but the majority had been forced to go there. They did not starve, but neither did they live in a paradise. Emily Hobhouse, an Englishwoman, gave a great deal of help to the inmates of the camp. The medical services were very bad and, in a place where so many people were congregated, epidemics broke out. My mother was sent to the 'Draadkamp' (prison camp) to do hard work for a month because she had infringed a regulation —she had done some washing outside the tent where she lived— and the whole household went with her. At the end of the month my mother decided to stay in the prison camp because it was much easier to get food there and the children got clothes and boots. We were in the prison camp for six months until the war ended. We were then free to leave and my mother decided to go to Bloemfontein with the children. There she obtained a job doing laundry work for the Imperial Club for which she received £15 a month.

Two years later my father and brother returned from Ceylon. Both were very bitter against the British.

My father started working as a labourer on the railways, and my sister and I went to the railway school, later called the Brebner School, until 1909. We were taught High Dutch and English.

At the beginning of 1911 I arrived in Johannesburg and obtained employment through a school friend of mine, Julia Makonik, whom I had known in Bloemfontein. She found me a job in a small workshop where she was a tailoress. I started at 10*s.* a week. The hours were from seven a.m. to six p.m. daily, with an hour for lunch, and seven a.m. to twelve noon on Saturdays. The workshop was terribly overcrowded and hot, with primus stoves going all day and the smell of paraffin filling the air.

For about three months I lived with my brother and sister-in-law and did not have to pay board. Then I went to Julia's people, where I also had nothing to pay. A month later my parents arrived in Johannesburg and my father got a job as a ganger on the railways. My family rented a house and I went to live with them.

Very often we had to take work home and sit up late at night finishing it. For this we received no extra pay. The boss of the workshop was Mr Schiller, a highly qualified tradesman, friendly, but fond of using bad language. There was no union in existence, as far as I know, and workers were entirely at the mercy of their employers. I worked for Schiller for one year and, during that time, I received a rise of 2*s.* 6*d.* and, a few weeks before I left, one of 5*s.*, making my wage 17*s.* 6*d.*

I then went to work in another tailoring workshop where I received 25*s.* a week to start with and, after six months, was earning £2 a week; this was considered a particularly high wage at the time.

At the end of 1912 I was married to Pieter Swanepoel, a labourer-fitter on the railways. His wages were about £6 a month, but we got a free railway house and he also earned about £6 a month in his spare time from boot-making. We moved to Germiston, and my husband changed his work several times in order to better our income. In November 1927 he died, leaving me with two children aged eleven and fourteen. We were practically penniless and my total income was 17*s*. 6*d*. a week, which I earned as an usherette at the Apollo Theatre, Germiston. One evening, Mr Schiller, my employer of sixteen years ago, came to a show at the Apollo. He told me that, if I wanted work, I should get in touch with him at the African Clothing Factory, Germiston, where he was now employed as a foreman. I did so and, on the 23rd January 1928, I started work there at 25*s*. a week, which in those days was the highest wage paid to any factory worker. We worked from seven-thirty a.m. to six p.m., with a lunch break of one hour, and on Saturdays from seven-thirty to noon. The African Clothing was the largest factory in the Transvaal and one of the largest in South Africa. There was a piece-work system in existence and we had to turn out a certain amount every day. Many workers would start work before time and work through their lunch hour to make up their quota. There were no rest intervals.

I found it impossible to live with two children on my wages of approximately £5 a month. I therefore continued working as an usherette at the cinema and also took in two young girls of the factory as boarders at 10*s*. a week each.

When I started working for the African Clothing there was a union of garment workers in Johannesburg and I believe they had a wages agreement, but the workers of Germiston were not organised. One day, about three months after I had started work, Mr Dan Colraine, who was then secretary of the Johannesburg union, visited our factory and spoke to us during lunch hour. The majority of the workers readily agreed to organise a union and Mr Colraine handed me several membership forms. Immediately he had left, one of the girls said to me: 'Don't take the forms round. You will get the sack. A union has been started once before in the factory and the workers who helped to organise it were all sacked.'

I took no notice of the warning and, with the help of three others, got over a hundred and sixty workers to sign the forms and enrol as members of the union. At the end of the week I found a week's notice in my pay envelope, and so did the three other girls who had helped. I at once got in touch with Mr Colraine and told him about it. He came the following Monday and wanted to address the workers, but only a few gathered to hear him. All the others were afraid. He called another meeting outside the factory for the following day and this time all the workers who had enrolled as members turned up. The workers there and then decided to strike for the right to belong to a union and for the reinstatement of the four of us who had been dismissed.

The following day all the workers turned up at the factory, but only about twenty went in to work. I automatically became the strike leader and the workers looked to me for guidance. At first the employers were bitterly hostile and said that they would sack all the strikers, but after four days an agreement was reached to reinstate all the workers, including myself. Everybody got a full week's pay, including the four days we were away and we were brought under the Johannesburg agreement, which fixed wages for women workers at £1 to start and £2 10*s.* after two and a half years. Many of the workers received increases in wages; my own were raised to £2 a week. We also succeeded in getting a ten-minute rest interval in the morning and the lunch hour was properly observed. All the factory workers now joined the union and I was elected shop steward. The workers used to come to me with their complaints, which I had to take to the employer and naturally I was not very popular with him. Most of the complaints were settled to the satisfaction of the workers, as the employers did not want to have any trouble. On one occasion there was an argument about singing in the factory. The workers found the work monotonous and strenuous and, to break the monotony, they would start singing popular songs. Mr Sam Kalmek, one of our employers, apparently did not like music and tried to stop it. He told me that, if I wanted to sing, I should go on the stage, where I would earn more money, and lodged a complaint against me with the industrial council for leading the singing. The Chairman of the council told Mr Kalmek that there was no ground for complaint and that, in his own factory, he encouraged the workers to sing as it meant more production.

Trade unionism spread quickly among the workers of Germiston, and within a short time all the garment workers were members of the union. The workers gained more and more confidence in the union when they saw that it was successful in getting them higher wages.

In 1931 the union called a general strike of all workers in Johannesburg and Germiston against the attempt by the bosses to cut our wages by 25 per cent. The workers loyally responded and there were no scabs.

After about three weeks the strike was settled, neither side winning a victory. But the employers started organising immediately to break the union and to reduce wages. They did not openly attack the union, but used all sorts of tricks to get the workers away from it.

I did not return to the factory as I had been appointed organiser of the union for the Germiston branch. There were about a thousand workers in Germiston at that time and the town had become an important clothing centre.

In 1932 the employers once again tried to cut the workers' wages and the union called a general strike for the second time in August 1932. This time the workers were not as united as in 1931 and there were a number of strike-breakers in some of the Germiston factories. We organised pickets and did everything possible to prevent scabs from entering the factories. The pickets had to be outside the factories early in the morning, even before five a.m., as the employers were doing their utmost to bring in scabs. The pickets did not use violence against them, but resorted to booing and singing uncomplimentary songs or pelting them with tomatoes and eggs. Later on the bosses called in scores of police to break the strike. The police must have had instructions from Mr Pirow, who was then Minister of Justice, to handle the strikers without kid gloves and many workers were beaten up and arrested. On one occasion one of the girl strikers standing outside one of the factories had her pockets filled with rotten eggs. One of the policemen came up to her and slapped her on the pockets, with disastrous consequences to her clothes. He then arrested her. I went up, got hold of the girl and tried to pull her away from the policeman, but suddenly I 'saw stars'. The policeman had slapped me violently across the face and, for a whole week, I proudly bore my badge of honour—a black eye.

One day when there was a crowd of pickets standing outside one of the factories about five or six mounted policemen rode up and told the workers to disperse. Before the workers had time to make up their minds what to do, one of the mounted policemen rode into the crowd and several of the girls were knocked down. There was a general commotion and some of the girls were severely injured. A few had to be taken to hospital and one of them suffered from an injured ankle for some years. The general treatment by the police of the girl strikers was shameful.

In the end the workers had to give in and after about two months they returned to work with a cut of 10 per cent in their wages. Many of them had lost their faith in the union, and the employers, taking advantage of the situation, did everything in their power to discourage union activities. Many workers were paid off and there was a great deal of unemployment.

In 1934 I gave up the position of union organiser and went to work for a factory in Johannesburg. After about a year I returned to work in Germiston. In 1936 I started to work for New York Clothing, where I was employed until 1951.

By 1936 the workers had forgotten their earlier defeat and the union once again began to make progress. For a year or two I was quiet, then I started taking an active interest in union affairs again. For the last ten years I have served on the Germiston branch committee, on the industrial council, the medical aid society and as a member of the central executive committee of the union.

In the last twenty years there has been a complete change for the better in our wages and conditions of work. My wages now are £5 4*s*. a week and I work a five-day week of forty hours. I get three weeks and six days paid holidays, as well as free medical attention and sick pay in case of illness. The small, overcrowded tin shanties of the earlier years have disappeared and today Germiston has a dozen large, modern factories, with cloakrooms and other amenities. But what is more important, perhaps, than any material improvement in our conditions, is the fact that we no longer feel like slaves, but like free men and women, and know that we have a strong union to depend on in times of need.

CHAPTER EIGHT

Capitalists without Money

IN 1928 the clothing industry presented a picture of primitive capitalism. There were about fifty factories on the Rand, roughly forty in Johannesburg and the rest in Germiston; of these only four employed a hundred or more workers and could be considered modern by South African industrial standards of that period. The rest were nearly all sweatshops, some large, some small. The making of garments requires little capital: a few willing hands, needles, scissors and the power of self-exploitation are all that is necessary. The majority of the manufacturers obtained their sewing machines on the hire purchase system and their materials on credit, when they could get it. They did not sell their products to customers directly, but worked for wholesale merchants or retailers on a cut-make-and-trim basis. Having little or no capital of their own, they were forced to lead a hand-to-mouth existence. Even the well-established wholesale houses took full and mean advantage of these penniless employers and paid as little as three shillings for cutting, making and trimming a dozen pairs of trousers and less for shirts. The Industrial Conciliation Act made provision for minimum wages to employees but at that time the fixing of contract rates by agreement was not included in the Act. Only in 1937, when the Act was amended, was provision made for the inclusion in industrial agreements of work given out on contract to any person by a principal or contractor and for the contract rates to be paid.

The struggle for existence forced the indigent manufacturers to engage in ruthless competition and reduced cut-make-and-trim prices to a fantastically low level.

Very few could afford patent machines for the sewing on of buttons, making buttonholes and other operations, and the band-saw was a luxury which was beyond their means. The cutting was done by scissors, buttons were often sewn on by hand and buttonholes were hand-made. Steam-pressing was unknown and, indeed, in at least one factory the pressing of cheap khaki trousers was done by workers sitting on bundles of these garments. Afrikaner workers are not of slender build and this primitive method served its purpose.

Most of these 'manufacturers' maintained a miserable existence by pilfering. A merchant would supply a roll of cloth to cut-make-and-trim, say, a hundred garments and the manufacturer would, by devious methods, squeeze out a hundred and five garments and keep the difference for himself. Wholesale pilfering of workers' wages was also common.

In spite of the existence of an industrial agreement which fixed minimum wages by law, scores of workers received no pay at all. They were told that they were 'apprentices' learning a trade and had to be content with the hope of one day earning some wages. Hundreds were paid a few shillings a week and only the big factories made any attempt at observing the agreement, but even there underpayments were common. In some factories every worker was underpaid, in others only a small percentage received the legal minimum. The organisation and methods of production in many factories were badly out of date. Hardly any of the cut-make-and-trim manufacturers had regular supplies of work. For a few days they would be very busy and then a long period would follow when they had to look desperately for work. Frequently factories were forced to cease operations because the employer ran out of cotton. The cut-make-and-trim manufacturer had to supply cotton and trimmings which he usually had to buy for cash—and cash was always short.

During the first six months of my secretaryship I spent a good deal of my time examining and checking wages and wage registers. I usually called at the factories during the lunch hour and often found the employer and some workers sharing their lunch of sandwiches or fish and chips. I introduced myself and asked the employer to produce his register. Some employers had registers, others looked at me with amazement and said: 'Registers? What's that?' In several factories employers pulled out from their pockets bits and pieces of paper on which they had recorded the wages paid and informed me that these were their 'registers'. In those factories where registers were well kept and workers signed receipts over an affixed stamp, the records were not infrequently faked and the workers did not receive the full amount for which they had signed.

I took statements from the workers individually and thus ascertained the wages to which they were entitled under the agreement. When I checked the employer's register I usually found that many workers were being underpaid. I then informed the employer that he had underpaid his workers and would have to pay back-pay, not forgetting to emphasise that underpayments constituted criminal offences which carried penalties of six months' imprisonment and a £100 fine. It would take me some time and effort to explain the legal position to the employer, and on at least one occasion, when I presented a statement of underpayment, the bewildered employer looked at me and said:

> Look, Sachs, I don't know anything about the law and I'm not a criminal. I pay the workers as much as I can. When Friday comes and I have to find wages, I have to chase after those bloody merchants who give me work to get an advance from them for the following week. This week I haven't got a penny yet with which to pay wages. I know the workers are poor and they have to live, but what can I do? Where can I turn?

On several occasions employers after telling me their tale of woe ended with the request: 'Sachs, can you lend me a fiver to pay the wages? I'll pay you back next week with interest.'

In this welter of misery, hours of work had neither beginning nor end. Often the employers would stay in the factory after the workers had left and continue working until midnight or later. Others made their employees take work away with them to finish and so turn their tiny overcrowded homes into workshops.

Conditions were terrible enough for the workers when there was a full week's work, but this was rare, and hundreds of them collected only a few shillings at the end of the week. The employers, not wanting to lose their workers, would beg them to come in every day, hoping to get work from merchants. Often the workers would spend the last few pence they had on tram fares to come to the factory, only to find that the employer had been unsuccessful in securing work or had been told by a merchant that Mr X, another cut-make-and-trim man, was making garments *1s.* or *2s.* a dozen cheaper and had got the work. Most of the garments produced were of the cheapest quality.

What the employers lacked in efficiency and organisation they tried to make up by driving the workers inhumanely, cursing and shouting at them. The majority of the factories were situated in slum premises, totally unsuitable for human beings. Lighting and sanitation were of the worst and the premises were usually extremely untidy. The inside of the workshops presented a most depressing picture. The 'capitalist' employer, without a penny to his name, seemed harassed, tired and miserable. The air was foul; there was no sign of any organisation or order. Bundles of garments, finished and half-finished, were strewn all over the place, together with pieces of cut or uncut cloth. There was constant shouting—the foreman or the boss shouting at the workers, the workers shouting for cotton or for parts of garments. Only the bright faces of the young women, patiently toiling away, humming or singing 'Sarie Marais' and other folk-songs, relieved the utter sordidness of these sweating dens.

As far as the workers were concerned, their life was one endless struggle and worry bereft of all pleasure. Many literally starved. They did not understand the mechanics of capitalist production and felt no particular animosity towards their individual employers. Indeed, many of them were on quite friendly terms with their bosses.

In the four larger factories, where nearly half of the total number of workers were employed, things were very much better than in the rest of the industry. But there, too, the foreman relied on getting production, not by efficient organisation, but by slave-driving the workers, shouting at them and abusing them.

There were a few Coloured women workers in two or three factories, whose average wage was about 7*s*. 6*d*. a week, but as they were not members of the union and afraid to join or give information for fear of losing their jobs, it was very difficult to enforce the provisions of the agreement on their behalf.

There were also several hundred African workers—all males—employed almost exclusively as pressers and on other heavy work. Their conditions of work were very poor, but in a way they were better off than the Europeans. Under their contract of employment, governed by pass laws, they had to be paid a full week's pay and could not be put off when times were slack. In addition, they were used to such very low standards of living that even the miserable conditions of the clothing industry were an improvement for them.

At the beginning of 1929 the prospect of obtaining higher standards for the workers in the clothing industry seemed hopeless.

It is always difficult to get employers to agree to improvements, even when they have abundant capital resources and make substantial profits; to demand higher wages and better working conditions from employers who themselves were penniless and struggling to make ends meet seemed futile.

The various committees of the union were not very helpful in formulating policies and tactics with which to combat sweating. Nearly all the committee members belonged to the group of higher-paid workers. They had received their training in class struggle in the small workshop and were far too preoccupied with their own problems to find the time and energy to study and analyse the highly complex problems of South Africa and its industrial revolution.

I knew little of the practical side of the clothing industry, but had a good knowledge of the economic and social problems of South Africa and the struggles which the workers in Britain and other countries had faced when the factory system was first introduced. I did not lack energy, and the terrible conditions of the workers fired me with a strong desire for action and left me no time for despair or hopelessness. I prepared lengthy memoranda for the committees, analysing the position and stressing that the problem was a national one and not only common to the clothing industry.

The choice before the union was either to succumb to the surrounding misery and patiently wait for better times, or to fight with zeal and determination against every evil. The plan of campaign which the general membership finally adopted was briefly as follows:

(1) First of all, the masses of Afrikaner women workers must be persuaded to join and play an active part in the Trade Union. Since they were complete strangers to trade unionism, we would have to undertake systematic educational work amongst them. The struggle could not be confined to purely trade union matters. The demand for improved working conditions must play a major rôle, but the problem of their poverty transcended the narrow field of trade unionism and was national in character.

(2) The industrial agreements, which provided minimum wages and other conditions of employment for workers, were to be rigorously enforced by criminal prosecution against employers who violated them and, where this proved ineffective, by strike

and other action. Employers who could conduct clothing factories only by exploiting themselves and pilfering the workers' wages, and who could not provide reasonable standards for their workers, had either to change their methods or to get out. They were of no use to anyone, not to the country, not the workers, not even to themselves. The Wage Act and the Factories Act, and all other laws dealing with questions of hygiene and sanitation, were to be enforced. In addition, the workers were to be taught the provisions of the industrial agreements and told to keep a check on their own wages and conditions of work and on those of other workers, to make sure whether all the provisions of the agreement were strictly observed. The workers were also to be invited to bring their wages to the union office to be checked and to lodge complaints. The union would undertake to protect every worker who might be victimised as a result of giving information, about contraventions of the agreement, to officials of the union or to the industrial councils.

(3) Several of the leading employers, both in the tailoring and clothing industries, were ready to co-operate with the union in eliminating sweating. Naturally, the employers who paid higher wages and observed the provisions of the agreement were anxious to eliminate unfair competition from the small 'rat' employers, and the union was to co-operate with the better type of employers. We were to start a national campaign, by means of demonstrations, publications and newspaper articles, to expose the appalling conditions of the women workers in industry. Their abysmal poverty was not to be hidden, but must be flaunted in the faces of the public so as to arouse the conscience and sympathy of the mass of the people and thus force the Government to take action.

In one respect, the union had been fortunate in its earlier struggles. Violent racial conflicts, which were later provoked by the propagandists of the Nationalist Party and dissipated so much of the energy of the union were then unknown. At that time there were two main racial groups in the union—several hundred Jewish workers and the rest nearly all Afrikaner women—and there was complete racial harmony. I recall an incident at a big general meeting in 1930 which illustrates this. The overwhelming majority of the members were Afrikaans-speaking and the union decided to introduce bilingualism in all spheres of its work. An Afrikaner woman, Mrs Booysen, got up at the meeting and said: 'It's all very well having English and Afrikaans, but what about the Jewish workers? Why shouldn't their language be recognised by the union?' But trilingualism had to be abandoned because nobody could be found who could speak and write Yiddish fluently and the task of translating technical terms of the industrial agreements into Yiddish proved quite hopeless.

CHAPTER NINE

The Struggle against Sweating

ALL SOUTH AFRICAN LABOUR LAWS have objectionable features which cause bitter resentment among the workers, and nearly all of them are punitive in character.

Before Union each of the four provinces in South Africa enacted its own laws. One of the earliest labour laws is the Master and Servants Act, Act 15 of 1856, of the Cape Province. In the Transvaal a Master and Servants Act was introduced in 1880 (Law 13 of 1880), when the British were in occupation of that Province. A similar measure was enacted in Natal under Ordinance 2 of 1850, and in the Orange Free State under Ordinance 7 of 1904. In 1911 the Native Labour Regulations Act was passed by the Union Parliament. Under all these laws non-European—and especially African—workers are guilty of criminal offences when absenting themselves from work without lawful cause.

In consequence of the industrial disturbances on the Rand in 1913 and 1914 an Act was passed, not for the purpose of preventing and settling disputes by conciliation but to give the police wider powers to deal with strikers and to afford maximum protection to strike-breakers. The Act is known as the Riotous Assemblies and Criminal Law Amendment Act of 1914. This Act applies to all workers, irrespective of race or colour. Smuts, who introduced it, could never rid himself entirely of the feudal conception of the 'master and servant' society and it was his belief that workers on strike were criminals who disturbed law and order. Thus, when he passed the Industrial Conciliation Act in 1924 (after the violent industrial strife on the Rand in 1922), which was the first labour law to introduce employer-employee instead of master and servant relationships, he made strikes, under certain circumstances, illegal and provided for penalties of three years' imprisonment and a £500 fine. In 1937 the Act was amended and a new repugnant principle introduced which, in effect, meant that a worker charged with striking was presumed guilty unless he established his innocence.

Another obnoxious feature of South African labour legislation is the wide discretionary powers given to the Minister of Labour and his departmental officials. Under the Industrial Conciliation Act the Minister may gazette agreements entered into between employers and trade unions only 'if he deems it expedient'. The industrial registrar is given wide powers to deal with trade union registration and can dictate to unions what they should include in their constitutions. The Wage Act, which has been held up by various Ministers as a piece of excellent legislation—almost socialist in character, has in fact proved a complete failure for, while the Wage Board established under the Act can report and make recommendations, none but the Minister has the power to make a recommendation of the Board legally binding as a determination.

The Unemployment Insurance Act is almost entirely under the personal control of the Secretary for Labour.

Bureaucracy, even when it is benevolent and efficient, is objectionable. In South Africa, where there is as yet no traditional respect for the rule of law, where Ministers are usually inferior politicians and seldom statesmen, and where departmental officials lack the tradition of service and efficiency, the enormous powers placed in the hands of individuals, powers which cannot be challenged in a court of law, have been a constant source of irritation to workers and to employers.

A further feature of South African labour laws is the clumsy, ambiguous and obscure manner in which they are drafted. This has proved disastrous to the workers' cause and of immense benefit to defaulting employers. On numerous occasions industrial agreements and wage determinations covering tens of thousands of workers have been invalidated by the courts, mainly because of bad draftsmanship in the statutes under which they were made.

Finally, there is the question of enforcement of the laws. The authorities and the police have always acted with promptness, efficiency and rigour when prosecuting workers, but the enforcement of the provisions of the various laws which accorded workers benefits has been left largely in the hands of incompetent, inefficient and frequently corrupt officials. Our efforts to secure for the workers their legal rights under the labour laws of the country invariably proved dilatory, exasperating and often futile. In some countries machinery created by law works expeditiously and determines wages for groups of workers within a short period. In

South Africa it has often taken the Wage Board three years, and even longer, to make a recommendation. Industrial agreements between employers and trade unions were held up by Ministers for months, in some cases even for years, before they were gazetted.

In seeking to secure for the garment workers the rights they were entitled to by law, the union concentrated on three main objectives:

(*a*) the enforcing of the provisions of existing agreements by prosecutions;

(*b*) repeated applications to the Wage Board to fix uniform wages and conditions of employment for the clothing industry on a national basis, thus eliminating unfair competition from coastal areas (Cape Town, Durban etc.);

(*c*) a campaign, in co-operation with other unions and with the South African Trades and Labour Council, for improved and more up-to-date labour legislation.

The enforcement of agreements through prosecutions was not simple. The vast majority of employers had no respect for law and few of them took the trouble to read the industrial agreements. To initiate prosecutions and to succeed in obtaining convictions, evidence was required from the employees and, here again, the union was faced with great difficulties because of the terrible fear of victimisation.

I would go into a small tailoring shop, where I needed no introduction, and approach a worker to check his or her wages and hours of work. In the friendliest manner I would ask for the full name. With the women there was generally no difficulty, but the older Jewish worker would reply: 'My name? What do you want my name for?'

I must confess that I found it somewhat difficult to explain why I wanted his name, but after some time he would grudgingly give me the information I sought.

Next question: 'How old are you?'

'How old am I? I don't remember. I think I was born ten years after the Turkish war.'

Knowing a little about European history, I guessed that he was born in 1887.

'What work are you doing?'

This was important, as there were different wage rates for different classes of work.

The answer would invariably be: 'Hmmm, what work am I doing? I do everything.'

I would then ask: 'Do you do cutting?'

'No.'

'Do you do pressing?'

'No.'

'Do you do fixing or shaping?'

'No.'

I would ascertain finally that he was really only basting out or basting under garments, or perhaps performing several operations, but not all.

'How long have you been in the tailoring industry?'

This question was important in order to establish whether he had had five years' experience and was entitled to the wage rate of a qualified man, or was still a learner.

The retort would often be: 'Why do you ask such silly questions? I've been a tailor all my life.'

After a little effort, we would mutually agree that he was not born with a needle or scissors in his hand, but had started in the tailoring industry at the age of ten or eleven, somewhere in Poland or Lithuania. I would also learn a great deal about his earlier life: that as a youngster he had worked for a few years without receiving any payment and that, while learning his trade, his duties had also included scrubbing floors, looking after children and doing all sorts of work which had not the remotest connection with tailoring, and that his hours of work had been from about five a.m. to midnight, or until he dropped exhausted.

Then I would come to the most important questions of all: 'What wages are you getting?'

The answers I received were more or less as follows: 'I'm getting the proper wage', or 'I'm getting the union wage', or 'Please don't worry, Mr Sachs, I'm getting the right wage.'

Far from convincing me, that always made me feel I had good cause to worry.

Sometimes the employer would chip in and answer for the worker, saying: 'Oh, he gets the proper wage.'

We had established a fairly well organised intelligence service in the industry and knew the exact wages of almost everyone, but in cases of underpayment we had to get an affidavit from the worker and his consent to appear in court to give evidence. This proved very difficult. Very few of the men told the truth. The majority of those who were underpaid were too frightened to give me the correct information and even more frightened to come to court, for the Jewish workers who had come from Czarist Russia had every reason to fear courts, policemen and magistrates. There was nothing I could do, even though I knew that I had received false information, but before leaving the shop I would call the worker aside and ask him to come up to the office for a friendly chat. Many of them came and talked more freely. Their stories were more or less identical:

> Mr Sachs, I know that you work for the workers. I know that the union is trying to do its best to help us, but what can I do? I am a first-class tailor and work very hard. I know that under the agreement I am entitled to £8 a week, but I only receive half that amount. You think I like it? I have a wife and family in the old country. I have to support them. In fact, I want to bring them here. I have also to support myself, and, if I told you the truth and my boss got to know, I'd soon get the sack and who would give me a job then?

Without the whole-hearted co-operation of the underpaid workers, our efforts to enforce agreements were hopeless. We had to become detectives to cope with the situation. Above all, we had to gain the confidence of the workers and bring pressure to bear upon delinquent employers in order to intimidate them and make them become law-abiding.

We decided to employ persuasive measures and to apply a little 'prodding', where necessary.

I raised the question of enforcing the provisions of the agreements, both at the Industrial Council for the Bespoke Tailoring Industry (of which I was secretary) and at the Industrial Council for the Clothing Industry. At the Bespoke Tailoring Council there was no difficulty and here I must pay tribute to the late W. J. Madden, one of the leading employers in the tailoring industry in Johannesburg, chairman of the Council and for some time also chairman of the Merchant Tailors' Association. Mr Madden, who was a devout Roman Catholic, came from the ranks and had experienced hardships in his youth. He was a man with a high sense of honour and had deep sympathy for the workers which was reflected in the way he ran his own workshop. I submitted a full report to him on the deplorable state of affairs in the industry, suggesting that energetic measures be taken against offending employers and received his wholehearted support.

Under the auspices of the Council, we convened a meeting of merchant tailors and middlemen tailors, and Mr Madden and I appealed to them to help us improve conditions in the tailoring industry. We pointed out how the whole industry would benefit from the elimination of sweating and unfair competition. We offered to help to adjust wage rates gradually, provided employers stopped faking registers and came to us with their difficulties in a straightforward manner.

The meeting lasted about two hours and was attended by over fifty employers. The remarks I overheard when the meeting dispersed made me realise that our speeches had had little or no effect. Mr Madden and I came to the conclusion that it was essential some order be introduced into the industry and, within a few months, twenty-seven employers were prosecuted, twenty-five of whom were convicted, the other two managing to escape conviction through technicalities. The English daily press was co-operative and gave much space to the court proceedings. In the first case the employer was convicted for several breaches of the agreement, fined £40 and ordered to pay a substantial sum in back pay. When the other employers received their summonses, they rushed to the Council or union offices, but I explained to them that, since they had not listened to the advice we had given previously, they would now have to deal with the magistrate. I also made it plain that the Council and the union were determined to enforce the agreement and would not abandon prosecutions until every employer had been made to realise that agreements must be honoured.

I warned them that, should they victimise any of their workers who gave evidence, they would get into trouble. There was a provision in the Industrial Conciliation Act prohibiting victimisation of employees who gave information to council officials or evidence in court. But it was almost impossible to prove victimisation. However, in one case where a merchant tailor, after being convicted, sacked two workers who had given evidence, the union called a strike and staged a demonstration outside his premises, in which over a thousand workers participated. Within a week the employer reinstated the workers, paid them for time lost and the strike was settled.

The results of a policy of action soon became apparent. The delinquent employers became terrified of the Council and of the union and, uninvited, came to seek advice. But what was more important was the new spirit created among the workers. Confidence in the union and themselves took the place of fear, and scores of underpaid and sweated workers came forward with their complaints. The union pledged support to the middlemen tailors in their efforts to secure full contract rates from merchant tailors; this was followed by vigorous action directed to convince the merchant tailors that the days of exploiting middlemen tailors were gone. Several merchant tailors, who refused to toe the line, had their work stopped and, in addition, were treated to a few lively demonstrations. One well-known firm of merchant tailors, which exploited middlemen, had a large shop in the centre of Johannesburg. For nearly a month, during the lunch hour, the union organised demonstrations outside the shop. Hundreds of workers and thousands of inquisitive people would be attracted to the demonstration and speakers from the union would climb on to a motor car bedecked with banners and address the crowd, not only exposing the wickedness of the firm, but commenting on the bad conditions in the industry generally. On one occasion the firm very foolishly called in the police, and the sergeant, accompanied by about half a dozen policemen, approached me angrily while I was speaking to the crowd, saying: 'What right have you to hold a meeting here? You are causing an obstruction.'

I had been arrested previously for addressing a meeting of strikers in the street and charged with obstruction. At that time the magistrate had seemed particularly anxious to convict me, but on the strength of a judgment in the Transvaal Provincial Division of the Supreme Court, declaring invalid the bylaw under which I was charged, had reluctantly discharged me. I thereupon told the sergeant that I was entitled to address the meeting and that he had no right to interfere with me. South African crowds always enjoy a crack at policemen and, when I offered to lend the sergeant a copy of the judgment, there was a roar of laughter from the crowd, which had increased to about three thousand. The men in uniform beat a hasty retreat.

Demonstrations proved very effective in exposing bad employers and forcing them to observe agreements. They also served in rousing interest and enthusiasm among workers and bringing them into active participation in the union's struggles.

meant that the demands for back-pay could not be enforced in the courts. A special Council meeting was called to consider the situation. The union delegates informed the employers that, unless the back-pay due was paid, the union would take strike action. Eventually, after much discussion, the union representatives agreed to accept two-thirds of the back pay, but only on the assurance of the employers that in future the agreements would be strictly observed.

Probably no country in the world shows so little respect for agreements and laws governing workers' wages and conditions as South Africa.

The Goodman judgment and a series of similar judgments of the Supreme Court which followed, invalidating industrial council agreements and wage determinations, led to disastrous consequences for the workers. The employers had never had much faith in legal wage instruments, and many of them now began to take full advantage of the situation. Claims for back-pay could no longer be enforced through the courts, and the salutary effect of the earlier rigorous enforcement of agreements soon wore off. The employers who were willing to pay the agreement wages were faced with unfair competition from those who exploited to the full the legal chaos created by the successive judgments.

The union determined to take energetic counter-action to meet this contingency. During the currency of agreements, strikes were prohibited under a penalty of three years' imprisonment and a £500 fine. Now that the agreements had been invalidated, strikes became lawful, provided the dispute was first submitted to an industrial council or conciliation board. Such submission was a mere formality which, though irksome, did not present insurmountable difficulties.

We decided to make an example of two of the worst factories, each employing about sixty workers. In the first factory, the employer, a cut-make-and-trim manufacturer, was in the habit of paying his workers a few shillings a week, the balance being 'carried forward'. Some workers did not receive any wages at all and six were even compelled to pay a premium of £3 for the privilege of learning how to make cheap khaki trousers. Two of them had had to pawn their belongings in order to pay the premium. The wage register was kept on scraps of paper which the employer's son carried about in his pocket. Repeated demands that the agreement be observed met with blank refusal or vague excuses; the union therefore decided to take strike action.

All the workers in the factory were called to a meeting and the situation explained to them; they readily agreed to stop work as soon as the legal formalities had been complied with. The evening before the strike was due to start, two union officials, one of them a woman, waited outside the factory to tell the workers they were to stop work the following morning. The woman organiser was violently assaulted by the employer's son. In the meantime the employer had been busy visiting the workers at their homes trying to persuade them not to strike and, the following day, many scabs reported for work. Early in the morning, however, the union officials mobilised an army of about a thousand workers who formed a picket line outside the factory. Within a few minutes twenty policemen appeared and this attracted a large crowd of passers-by. The factory area of Johannesburg became very lively of a sudden. The Riotous Assemblies Act makes it a criminal offence to 'molest' or 'intimidate' strike-breakers, but the mere presence of a thousand garment workers and probably two thousand onlookers had the desired effect on any would-be scabs.

A small core of workers, led by two sisters who had been forced to pay a premium, were determined to scab. I interviewed the two ring-leaders, who seemed intelligent and tenacious. They lived in appalling poverty, yet they were determined to perpetuate a system of sweating and misery for themselves and their fellow-workers.

The union learnt that the firm which supplied this rat-shop with work was one of the leading wholesale houses in Johannesburg. Two thousand garment workers, followed by an equal number of inquisitive sightseers, demonstrated outside the firm's premises. I told the crowd that the magnificent building where the firm had its offices and warehouse was really built, not of brick, but of the sweat and toil of young women workers. The following morning I received a message from the general manager of the firm asking me to come and see him. When I presented myself, he seemed resentful and I quickly made to leave. He called me back politely and asked me why we had held a demonstration outside his firm. I told him of the disgraceful conditions in the factory which his firm was supplying with work and also made it clear that we would continue with the demonstrations until the firm gave its work only to those employers who treated their workers fairly. The manager asked for time to consider the matter and, within a few days, I was called in again and advised of the following decision:

(*a*) that in future the firm itself would be responsible for the proper payment of wages and the conduct of the factory;

(*b*) that, should the union find the employer reverting to his old practices, the firm would give the work elsewhere.

These terms were conveyed to the employer, who had been kept waiting outside. The manager expressed his regret and assured me that he had not been aware of the conditions in which the work had been made up.

In the second factory the position was more complicated. It was run by a vicious woman with the assistance of her husband and son. Every clause of the agreement was treated with contempt. Wages were paid if and when cash was available. Hair-pulling, face-slapping and abusive language were common.

One evening the workers were told by the union that a strike would begin the following day. At five in the morning sixty-three workers turned up in pouring rain to form a picket line outside the factory. This proved unnecessary, as there was not a single scab. At about seven a.m. the strikers marched to the Trades Hall where still full of high spirits despite their drenching they started dancing. During the lunch hour the workers marched back to the factory and held a meeting. A large crowd collected and, standing in the doorway of a building, I began to address them. Within a few minutes a sergeant of police, accompanied by two constables, rushed up and angrily told me that I was causing an obstruction. I pointed out to him that I was standing on private premises and was not causing any obstruction; that if there was an obstruction, it was caused by the crowd. I also suggested that the citizens of Johannesburg were entitled to use public places to discuss public affairs and we were discussing something of national importance —the inhuman exploitation of large numbers of women. This brought laughter and cheers from the crowd, but the sergeant was not impressed.

He arrested me and led me through the centre of Johannesburg; hundreds of workers followed, using language about the police which was not altogether complimentary. I told the sergeant that there was no need to stage this demonstration and that I would report to Marshall Square to be charged, or he could bring me to court by summons. He was too angry to yield and so the procession continued through the city to Marshall Square. There, bail was fixed at £2.

A few days later, the employer surrendered and an agreement was signed which opened with the clause:

> The employer undertakes not to use abusive language towards employees in the factory. For every occasion when the employer or his representative uses abusive language against one or more workers, he shall pay a fine of £2.

We asked the employer, as a guarantee, to deposit £50 with the union but, as he had no cash, we accepted promissory notes. The woman who was in charge of the factory proved incorrigible, but the main abuses were eliminated. For many years, however, there were constant disputes in this factory and it was only when the woman retired from business and her son took over that harmony was established.

Some weeks after the strike I received a summons to appear in the Magistrate's Court, Johannesburg, to answer a charge of obstruction. I defended myself and pleaded 'not guilty'. The prosecutor called three policemen as witnesses. The case lasted two days and I made use of the opportunity to experiment in cross-examination. The Crown then closed its case and the magistrate seemed ready to convict and punish me. I told him that I was applying for my discharge on the ground that the by-law under which I was charged was invalid, and I quoted the case of *Naidoo* v. *Pretoria Municipality*, T.P.D., 1927. The magistrate angrily inquired why I had not raised the point at the opening of the proceedings before the Crown called evidence. I explained that I was not a lawyer, but only a trade union official. Although the quoted case was perfectly clear, he would not give judgment immediately, but made me appear again the following week.

There was no smile on his face as he discharged me.

Every little victory the union scored, however remotely connected with the workers' conditions, had a tremendous effect on the morale of the workers. This case received much press publicity and, when the workers learnt that I was discharged, there was great rejoicing.

CHAPTER ELEVEN

Court Cases

In 1931 a strike started in a factory over the dismissal of a number of workers. The workers were divided and about one-third refused to strike. The strikers, with the help of hundreds of other workers, picketed the factory. After about two weeks we were served with an interdict, the firm being the applicant; the Garment Workers' Union, Mr G. Malan, an organiser of the union, and myself the respondents. This was the first time in the history of the labour movement of South Africa that an injunction had been applied for in industrial disputes. The employer obtained a temporary interdict restraining us from 'molesting or interfering with the employees of the factory'. During the strike we held regular meetings outside the factory in the lunch hour and after work each day; the day the interdict was served, a squad of policemen and an inspector stood waiting outside the factory, presumably to arrest us for refusing to abide by the court order. At five-thirty p.m. I mounted a little platform in the usual way and, as the inspector approached, I addressed him and the crowd which the presence of the police had attracted. I read the terms of the temporary interdict and assured the inspector that we had no intention of molesting or interfering with the employees of the factory and, indeed would never engage in such practices. I took the trouble to explain that there had been no need for the firm to apply for an interdict, as molesting and interfering with scabs was a criminal offence under the law. The inspector, who seemed quite human, appeared nonplussed and took no action. I then went on to say how energetic the police were in protecting the property and rights of the employers but how they never took action to enforce the law when hundreds of exploited workers were being illegally underpaid by their employers. After denouncing the practices of sweating, I continued with a lecture on class justice and ended by saying that there was no justice in South Africa. I made a passing reference to the conviction of a union leader on a frame-up a month previously and hinted that the police were not descendants of George Washington.

Six weeks later I received a summons to answer a charge of contempt of court for attacking South African justice. In the meantime the employer's application for the interdict was argued in the Supreme Court and Judge de Waal gave judgment against us. However, as there was a dispute on the facts of the case, the matter was sent for trial. A few days before the trial was to begin, the employers' association approached the union, asking us to drop the action; each side to pay its own costs. We knew that the employers had no case and told them that, since a member of their association had started the action, he could withdraw it, but he would have to pay all the costs. At first they refused, but the day before the case was due to be heard the firm withdrew the application and paid all the costs.

I was now due to appear in the Magistrate's Court, Johannesburg, on the charge of contempt of court. Johannesburg magistrates usually accept the word of a policeman rather than that of a trade union official and I knew that, on evidence, I must be convicted. I decided to take two exceptions to the charge: firstly, that the charge of contempt of court must be tried by a Superior Court and not by a Magistrate's Court, which is a creation of statute; secondly, that the charge disclosed no offence. I quoted numerous South African and English cases in support of both exceptions.

Mr van Schoor, the magistrate, seemed to pay little attention to my legal arguments. He adjourned the proceedings and, the following day, when the court resumed, he informed me that he had consulted some of his fellow-magistrates and that, although they agreed my submission had some grounds, he had decided to proceed with the case. I knew at once that the matter would have to go to appeal.

The chief witness for the prosecution was Detective-Sergeant Toerien, an Afrikaner who spoke slowly in halting English. He knew no shorthand and admitted in his evidence that I had spoken rapidly for about half an hour, yet he gave the court a verbatim report of my speech. His story was accepted by the magistrate and I was found guilty.

As soon as the verdict had been announced, Mr van Schoor, who had been most amiable throughout the proceedings, changed his demeanour entirely. He began by delivering himself of a homily which ended in him telling me that, if I did not like the justice of

South Africa, I could go elsewhere. Then, he asked me the extraordinary question: 'Sachs, did I give you a fair trial?' I was not prepared to answer this question in the affirmative and, had I answered negatively, I should have been guilty of contempt of court. I therefore declined to reply. He repeated the question angrily, and then I told him that, as I was the accused, it was not for me to say whether my trial had been fairly conducted or not. This apparently made him all the more angry. He then asked Toerien if I had been convicted previously. I had been convicted twice in the Magistrate's Court, but had appealed in each case, and both convictions had been set aside. Toerien knew this, but still produced evidence of these convictions in court. I protested strongly and told Mr van Schoor that both my successful appeals were recorded in the Law Reports and he could verify this for himself. I said that, as the Court had itself expressed the view that there were interesting legal points involved, it was my intention to appeal. This annoyed Mr van Schoor intensely and he warned me that, if I were not careful, I should be committed for contempt of court. He fixed bail at £25. It was late in the afternoon and I had only £20 on me, so the detectives took my finger prints and rushed me off to prison. At about eleven p.m. when I was already asleep, there was a knock on the door of my cell and I was released. The warrant for my release had been obtained by my friends.

In due course my appeal was heard in the Transvaal Provincial Division of the Supreme Court. It was upheld and my conviction and sentence set aside.

At about the same time, I became involved in two more court actions.

In one of the tailoring shops, where the employer professed to be progressive, the workers came out on strike. To discredit the union and its general secretary, the employer hired the services of two extremely able and unscrupulous men, who had been running a low type of weekly paper called *L.S.D.* Suddenly, their rag came out with posters and banner headlines, 'exposing' E. S. Sachs. They accused me of 'dancing all night with skokiaan-reeking Zulu queens', and many other disgraceful acts. I have never danced in my life and this was nothing but a crude attempt to exploit race hatred and discredit me and the free trade union movement. One of the editors of the paper told me that he had been promised £25 for the 'job', but that the employer was a 'scoundrel' and had paid him only £5.

I was not afraid of blackmail and I sent an affidavit to the Attorney-General, requesting that the editors be prosecuted for criminal libel. Both were convicted on seven counts of criminal libel and also on five counts of public indecency. One was sentenced to twelve months' imprisonment and the other to six months', and their paper was closed down. Many business men thanked me and were deeply grateful that I had rid Johannesburg of a pest.

After the strike of 1931 most of the employers began to show hostility to the union and did all in their power to weaken the union and to hinder the officials in their work. During one of my routine visits to factories, I was chatting to a group of about a hundred garment workers, when the employer, who had formerly been friendly, became abusive. His brother, another director of the firm, rushed in, shouting: 'What did the *L.S.D.* say about you? If the girls knew what the *L.S.D.* said about you, you would not be secretary for long!' I told the gentleman that he would regret this slander and left the factory.

As a trade union leader I have always fought vigorously, often ruthlessly and perhaps crudely, for the cause of the workers who had elected me and whose misery I felt keenly; but I never indulged in personal abuse. The two brothers had, up to this time, utterly condemned the filthy attacks upon me in the *L.S.D.*, but now that relations in the industry had become disturbed, they readily drew on the slander published by that paper.

I issued a summons for defamation and the case was set down for hearing in the Witwatersrand Local Division of the Supreme Court. Before the case opened my counsel asked me whether I would be prepared to accept a settlement. I told him that I had no wish to proceed with the action, as the employer had been quite reasonable before this trouble started, and that I would be prepared to waive the claim for damages and agree to each party's paying its own costs. I wanted no formal apology, but merely that the employer should go to his workers and, in his own words, retract the statement. But it appeared the employers' association had now taken a hand in the matter and urged the employer not to settle the case, hoping that, if I lost, the damage to my reputation would deal a serious blow to Trade Unionism.

The proceedings lasted eight days and, under cross-examination, the employer showed up very poorly. I was awarded £75 damages and costs, which amounted to over £2,000. I was never happy about this case and it was only the obstinacy of the employers' association and the stupidity of the defendant that forced the issue.

CHAPTER TWELVE

The General Strike of 1931

THE WORLD-WIDE DEPRESSION, which started in 1929, had a serious effect on South African economic life. By 1930 industrial production, which was only in its infancy, began to decline and large-scale unemployment followed. As there was no social insurance of any kind in the country, the unemployed workers suffered great distress. For the hundreds of garment workers who had no savings at the back of them life became unbearable and many literally starved. The union spent large sums in buying essentials, such as flour, sugar and bread, for distribution among members, but our funds were totally inadequate to cope with the problem.

The agreement with the clothing industry expired early in 1931 and negotiations for a new agreement started under circumstances which were by no means favourable for the workers. The employers demanded a reduction of 25 per cent in wages and this demand was countered by a request from the union for a substantial increase in wages. During the years 1929-30, the union was very active and aroused a tremendous spirit of militancy among the workers. A great many small-scale strikes, involving one or two factories, had recently taken place, though most of them were not concerned with questions of wages and hours but directed against minor abuses prevalent in the industry at the time. Nearly all these strikes were successful and this helped to inspire the workers with confidence.

Negotiations between the union and the Transvaal Clothing Manufacturers' Association dragged on for months, and both sides were adamant. Finally, when complete deadlock was reached, a mass meeting of garment workers, attended by about twelve hundred, was called and the workers, with great enthusiasm, voted unanimously to come out in a general strike. Tactically, the strike may have been an error for, as a result of the depression, orders for garments to the factories declined considerably. There was a good deal of division, however, among the employers. Some of them were prepared not only to drop thc dcmand for a reduction in wages, but to consider minor increases.

In July 1931, 2,289 workers in Johannesburg and Germiston stopped work. There was not a single scab in their ranks. Fortunately we succeeded in splitting the employers and one of the largest manufacturers came to an agreement with the union to carry on work under the old conditions pending a settlement. This scabbing on the part of a large employer caused grave misgivings in the ranks of the manufacturers.

The union officials had ample experience in handling small strikes, but the general strike presented numerous unforeseen problems.

In Johannesburg about fifteen hundred strikers assembled at the union headquarters, where the largest hall could seat only seven hundred. As there were no scabs, there was no need for picket lines and we were faced with the problem of what to do with such a large crowd. It was essential to keep the workers together for the first few days of the strike at least, for we knew from experience that there was a much finer spirit amongst the workers when they were together than when they remained dispersed in their homes. Then there was the problem of feeding them. Nearly all the workers lived far away from the centre of the city and a trip home would have involved them in extra expense. Besides, most of the cupboards at home were bare.

A strike committee was elected and we promptly got down to business. Banners were hastily improvised and we led the strikers in a demonstration through the streets of Johannesburg, singing folk-songs and shouting slogans. The repertoire of labour songs in South Africa is very limited, but the workers soon made up songs of their own to the music of popular tunes. While the strikers were demonstrating, a group of highly efficient women hastily prepared sandwiches. But we were still faced with the problem of finding useful tasks for idle hands and the committee decided to organise teams to try and collect money for the strike.

At five o'clock every morning hundreds of women and a few men used to assemble at the Trades Hall and, from there, disperse along the Reef. We soon found that there was warm support for the strike among the miners, and small groups of women collectors would stand outside the mine shafts to meet the workers as they came off shift. Several hundred more strikers went round collecting in the city. The organisation of mass collections served several useful purposes. Firstly, it relieved the congestion at the Trades

Hall; secondly, it kept large numbers usefully occupied; thirdly, it brought in some much needed cash. Last, but not least, the young women collectors were able to rouse a great deal of public sympathy for the workers' cause.

The officials and the strike committee sat at the Trades Hall all day and usually till about midnight to await the return of the collectors and to hear and examine their reports. Generally the collectors were well received in the city, and only in a few instances did they meet with rudeness. The first day's collection brought in over £700, mostly in coin. The five hundred workers of the bespoke tailoring section, who were not on strike, unanimously resolved to donate 25 per cent of their weekly wages to the strike, but the response from the trade union movement as a whole was not very inspiring.

After about a week many of the workers dispersed to their homes, and only visited the union headquarters in order to sign the strike register. But hundreds of others came every day to Trades Hall, where they quickly got together a dance band and passed the time happily dancing to it. This caused considerable annoyance to the union officials and their staff who had their offices in the building.

The employers refused to yield, but the fact that one large factory carried on operations began to worry them considerably.

At this stage one of the union officials committed a grave tactical blunder. Before the strike the employers had agreed among themselves to help each other out in case of need. Accordingly many manufacturers, whose factories were on strike, began sending rolls of cloth to the unaffected factory to be made up into garments. The workers showed some ingenuity and, without any directives from the union, determined to thwart the efforts of the outside employers to get their orders executed. They mixed up the sizes of different parts of garments and often the colours, with the result that the finished articles presented a somewhat strange appearance, with one leg of a pair of trousers being of blue serge and the other of worsted grey, or a size three being sewn together with a size six. On one occasion the workers got up from their machines and threw the rolls of cloth into the street. The employers very naturally felt indignant, but there was nothing they could do. The union officials had to exert great pressure on the several hundred workers in the scab factory in order to stop them joining their fellow-workers who were on strike. It was very difficult for masses of young women workers to appreciate fully the advantages of 'divide and rule'. During the third week of the strike, in a moment of excitement and irresponsibility, one of the union officials led a demonstration of several hundred workers outside the scab factory. The demonstrators cheered and sang songs and the workers inside became restless. Suddenly, they got up from the machines, walked out and joined the strikers.

This was what the employers were waiting for. Now the whole industry was at a standstill and no employer could execute urgent orders. Signs of demoralisation also became apparent among many strikers who would continually ask: 'When are we going back to work?'

The situation became somewhat difficult for the union and fresh negotiations were opened with the employers. After several meetings an agreement was reached whereby the employers withdrew their demand for a reduction in wages and the union withdrew its demand for an increase. All that the workers received was a contribution of threepence a week to the voluntary sick fund of the union, which the employers undertook to pay. The workers returned to work with their spirit unbroken, but without the flush of victory.

The new agreement ended the strike but did not establish peaceful relations. It was due to expire after only nine months and both sides, though anxious to avoid trouble, fully expected another clash as soon as this happened and began to make their preparations accordingly. All the advantages were on the side of the employers. The economic position of the country had deteriorated still further, and most of the factories in the clothing industry were on short time. Unemployment was rife, with the result that union funds were soon seriously depleted and our position gradually grew weaker. Many individual employers began to show open hostility towards the union. Active trade unionists were dismissed and numerous obstacles were put in the way of union officials in the conduct of their work. In the ranks of the workers there was a good deal of apathy and demoralisation and many members stopped paying their contributions and lost interest.

On the other hand, three years of vigorous, militant trade union struggles led to hundreds of young Afrikaner women taking an active part in union work. The numerous small strikes, and more especially the general strike of 1931, did much to inspire confidence and a spirit of unity, loyalty and sacrifice among large numbers of workers. Many factories elected factory committees and shop stewards and these dealt actively and regularly with workers' complaints, enrolled new members and inculcated the spirit of trade unionism among their fellow-workers. Above all, the voice of the young workers began to make itself heard. Formerly they had been too shy and inarticulate; now one could hear women expressing with youthful exuberance the true spirit of trade unionism. Several of the more promising Afrikaner women were elected to the various committees of the union. At first they felt more at home leading demonstrations, addressing meetings of strikers or standing on the picket lines, and found the routine of committee meetings rather dull and monotonous. But gradually some of them began to understand the importance of committee work. Many Afrikaners, especially the women, are born orators. They cannot express themselves adequately in English, but in their own language they are magnificent and inspiring. The older men in the union soon changed their opinions about 'these girls' and, while the technical work of the union, such as finances and other purely administrative matters, still remained the preserve of the 'old guard', the spirit of the union, the fiery cross of trade unionism, the struggle for a new life and for social justice, were taken over entirely by the young girls from the Platteland.

CHAPTER THIRTEEN

General Strike 1932

LENGTHY NEGOTIATIONS took place between the union and the employers' association before the agreement expired in the middle of August 1932, but these proved futile. The employers again demanded a reduction of the workers' wages by 25 per cent to bring the wages on the Rand into line with coastal rates. The union, on the other hand, considered the existing wage for women workers of £1 a week to start, rising to £2 10*s.* a week after two and a half years, as quite inadequate. Four pounds a week was considered to be the minimum on which a woman worker could live. Whilst we realised that it was unrealistic to ask for this figure with the industry in its present parlous state, the union felt that any reduction in the existing wage would not only cause immediate hardship, but would also handicap any future efforts to secure a decent living wage.

At the beginning of August the employers issued a pamphlet to the workers, denouncing the union and urging the workers to accept the terms they offered. Scabs were promised police protection. The employers also made efforts to strengthen and unite their own ranks. This time, leaders of the employers displayed more vigour and confidence than in 1931. The union, on the other hand, entered the struggle not too hopeful of victory, but resolutely determined to fight to the bitter end against any lowering of standards and to go down fighting rather than surrender.

A strike committee was elected, composed almost exclusively of women workers. As the workers' ranks were divided, it was decided not to call a general strike, but to withdraw labour at first only from those factories where all, or the overwhelming majority, of the workers were loyal. Such tactics, we felt, might lead to a split among the employers and would not overtax the financial and organisational resources of the union. The workers who did not come out could give financial support to those who were on strike. Above all, we were not sure what the response to a general strike would be. Accordingly, acting on the reports of shop stewards, a group of about ten factories was chosen for strike action.

One Monday in August, on instructions from the union, the workers in the selected factories stopped work and assembled outside their respective premises to form picket lines. In one factory, where about a hundred and twenty workers were employed, the forewoman and two other workers tried to break through the picket line to go into the factory. The forewoman's sister, a girl of sixteen, was a militant striker and, when she saw her elder sister attempting to scab, she became furious. Saying 'I would rather see you dead than scab', she grabbed her and a scuffle ensued, with the older sister getting the worst of the argument. Within a few minutes, a lorry-load of police appeared, led by a brute of a sergeant. He tried to clear the entrance to the factory by force and, in the process, he violently slapped the face of a little woman striker who was standing by watching. She fell and the crowd of pickets became infuriated. Within a few minutes a fight had started between the girls and the police. Some of the police used their fists freely, others refrained from assaulting the infuriated women. It was early in the morning, but a large crowd soon collected. The sergeant, a big, hefty man, distinguished himself by knocking out about half a dozen women. The battle came to an end when the employer, a respectable Johannesburg merchant, arrived, begged the police to go away, and assured the pickets that no scabs would be employed in his factory.

The police remained, however, but within an hour the scene had changed completely. Nearly all the policemen were young Afrikaners and, like the girls they had been beating up, had been driven off the land through poverty to find employment in the cities as 'protectors of law and order'. The erstwhile combatants commiserated with each other, in a most friendly manner, the policemen pointing to scratches on their faces and to missing buttons on their tunics and the girls to their multiple injuries. A few nights later, twenty-two policemen turned up in 'mufti' at a strikers' dance and the bitterness of the fight outside the factory was forgotten in the music of the *boere orkes*, playing Afrikaans dance tunes. Nevertheless several of the girls were later arrested and convicted.

Once again the stupid action of the authorities in sending hordes of policemen to beat up girl strikers had an entirely different result from the one they expected. The strikers became embittered and even more determined; would-be scabs lost their nerve, and the employers were filled with fear lest disturbances occur outside their factories. Most important of all was the effect of the police action on the mass of workers. Hundreds of apathetic and even hostile garment workers were roused to action. Public sympathy, too, was on our side. For several weeks the strike continued on its stormy course, more factories being called out or coming out of their own accord. The employers, determined to break the strike, sent out teams to recruit scabs and picketing became extremely important.

Our fortunes fluctuated. In some cases the employers succeeded in getting their workers back to the factories. In others workers who had at first refused to come out now joined the strikers. In Johannesburg almost the entire industry was brought to a standstill, but in Germiston there were hundreds of scabs. We therefore decided to back up the strikers in Germiston by sending pickets from Johannesburg. The employers were beginning to feel worried. On Monday, the 4th September, the strike committee decided to proclaim a general strike in the industry and notices to that effect were posted up on all factories. The response was good and the prospects of a negotiated settlement seemed fair. We knew that we could not expect a victory and would have agreed to call off the strike on the old conditions.

Suddenly Mr Oswald Pirow, then Minister of Justice in the Nationalist Government, began to take a hand in the strike. There was a by-election pending in Germiston and the Nationalist Party was anxious to win the seat. Pirow feared that the strike might impair the chances of his party. Here were masses of Afrikaner women fighting against starvation wages, and the Nationalist Government, the so-called friend of the Afrikaner people, was doing nothing to help them. Germiston is largely a working-class district and most of the garment workers were the daughters, wives or sisters of miners, railway workers and labourers. The workers' vote would be decisive. Pirow, instead of trying to gain the workers' support for the Nationalist Party by showing sympathy for them, decided to use ruthless methods to break the strike. Large numbers of foot and mounted police were mobilised to protect scabs and break the picket lines. Scores of girls were arrested and, in Germiston, a group of mounted police rode into a crowd of pickets and several girls were badly injured. This high-handed action caused widespread indignation among the workers of Germiston and thousands attended a mass meeting called by the union to protest against Pirow's action. On one occasion we received a message that two young girls had been arrested in Germiston. The union solicitor and I called at the Germiston police station to try and find out the nature of the charges and to secure their release on bail. The sergeant in charge was not only very abusive, but threatened to arrest me if I did not 'get out'. That night I addressed a public meeting in a hall in Germiston which is meant to hold about five hundred people, but over a thousand crowded into it. I had been on duty since three a.m. that day and, at seven-thirty p.m., when I arrived, I was so exhausted that I could hardly stand, but the hall, including the platform, was so crowded that there was no room to collapse. Incensed by the outrageous attitude of the police, I told the audience that, while we were holding the meeting, two young girls were being kept in jail and terrorised and that the police refused to release them on bail. A wave of anger swept the crowd and they wanted to storm the jail there and then. I appealed to them to try peaceful means first and a deputation of five was appointed to secure the girls' release. The crowd shouted in Afrikaans to the members of the deputation before they left: 'Bring the two girls here or we shall come and fetch them.'

The meeting lasted for hours and sometime after eleven p.m. the two girls were brought in, half asleep. Their release had been obtained only when the deputation informed the police of the mood of the crowd. When they were hauled on to the platform, there was a roar of cheering which nearly brought the roof down. They were asked to say a few words.

Gertie Guites, who looked about fifteen, made a short speech in English, which was very well received.

Then came Johanna Cornelius, a young girl from Lichtenburg, dressed in a school blazer, dark and attractive. She spoke in Afrikaans and told the crowd what the girls were fighting for:

> We Afrikaner girls, the daughters of our fathers who fought for freedom, are not frightened of Mr Pirow and his police. We are tired of slaving for a few pence and of starvation, and will carry on the fight for a living wage to the bitter end. The police threatened us and said that we would be charged with murder. But we are not afraid. Our fathers rebelled for freedom, and we are their daughters.

When she finished, there was tense silence in the hall, broken only by sobbing. Johanna is a born speaker, and I saw immediately that here was a girl who, given the opportunity, could become a great leader. And a leader she became. Twenty years later, when the Malan Government removed me from my position as general secretary, Johanna Cornelius was elected by an overwhelming majority general secretary of the Garment Workers' Union against a Nationalist opponent, and this position she still holds. Like many other Afrikaner women, Johanna began her trade union education on the picket line and in prison.

Pirow, meanwhile, was busy with the employers. Years later one of the leading employers of Germiston told me that Pirow had called the Germiston employers to a private meeting and had told them that the strike was having a serious effect on the by-election and must be settled. The employers had said that they were willing to settle the strike, but Sachs was the obstacle, whereupon Pirow promised to deal with me.

A few days later, on a Sunday night, at about eleven o'clock, there was a knock on the door of my flat. Two men entered and introduced themselves as Mr Moll, Transvaal organiser of the Nationalist Party, and Mr Wentzel, also a leading Nationalist. When I asked them the purpose of this nocturnal visit, Mr Moll told me that they had come to ask me to settle the strike. I told them that nothing would give me greater pleasure than to have the strike settled. The workers would return to work immediately, providing they were assured that their wages would not be cut.

Mr Moll informed me that if I did not settle the strike Mr Pirow would deal with me. I explained to them the terrible hardships which thousands of Afrikaner girls had to endure in the factories and suggested that here was an opportunity for the Nationalist Government, which claimed to be the only friend of the Afrikaner people, to show its sympathy for masses of suffering Afrikaners. I told them that in no circumstances would I advise the workers to accept a cut in wages nor was I going to be intimidated by Pirow's threats. The two spokesmen of the Nationalist Party however were interested solely in the results of the Germiston by-election. The poverty and suffering of large masses of workers did not concern them in the least.

Then, for the first time, Mr Pirow and the Nationalist press introduced the communist bogy into South African politics and exploited it on a big scale in the Hitler fashion. The grave economic problems that were facing the country, the mass unemployment and starvation, were completely ignored. At political meetings in Germiston, the 'menace of communism' was flogged to death and I, of course, was held up as the 'arch-communist conspirator', out to destroy white civilisation and put the 'kaffirs' in power. It was well known that I had been expelled from the Communist Party in September 1931—my expulsion and the expulsion of others had received widespread publicity—but facts and truths have never bothered the unscrupulous politicians of the Nationalist Party. These Nazi tactics failed in their purpose and the Nationalist candidate was hopelessly defeated by Mr J. G. N. Strauss, who is today the leader of the United Party, the major opposition party in South Africa. The union leaders had asked the people of Germiston to show their disgust with Mr Pirow and his mounted police by voting against his candidate, and they responded magnificently.

The struggle against wage cuts continued for two months under the greatest difficulties. The funds of the union grew desperately low and, at the beginning of October, we were only in a position to pay a few shillings a week strike pay. At one meeting called by the strike committee to discuss the critical situation hundreds of women workers got up and offered to give up the money to which they were entitled so that their few shillings could be given to those who had children to support.

Starvation, physical exhaustion, lack of adequate support from the rest of the trade union movement and, last but not least, police violence, sapped our strength and, by the middle of October, there were only five hundred workers left out of a total of three thousand who were prepared to carry on the fight to the bitter end. We saw that we had no hope of winning and resolved to surrender as a defeated army, rather than allow the strike to fizzle out. By the middle of October, Colonel F. H. P. Creswell, leader of the Labour Party, who was then Minister of Labour in the Nationalist Government, intervened—not on the side of the workers—and suggested that the workers should return to work and the dispute should be submitted to arbitration. We put the position clearly to the strikers and left the decision to them. We stressed the fact that we had no confidence in the arbitrator whom the Nationalist Government would appoint, but also emphasised that our forces were exhausted and that, by accepting arbitration, we would at least go back as an organised body. I remember addressing a meeting of several hundred strikers in Germiston one night in an open field, which was almost in complete darkness. I put the position squarely to them. Scores were in tears, heart-broken, but I could see that, although we had lost the struggle, they were still full of courage.

Defeat was terrible to accept, yet there was no choice but to agree to arbitration. We knew that all our efforts would be futile, yet we worked hard to prepare our case. The Government appointed a single arbitrator, the late Mr Britten, Chief Magistrate of Johannesburg. He gave the impression of being a devout Christian gentleman, but completely ignored the plea of the union and gave an award 100 per cent in favour of the employers. The employers had withdrawn their demand for a 25 per cent reduction in wages, but had insisted on a 10 per cent cut. In his anxiety to help the employers the arbitrator had first issued an award which, in effect, meant a reduction in wages in excess of 10 per cent but when we drew his attention to the fact that he was going beyond the terms of reference, he amended his award. It was all a foregone conclusion, but at least we signed the 'terms of surrender' as a union.

But Mr Pirow was not satisfied with the crushing defeat he had helped to inflict on the workers and, on Saturday morning, 5th November 1932, when I came to the Trades Hall, Detective-Sergeant Toerien served me with an order, which read:

To:

EMIL SOLOMON SACHS

In terms of the provisions of sub-section (12) of Section One of Act No. 27 of 1914 as amended by section One of Act No. 19 of 1930, you are hereby notified that WHEREAS I find that you are creating feelings of hostility between the European inhabitants of the Union on the one hand and the Coloured and Native inhabitants, on the other hand, in the Magisterial districts of Benoni, Boksburg, Brakpan, Germiston, Johannesburg, Krugersdorp and Springs, in the Province of the Transvaal, I HEREBY prohibit you from being present within the aforementioned Magisterial districts of Benoni, Boksburg, Brakpan, Germiston, Johannesburg, Krugersdorp and Springs, in the province of the Transvaal, for a period of twelve months as from the seventh day after the delivery or tender to you of this notice.

O. PIROW,
Minister of Justice

I had devoted years of my life to the promotion of harmony between the European and non-European members of the Union and now, without any semblance of a trial, without even a hearing, I was told peremptorily to get out of the Witwatersrand for a period of twelve months because I was creating inter-racial hostility. Such tyranny had to be fought at all costs. Pirow's action caused widespread indignation, not only in the ranks of the trade union movement, but among all fair-minded people.

I decided to make application to the Supreme Court to have the order set aside and engaged the services of Colonel C. F. Stallard, K.C., then leader of the Transvaal Bar, who, in addition to being a lawyer of outstanding ability, was also an active politician, conversant with the South African political structure. I knew that the decision of the court would be of great importance, not only to me personally, but that it would vitally affect the liberty of every citizen in South Africa.

On Tuesday, the 24th November 1932, my application was heard in the Transvaal Provincial Division of the Supreme Court before Judges de Waal, Tindall and Barry (*E. S. Sachs* v. *O. Pirow*, N.O., 1933 T.P.D. pp. 141-169). J. Murray, K.C., now Justice Murray, a formidable opponent, appeared for Pirow.

Judge Tindall and Judge Barry were both lawyers of great ability, who had long maintained the high tradition of the South African Bench. I did not like Judge de Waal, who had been one of the judges of the Special Criminal Court which, in 1922, had passed the death sentence on Taffy Long, the miners' leader.

The three judges in Pretoria gave judgment in favour of the Minister, but awarded me a portion of the costs.

I gave notice of appeal to the Appellate Division of the Supreme Court and, on the 26th September 1933, the appeal was heard before A. C. J. Stratford, J. A. Beyers, J. A. de Villiers and A. J. A. Gardner. I had no money to engage the services of senior counsel, and Advocate Julius Lewin, who is now Senior Lecturer in Native Law and Administration at the University of the Witwatersrand, very kindly appeared on my behalf *pro deo*; Mr J. Murray, K.C., again appeared for the Minister. My appeal was dismissed. (*E. S. Sachs* v. *O. Pirow*, N.O., 1934 A.D. p. 11)

The banishment order against me was, however, never enforced. Early in 1933 General Smuts became Minister of Justice and he withdrew the order.

On the 17th December 1932 the Transvaal Provincial Division of the Supreme Court dismissed my application to set aside Mr Pirow's banishment order. A few days later, Mr Justice Barry, in the Witwatersrand Local Division of the Supreme Court, gave judgment in my action for defamation (see page 82) and awarded me £75 damages with costs. Months of intensive struggle had left me exhausted and, as the time was not propitious for attempting to revive the union, I left for England to recuperate. I intended to tackle the big task of rebuilding the union with renewed energy on my return.

Mr Pirow, however, was determined to harass me and, when I landed in Southampton, I was declared an 'undesirable alien' and detained in Bargate Gaol in Southampton for five days. No one could tell me why I was detained, but from one of the detectives I learned that the authorities had received a request for my detention from South Africa. The British Trade Union Congress intervened and I was released. I spent a few weeks in London and then went to Berlin, where I stayed for a momentous week, when Adolf Hitler was appointed Reichs-Chancellor of Germany on 30th January 1933.

CHAPTER FOURTEEN

Rebuilding the Union – Conciliation

When I returned to South Africa in March 1933 I found the stillness of the grave in the union office. The mass of workers in the factory section had lost interest in the union and were completely demoralised. The few hundred members who had borne the brunt of the struggle were exhausted. In the bespoke section the majority of the workers continued paying the union contributions, but there was widespread apathy. The prolonged and bitter struggle, however, had thrown up a small group of Afrikaner women workers, at the head of whom stood Johanna Cornelius, who were prepared to do all they could to rebuild the union. For a few weeks, hardly any members called at the office and it was almost impossible to address workers in the factories. The employers were bitterly hostile and active trade unionists suffered badly from victimisation.

The union resolved on two lines of action. First, we started injecting life and activity into the bespoke section, which had not taken any direct part in the strike, and undertook an energetic campaign to enforce the provisions of the agreement. This led to several successful prosecutions, whilst substantial amounts of back-pay were also collected without court action. Every little victory helped to re-establish confidence and inspire hope.

In the factory section a lengthy appeal was addressed to individual workers at their homes, and this was followed by numerous home visits. Over four hundred workers' homes were visited by officials and volunteers, and everywhere the representatives of the union were cordially received. Hundreds of workers who had left the union rejoined, and many of them soon became active again. Like many other countries South Africa began to recover from the depression and, when the country went off the gold standard at the end of 1932, industrial development was stimulated. New factories sprang up and some of the older ones expanded production. This improved the employment position and made the workers a little more independent.

When the Britten arbitration award expired in 1933 negotiations were started between the union and the employers for a new agreement. We felt that time could wipe out the feeling of hostility between the employers and the union which had been created by the strike, but some employers resolutely refused all dealings with the union. Gradually, however, the atmosphere became more friendly and the employers offered a 5 per cent increase in wages on the scale laid down in the arbitration award. The representatives of the union pressed for a return to the old wage scale, but the employers were adamant. I had come to the conclusion that it was far more important to rebuild the union than to try to obtain a 5 per cent increase for, once the union was strong again, we would be in a position to demand higher wages and better conditions. I also knew that any improvement we could secure for the workers would have a tremendous effect on their morale and would inspire confidence in the union once again. Above all, I was quite convinced that we had neither the forces nor the means with which to start another strike. The majority of the central executive committee, including Johanna Cornelius, opposed my advice and insisted that we should take strike action. The union has always been based on true democratic principles and we decided to call a general meeting and let the members decide whether to accept the offer of the employers or to go on strike for a 10 per cent increase. About four hundred members attended and both points of view were fully discussed. A secret ballot was taken and, by a majority of more than two to one, the meeting decided to accept the employers' offer. An agreement was entered into and, once the workers saw that the union could still further their interests, they started flocking back. Within six months, about 90 per cent of the workers, over three thousand altogether, were members of the union.

On 16th July 1934 the members of the Bespoke Tailoring Section seceded from the Garment Workers' Union and registered a union of their own, known as the Tailoring Workers' Industrial Union. There were several reasons for the breakaway. The most active members in the factory section, consisting almost entirely of young Afrikaner women who had played a leading rôle in the two general strikes and in many other disputes, began to find the 'paternal' attitude of the men in the bespoke section irksome and unbearable. On the other hand the men were overburdened with difficulties of their own and could no longer be bothered with the numerous problems of the factory section. At joint general meetings the women workers often felt disgusted with the attitude of the tailoring workers, who were habitually bickering and frequently engaged in petty quarrels, without giving due attention to the business on the agenda. There were also many personal intrigues, which are not worth recording. The workers in the bespoke tailoring industry had a different background and different traditions from those in the clothing section and their industrial agreements provided for higher rates of pay and better conditions generally than the agreements for the clothing industry. Matters came to a head when Johanna Cornelius and a large group of shop stewards from the factory section advised me that, unless the two sections separated, the shop stewards would resign, as they would no longer tolerate the intrigues and quarrels of the bespoke workers. By mutual agreement the clothing section took over the union, and the tailoring section was given an adequate amount of the union's funds to enable it to start on its own. In the main both sections benefited from the secession, as it allowed each group of workers to devote all their attention to their respective problems. In subsequent years the relationship between the Tailoring Workers' Industrial Union and the Garment Workers' Union has been, in the main, cordial and co-operative. There have been minor conflicts between the two bodies, but they never assumed serious proportions or lasted very long.

In 1934 a new era began for the clothing industry and for the workers. The economic position of the country had improved considerably and secondary industries began to attract large capital investments. A number of large, up-to-date factories were built and the modern capitalist employers began to play a leading rôle in the industry. They realised that they could not build an industry, make profits and pay dividends by pilfering from the workers' wages; the more intelligent ones also saw that the industry would never develop satisfactorily by producing shoddy garments and that the quality of production would have to be improved considerably if they were to find buyers. Their attitude to the union and to the workers changed too. Strikes and disputes are very costly for the employer and the advantages of having contented workers soon became apparent. These new capitalists were anxious to eliminate unfair competitors and to stop the practices of the unscrupulous employers who thrived by robbing their workers. The cut-make-and-trim manufacturers, who accepted very low contract rates from merchants, were also in unfair competition with the big manufacturers, and the union, in co-operation with the employers' association, helped the cut-make-and-trim people to organise and secure fair contract rates.

The union did not abandon its militant policy, but decided to take advantage of the new circumstances and make full use of conciliation in order to secure the maximum benefits for the workers. The Industrial Council for the Clothing Industry, which had ceased to function during the strike of 1932, was re-established and, in due course, the conciliation machinery for the industry began to operate extremely well. The employers' representatives on the council were as determined to enforce the provisions of the agreement and to eliminate underpayments as the union. Indeed, for several years, while still secretary of the union, I was appointed director of the council, with power to enforce observance of all the provisions of the agreement.

Most of the employers now adopted a friendly attitude towards the union and gave union officials every help in the organisation of the workers and in the collection of contributions.

Within a few years a closed shop provision was inserted in the agreement. Much criticism, most of it based on ignorance, has been levelled against the closed shop. The attitude of the workers, who are members of unions, in the matter is simple and logical. They say:

> We, through our efforts, struggles and sacrifice, have secured improved conditions, from which all workers in the industry benefit. We would never have succeeded if we had not had a strong union. Our union is democratic and under the direct control of the membership. We, therefore, expect every worker to become a member. A worker has a perfect right to refuse to join, but we, on our part, also have the same right to refuse to work with him.

The closed shop provision never caused the slightest trouble to the workers or employers in the clothing industry. Indeed, the employers preferred to deal with an organised body and not to be bothered with individual members, and the only violent opposition to the closed shop principle emanated not from employers, but from the Nationalist Party. In 1949 Mr B. J. Schoeman, the

Nationalist Minister of Labour, refused to gazette an agreement for the clothing industry because it contained a closed shop provision. We were not in the least perturbed and advised the employers that we were quite prepared to have the agreement gazetted without the closed shop provision, but the employers insisted on its inclusion. At about the same time a number of workers, under the influence of Nationalists, began to make mischief in the ranks of the union. The central executive committee of the union issued a circular to all members, advising them that those who did not wish to be members of the union were free to resign and that the union would not enforce the closed shop provision. Not one member resigned.

Workers' complaints were promptly attended to by the union or the council and this helped to establish and increase the confidence of the workers in the union. On the other hand, the making of agreements always presented difficulties. Many of the employers have often proved generous, as individuals, but as a body their loyalty to class interests dominated their outlook. Since 1934 about twenty industrial agreements have been made between the Garment Workers' Union and the Transvaal Clothing Manufacturers' Association. The agreements were usually for one year and, on almost every occasion, negotiations broke down because of the employers' adamant attitude. When the terms of an agreement were accepted, it was nearly always under the threat of strike action.

The Garment Workers' Union may claim, with every justification, to have had the the 'best of two worlds'. We are very proud of the numerous strikes we led in the past and of our militant tradition; but we are also not ashamed of having taken full advantage of conciliation and the labour laws of the country. Leaders of the union continually impressed on the workers the need for building a great industry and for producing garments of good quality and workmanship; on the other hand we always demanded a just share for our members in the prosperity which their efforts had helped to create.

The Industrial Council for the Clothing Industry, Transvaal, became a model of efficiency in preventing and settling disputes. Several full-time inspectors were employed and paid by the Council to inspect wage registers and to enforce strict observance of agreements. Disputes were dealt with promptly and efficiently.

A Complaints Sub-Committee was elected by the Council to deal with all minor disputes and this body would meet regularly, often at an hour's notice, to hear complaints from workers and employers. Red tape and legal technicalities were eliminated and the decisions of the committee were invariably accepted by the parties to the dispute. In case of a deadlock on the committee or where a question of principle was involved, the matter would be referred to a full council meeting. The union and the employers' association co-operated to promote peace and the welfare of the industry generally.

From 1936 onwards employer-employee relationship in the industry was excellent, and there was all-round progress. Workers' efficiency and productivity increased enormously, factory organisation improved, the industry began to produce better quality garments and all connected with the industry began to feel that we were entering a period of prosperity, progress and peace.

Our hopes for a peaceful future were soon dashed to the ground when two problems peculiar to South Africa began to make their impact felt upon the industry and the economic life of the country generally.

Large numbers of non-Europeans began to enter the factories, and this brought us face to face with the crucial problem of race relations in industry. This problem however was soon resolved to the benefit of Europeans and non-Europeans. The second problem robbed our union, our industry, our entire country of peace and tranquillity. The rise of Nazism in Europe had a tremendous influence on the political development of South Africa, and from 1933 onwards certain sections of the Nationalist Party enthusiastically embraced Nazi philosophy, policy and technique.

The rest of the book is devoted to those two problems. After 1936 the history of the Garment Workers' Union is no longer one of bitter struggles over wages and conditions; our everyday economic problems were solved in a peaceful, unexciting manner. Henceforth, while not neglecting this important aspect of our job as a Trade Union, we had to concentrate all our energy and attention on maintaining racial harmony in the industry and on countering the furious attack of the Nationalists upon our union, the trade union movement as a whole and democracy itself.

CHAPTER FIFTEEN

The African Worker – A Policeman and Pair of Handcuffs always Waiting

THE BASIS of South African national policy for the last sixty years has been the maintenance of a vast reservoir of cheap African labour for the farms and mines owned by Europeans. The African people are attached to their homes and normally have no desire to leave them, but successive Union governments have introduced various methods to 'persuade' Africans to become labourers for Europeans. In the nineteenth century a poll tax and a hut tax were imposed, not only as fiscal measures, but also to compel the African to work for wages. Since African agricultural economy is too poor to yield even a bare minimum subsistence, adult males were forced to take employment with Europeans in order to meet these tax obligations, which had to be paid in cash. According to the report of the Industrial Legislation Commission of Enquiry (U.G. 62, 1951, par. 151), in 1936 the per capita annual income of 45 per cent of the Africans who lived in Reserves was £2 16*s.* 7*d.* For an African to pay two kinds of taxes, amounting to about 30*s.* a year, out of such a pittance was an impossibility, and he could escape going to gaol only by selling his labour to some white master.

In 1913 the Native Land Act was passed, which divided the entire country into 'black' and 'white' areas. Europeans were prohibited from holding land in areas demarcated as 'black' and Africans from holding land in areas demarcated as 'white'. However, a 'slight' arithmetical error crept into the process of demarcation. Seven per cent of the land was assigned to the African people—more than two-thirds of the population—and the balance to the Europeans. The act was obviously designed to dispossess the Africans of their land, create overcrowding among them, and thus force large numbers of them to become labourers. Corporations were established throughout the country to recruit Africans for work on farms and mines. Today there are nearly one million African agricultural labourers, and over four hundred thousand are herded in compounds on the mines. There they have to live like cattle, deprived of social and cultural amenities, away from their families, with no possibility of advancement. The average annual cash wage for African agricultural workers is under £30, for mine workers about £47—roughly one-twentieth of the wages of the European miners, who do not consider themselves overpaid. The cash earnings of Africans in the mines sixty years ago were about £55 per year. Considering the lowered purchasing power of the pound, the real wages of African miners are now less than half what they were in the nineties of the last century. Through a number of oppressive measures the mine owners have succeeded in keeping the wages of African miners down to a minimum.

In the last thirty years large numbers of non-Europeans, African, Coloured and Indian, have left the rural areas for the towns.

The process of urbanisation among Asians has been relatively more rapid than among other racial groups, followed by that of Europeans, whose ratio of urbanisation is the greatest. In absolute figures, urbanised non-Europeans outnumber Europeans considerably, in spite of the policies of segregation, repression and restriction enforced by successive Union governments.

The following table shows the increase in the number of workers in each racial group in the manufacturing industries during the period 1925-48.

TOTAL NUMBER OF WAGE EARNERS (ACCORDING TO RACE) EMPLOYED IN THE MANUFACTURING INDUSTRIES, 1925-48.

Table No. 23A, p. 18, *same report.*

	Europeans	*Africans*	*Asiastics*	*Coloured*
1925	56,433	82,608	10,026	27,391
1930	73,193	90,467	9,482	27,179
1935	92,919	112,091	9,879	27,352
1940	114,272	161,765	13,897	40,442
1945	128,071	245,538	17,492	53,205
1948	162,201	307,597	18,003	74,487

The total number of workers (all races) grew from 176,458 to 562,288 and the number of all non-European workers from 120,025 to 400,087.

According to the report (January 1954) published by Dr Guy Routh, PH.D., Secretary of the Industrial Council for the Clothing Industry, Transvaal, the labour force in the clothing industry in the Union of South Africa during the period 1937-8 to 1952 grew as follows:

	1937-8	*1952*
European males	985	1,503
European females	8,896	10,406
Coloured and Asiatic males	1,509	4,850
Coloured and Asiatic females	3,441	17,953
African males	1,228	3,214
African females	101	2,497
TOTAL	16,160	40,423

This shows that the number of European workers rose from 9,881 in 1937-8 to 11,909 in 1952 and that, during the same period, the number of non-European workers rose from a total of 6,269 to 28,574. The proportion of Europeans, however, fell from 61·2 per cent in 1937-8 to 29·4 per cent in 1952, while the proportion of non-Europeans rose from 38·8 per cent to 70·6 per cent.

For the clothing industry in the Transvaal Province alone, the figures are as follows:

	1937-8	*1953* (*August*)
European males	569	412
European females	5,923	7,333
Coloured and Asiatic males	73	550
Coloured and Asiatic females	250	5,767
African males	1,101	2,631
African females	8	2,742
TOTAL	7,924	19,435

These figures show the following:

(1) In 1937-8 the non-European workers constituted only about 22 per cent of the total in the Transvaal. In 1953 they formed 60 per cent.

(2) The number of European workers increased from 6,492 to 7,745.

(3) A very big increase in the number of African women workers, also in the number of Coloured and Indian workers.

(4) A decrease in the number of European men workers.

It is now common knowledge that the efficiency and productivity of the non-European workers, as well as the European workers, increased considerably over the years. According to the widespread opinions held by Europeans, including many trade union leaders, the influx of non-Europeans into industry and their advancement in skill and efficiency should have led to a decline in the standards of the European workers and to their dismissal and replacement by non-Europeans. The facts show an entirely different picture.

The following figures are taken from Dr Routh's report. They exclude African males, who are not 'employees' and not covered by the industrial agreements for the clothing industry. Figures for Germiston are not given either, and apparently they were not available; but this is of no consequence as Germiston is, in all respects, identical with the rest of the Transvaal, except that, in that centre, about 2,000 Europeans are employed, as against only a few hundred Coloured workers. The inclusion of Germiston would in no way affect the conclusions to be drawn.

TABLE VI:

Average Weekly Wages, Transvaal (excluding Germiston)

	1941 £ *s. d.*	*1942* £ *s. d.*	*1943* £ *s. d.*	*1945* £ *s. d.*
European males	6 10 11	8 0 8	9 2 6	10 11 1
European females	2 15 7	3 5 6	3 17 4	4 8 8
Coloured and Asiatic males	2 0 0	3 4 4	4 12 10	6 7 9
Coloured and Asiatic females	—	2 2 10	2 10 10	3 7 8

	Average Weekly Wages, Transvaal (excluding Germiston)		*Wage Board Figures (including Germiston)*
	1946 £ *s. d.*	*1947* £ *s. d.*	*1955* £ *s. d.*
European males	10 8 4	11 2 0	—
European females	4 18 4	5 2 0	7 8 9
Coloured and Asiatic males	7 6 9	7 6 0	—
Coloured and Asiatic females	3 8 3	4 0 1	6 14 4

These figures prove conclusively that the usual theories which are brought forward, in order to give a reason for excluding Africans from industry, have no basis at all in fact and that industrial and economic development follows its own course and laws. There is nothing singular about the clothing industry and a study of the development of any other manufacturing industry in South Africa will show a similar trend, establishing beyond a shadow of doubt that the introduction of non-European workers into industry and the rise in their standard of living which must inevitably result, constitutes no danger at all to the white worker; on the contrary it benefits all sections. It should be observed that the minimum wages, as laid down in the industrial agreements for the industry, cover all workers except African males, and the disparity in wage rates, as between Europeans and non-Europeans and between males and females, is explained by the following:

The basic factors governing wage rates are the standard of living of the various groups of workers and their productivity. The two naturally go together. Even in mass-producing industries there are different classes of work, which may be roughly divided into various categories—highly skilled, skilled, operative or semi-skilled, and unskilled.

In the clothing industry the first category includes cutting and designing; the second, tailoring by hand (e.g. basting, shaping, fitting etc.), and the machining of the better class of garments, such as men's coats and jackets and ladies' coats and costumes; the operative and semi-skilled would include all plain and patent machining or machining of one or two parts of a garment only, machining trousers, ladies' dresses and blouses, more simple operations of hand tailoring, pressing, machine cutting etc.; unskilled work is confined to cleaning, i.e. cutting off ends, folding, affixing labels or tickets, etc.

In the manufacturing industries, there is no legal colour bar and non-European workers may perform any class of work. In practice, however, every racial group fits into industry according to its standard of development and living, education, industrial training, cultural background, tradition, none of which are the attributes of any particular racial group.

We find the following distribution of workers in the clothing industry: the head cutters and designers are generally men and women from Europe, with a long industrial tradition and highly specialised training. But many Afrikaner men and women have, over a period of years, acquired sufficient training and skill to do cutting and designing and recently a few Coloured workers have succeeded in entering this branch of the industry. The second category is composed largely of Jewish tailors and machiners, but a substantial number of Afrikaner men, Malay workers who have a craft tradition, and even some Coloured and Indian men workers, have also successfully undertaken this work. The operative or semi-skilled work is performed almost entirely by women, the more difficult operations and the work on the better quality garments being performed by European or Coloured women, who have had a longer experience in the industry and possess a higher degree of skill. The more simple work of this nature and the work on the cheaper class of garments, such as shirts, khaki trousers, cheap suits and work-wear, is done by the less efficient Europeans and the mass of Coloured, Indian and African women workers, who have come into the industry comparatively recently. There is nothing predestined or immutable about this process and, in time to come, workers of all racial groups will be able to perform all classes of work, including the highly skilled and skilled.

In earnings we observe a similar tendency. All workers must receive not less than the legal minimum, but about half of the European workers, men and women, and a number of Coloured workers, which I would estimate at about 10 per cent of the total, receive from 5 per cent to 75 per cent above the minimum. This is reflected particularly in factories which operate a bonus system. The more oppression the workers of the different racial groups suffer, the lower is their standard of living, and the less is their opportunity of entering industry and acquiring skill and efficiency. Experience has shown that skill and efficiency are not determined by the colour of a worker's skin, but only by the opportunities afforded to him or her to advance.

Of course trade union action and the general economic development of the country played major rôles in improving wages, but oppression and lack of opportunity are coincidental with race and colour in South Africa. Hence the lower wages for non-Europeans.

The statistics of the office of the Industrial Council for the Clothing Industry, Transvaal, also show that, in times of trade recession, the tendency on the part of employers is to dismiss non-Europeans and retain or engage the services of Europeans.

An African who comes from the land to an industrial area is faced with difficulties which few can appreciate. He is not only a stranger in the big city, he is an outcast subject to countless oppressive laws and regulations. His own black skin is his mark of inferiority, of cruel oppression, of helotry. The cultural, social and civic amenities are not for him. Wherever he turns, he sees notices displayed: 'for Europeans only.' If he is tired, he cannot sit down on a bench in the street or in a park, for it is marked: 'Slegs vir Blankes' (for Whites only); should he feel hungry or thirsty, he cannot enter a restaurant or café. He would be thrown out. He cannot use the public convenience and will often have to walk miles to find one marked: 'Non-Europeans.' He cannot even walk on the pavement without the risk of being kicked off by some brute. No hotel will admit him and, in all but a few towns, he will not be allowed to use the same public transport as white citizens. He must travel in a bus or tram marked 'Native' and these run at long intervals and are intolerably overcrowded during peak hours. He may, in theory, sit upstairs in one of the few seats at the back of a European bus; but, if the conductor is one of those ill-mannered 'saviours of white civilisation'—and most conductors in the Transvaal are—he will not be allowed to board the public vehicle at all and will often be pushed off. The African does not even enjoy the 'privilege' of sleeping under the bridge or in the park. The law in effect considers an African a vagrant until he proves that he is not, and vagrancy is a crime. Under the various Urban Areas Acts he is prohibited from residing in the city altogether, unless he is a domestic servant, and then he may only live on his employer's premises. He must carry numerous passes and is liable to be stopped by any policeman, white or black, and be asked to produce them. Should one be missing, he is arrested and usually sent to gaol, as he cannot afford to pay the fine of £1 or £2. While seeking work he must have a work permit and, if he cannot find employment within a few days, he may be considered a vagrant. His permit may be extended, or he may be deported, not necessarily back to his home. If he wishes to avoid conviction he can accept work as a labourer for some white farmer. He usually finds lodging with some friends in a location, an area reserved exclusively for Africans, or in some Native township. These are invariably overcrowded, and lack the ordinary communal amenities, such as sanitation, lighting etc. The overwhelming majority of urban Africans are forced to live in slums, compared with which the worst slums in Europe and America would seem luxurious. Even if the African has enough money to build himself a decent house, he cannot do so, for he is not allowed to own any land in urban areas. In addition entire African communities may, at any time, be uprooted from the land on which they have lived for years and transplanted elsewhere. Some municipalities, among which Port Elizabeth is most prominent, have given much attention to the housing of Africans; but, in the main, the scandalous housing conditions for Africans in urban areas are examples of criminal neglect on the part of their European 'masters'. Even in his shanty town the African does not enjoy peace. For many years it has been a regular habit for the police to raid African homes in the middle of the night, usually on a Saturday. The pretext is the search for illicit liquor, or passes, or tax receipts, but the real motive is to show the African that, at any time, night or day, the white man is absolute master.

In the eyes of most Europeans the African can never do anything right. If he is illiterate and dresses shabbily, he is a 'dirty kaffir'. Should he acquire some education and dress and speak like a European his efforts will not be praised. On the contrary he is 'the cheeky kaffir, who thinks that he is a white man'. If he tries to be friendly he is 'impudent'. If he expresses resentment at the abuse constantly hurled at him he is again 'cheeky' and is often beaten up and arrested. If he shows neither friendliness nor resentment, but silently bears his suffering with the proud dignity so common among Africans, then he is regarded as simply 'one of those kaffirs you cannot trust, who are always treacherous and dishonest'.

The African is shackled with so many laws and regulations that it is impossible for him to obey them all. About one million are sent to gaol every year—a very high proportion. But what is really surprising is how the other millions succeed in keeping out of gaol. According to figures published in the Official Year Book No. 25 (p. 444), the number of Africans convicted in 1949 of petty 'crimes' alone, was as follows:

Trespass	57,028
Drunkenness	65,257
Possession of illicit liquor	137,913
Breaking location rules	32,288
Master and Servants Act	18,397
Municipal offences	38,360
Native Labour Regulations Act	10,509
Pass laws	44,903
Urban Areas Act	8,303
Curfew regulations	44,294
Registration and production of documents	55,673
Native taxation	21,381
TOTAL	534,306

Apart from this legalised oppression, the African is also very often the victim of lawless brutality on the part of Whites and wanton assaults on Africans are frequent.

In this atmosphere of oppression, humiliation and degradation, the African starts looking for work. He is denied almost all chance of education and only a small percentage of the new arrivals can read and write. Vocational training? In the Reserves or on the European farms he has no opportunity for learning a trade. With a smattering of English, sometimes without any knowledge of the language at all, he goes from door to door, asking for work. Often he is rudely chased away. When, at last, he succeeds in finding work, more troubles are in store for him. The European boss is usually not very friendly. Even the white worker, who claims to be a good trade unionist, is often hostile and treats him as a kaffir, abusing and assaulting him. There are exceptions, of course. There are decent employers and white workers, who show sympathy and understanding. But they are in the minority.

Even Europeans, when they have had no industrial tradition, find the factory bewildering at first. To the African, the strange, complicated machinery of a modern factory and the hostile faces around him, are utterly confusing and frightening. He usually starts as an unskilled labourer, sweeping floors, carrying materials or parcels and doing only menial jobs. He earns very little at first, about 30*s.* a week, but now he is no longer living in a primitive tribal society, but under a modern capitalist system. Transport and housing are his two major problems and food and clothing come next.

In Johannesburg it takes many thousands of Africans from two to three hours—often longer—to get to work and back home. From sunset to sunrise he must carry a special pass from his employer to enable him to go to work, to get home, or to visit friends, and these special passes are issued daily.

It is a great tribute to the Africans' patience and ingenuity, to their fervent desire to advance and their devotion to their families, that, in spite of all the obstacles in their way and the bitterly hostile world in which they live, over a million have found employment in the manufacturing industries, in transport, commerce, and other spheres. And their numbers are still increasing. Although they have no facilities to help them learn skilled trades, tens of thousands have already become skilled operatives or semi-skilled workers, very often handling complicated machinery. No one can stop their economic advancement; the entire economy of the country depends upon it. There is a violent and constant conflict between the backward political philosophy of the country, known as apartheid, and its rapidly developing economic life. A modern economy cannot be built on the fantastic theories of the champions of the master race.

Despite the increasing part played by the African in South Africa's industrial development, his status remains that of a serf. His contract of employment is governed by several Master and Servant Acts, by the Native Labour Regulation Act of 1911, and other restrictive laws.

In 1924, when the first Industrial Conciliation Act was passed—the Act was amended in 1937—to regulate the relationship between employers and employees and to provide a measure of collective bargaining for workers, Africans were excluded. A direct colour bar in the Act might have evoked criticism from abroad, so a new definition of 'employee' was introduced, which reads:

> 'employee' means any person employed by, or working for an employer, and receiving, or being entitled to receive, any remuneration, and any other person whatsoever who in any manner assists in the carrying on or conducting of the business of an employer but does not include a person whose contract of service or labour is regulated by Act No. 40 of 1894 of Natal, or, in terms of section two of the Masters and Servants Law (Transvaal and Natal) Amendment Act, 1926 (Act No. 26 of 1926) is regarded for the purpose of Act No. 40 of 1894 of Natal as a contract between master and servant, or is regulated by the Native Labour Regulation Act 1911 (Act No. 15 of 1911) or by the Natives (Urban Areas) Act 1923 (Act No. 21 of 1923), or by any amendment of, or any regulation made under, any of those laws; and 'employed' and 'employment' have corresponding meanings.

Section 24 of the Act prohibits differentiation or discrimination in any industrial agreements made under the Act on the grounds of race or colour, and section 48 (4) of the Act provides that the provisions of the agreement may be extended by the Minister to apply to Africans, on an application by an industrial council. In several industries this has actually been done but the Garment

Workers' Union tried for many years, without success, to have our agreements extended; the employers always refused, pleading the unfair competition which resulted from the low wages paid in coastal areas.

The African workers themselves have no voice whatever in the making of industrial agreements and in determining the wages and conditions under which they have to work. Under the Industrial Conciliation Act Africans are not allowed to be members of registered trade unions. Since 1928, however, our union has helped to organise a separate union of Africans, known as 'The South African Clothing Workers' Union', and has assisted the African workers in many ways. Officials of the union often helped the South African Clothing Workers' Union in making representations to the employers, and on several occasions the union threatened to take strike action to help them. In some instances, when African workers stopped work, European workers, although generally antagonistic to the Africans, were prepared to go on strike in order to help these less fortunate workers.

Since 1932 the wages and other conditions of employment of African workers in the clothing industry in the Transvaal have been governed by Wage Determination Nos. 42 and 120. The minimum wage provided by these determinations is much lower—often less than a third—of that provided in the industrial agreements for similar jobs. The weekly hours of work are more and the paid holidays less.

The absurdity of South African labour legislation is shown by the following:

Before the Second World War there were hardly any African women at work in the clothing industry, or in industry generally, although the number of African men employed was growing all the time. Their work was confined almost entirely to those occupations which required greater physical strength, such as machine or hand pressing and machine cutting. In the early thirties, the Government tried to introduce a 'white labour policy' in State services and private industry, and manufacturers were urged to dispense with the services of African workers and replace them with Europeans. For a time large numbers of European youths were engaged as pressers and choppers-out, but they did not stay very long and either found more congenial occupations in the clothing industry or left altogether. From 1940 onwards the industry expanded rapidly and there was an acute shortage of labour. African women, who had always worked as domestic servants, now began to take employment in factories. They wanted more freedom and more pay. By 1944 over a thousand African women were employed in the clothing industry in the Transvaal. Since 1924, when the first Industrial Conciliation Act was passed, it was taken for granted that African women, like African men, were not 'employees' in terms of the Act and did not come under the industrial agreements for the industry. Their wages and conditions of employment were governed by Wage Determination No. 42 and were much lower than those enjoyed by the workers who came under the agreement. By that time the union was expert at finding flaws in the oppressive South African legislation. I had made a careful study of the definition of 'employee' in the Industrial Conciliation Act and of the various Acts referred to in that definition, and came to the conclusion that African women were not covered by the proviso in the definition of 'employee', as the Acts mentioned applied to men. The union informed the employers of our view on the matter, but they refused to accept it, relying on the advice given them by the Labour Department and on the general assumption throughout South Africa that all Africans, men and women, were excluded from the provisions of the Act. We persisted, however, until the employers ultimately agreed that the Industrial Council should seek a Supreme Court ruling on the matter. Accordingly, an African woman, Christina Okolo, who had been working in the clothing industry for about a year, applied to the Transvaal Provincial Division of the Supreme Court for a Declaratory Order, asking the court to rule that she and all other African women were employees under the provisions of the Industrial Conciliation Act. The Industrial Council for the Clothing Industry, which was the respondent, engaged eminent counsel to appear both for the applicant and itself. The case was argued at great length and involved the careful scrutiny of several statutes and numerous regulations. On the 22nd December 1944 the Acting Judge-President Saul Solomon, gave judgment, holding that Act 21 of 1923 and Act 15 of 1911 did not apply to native females.

In the course of his judgment, the learned judge said:

A gap appears to have been left in the legislation hitherto passed and the second applicant has found her way through it.

> The result may be anomalous, but the court declares that the terms of the clothing industry agreement apply to her, as her contract of service or labour is not regulated by either Act 15 of 1911 or Act 21 of 1923. She, therefore, does not come within the exclusion. The costs of the proceedings will, by consent, be paid by the respondent.

This judgment did not cause any serious disturbance in the industry and in the course of a few weeks the African women had their wages increased by substantial amounts—in many instances from £1 to £2 per week. Their hours of work were reduced from forty-six to forty-four, as was provided in the agreement, and all the other privileges of the agreement were extended to them. The adjustment was effected without the slightest difficulty—only a few employers grumbled. Shortly afterwards all the African women workers were enrolled as members of the union and readily showed their gratitude to the union by being loyal members. And so, probably for the first time in history, and in an extremely backward country, a group of women enjoyed greater privileges than their menfolk, many of whom had worked in the clothing industry for over ten years. African men started at a weekly wage of £1 for a forty-six hour week, rising by yearly increases to £3 after five years, but their wives, daughters and sisters received £2 5*s*. per week for a forty-four hour week to start with, rising by quarterly increases to £4 12*s*. per week after two and a half years. In addition the women became entitled to four weeks' paid holiday per year, instead of the two weeks for African men, and could become members of our union, while the men were excluded from joining by law. The judgment of the Supreme Court also brought African women within the scope of the Unemployment Benefit Act, which had a definition of 'employee' similar to the definition in the Industrial Conciliation Act.

In 1953 the Nationalist Government passed the Native Labour (Settlement of Disputes) Act, which not only specifically excluded all African men and women from the Industrial Conciliation Act, but also deprived Africans of any rights of collective bargaining and negotiating with employers. Under this law, committees have been set up with absolute discretion to settle any dispute, involving Africans, as they think fit. Africans are, of course, excluded from serving on these committees but, in addition, even their right to make representations may be denied to them by these bodies, and they are powerless to do anything about it. Resort to strike action is impossible for this is prohibited by law and carries penalties of three years imprisonment and a £500 fine.

The Garment Workers' Union, however, decided to defend the interests of its African women members. It therefore notified the employers and the Government that no lowering of African women workers' standards would be tolerated and that these workers' wages and conditions must be governed, as in the past, by the industrial agreements for the industry. Strike action was threatened by the union should the employers decide to alter the conditions for African women workers. The employers who, like most industrialists, are opposed to the Government's 'apartheid' policy, agreed to the union's demands. Later a separate union was established for African women workers, which still works in closest co-operation with the Garment Workers' Union.

Where workers are united and determined to fight for their rights they can successfully challenge oppressive legislation.

CHAPTER SIXTEEN

Coloured and Indian Workers

IN THE CAPE AND NATAL the overwhelming majority of garment workers have always been Coloured, Indian and Malay, while in the Transvaal, until the Second World War, the European workers, of whom at least 80 per cent were Afrikaners, were predominant. In 1935 the union began to pay special attention to the organisation of coloured workers. At that time there were not more than a few hundred of them in the clothing industry and they were only employed in six factories—the largest being in Pretoria—on the manufacture of garments of the cheapest type. The definition of 'employee' in the Industrial Conciliation Act included these workers and they had the same legal rights of organising and collective bargaining as the Europeans. Indeed, the successive agreements for the industry, made by the union and the employers' association through the industrial council for the industry, always covered the employment conditions of these workers, as nearly all industrial agreements were extended to cover non-parties—i.e. employees who are not members of trade unions and employers who are not members of the employers' organisation. There has never been a colour bar in the constitution of the union but despite this very few of the Coloured or Indian workers joined the union and they worked under deplorable conditions.

Towards the end of 1935 I addressed a meeting at a factory where twenty-five Coloured workers, men and women, were employed. I was very cordially received. The workers understood the advantages which the union offered to its members and realised they were eligible to join. But they were anxious to find out whether they would have full rights of membership in practice, as well as in theory, whether they would be allowed to attend general meetings along with the European members, and whether they could be elected to serve on committees. Above all, they wanted to know whether they would be able to work in factories where white workers were employed. I assured them that, under the terms of the constitution of the union, they would be entitled to full membership, with exactly the same rights and obligations as the Europeans. I also told them that the central executive committee and the officials and staff of the union would treat them with all the attention and courtesy accorded to European members. But I could not speak for the mass of the white workers who, although they had proved themselves loyal trade unionists and courageous fighters, were nevertheless imbued with violent prejudices against non-Europeans.

We called meetings of shop stewards and of the general membership to discuss this important question. About 10 per cent were in favour of complete equality, without any racial discrimination. Over 80 per cent were in favour of a parallel organisation, which meant that the Europeans and non-Europeans would belong to separate branches, each branch having its own committee and holding its general meetings separately. The overwhelming majority would not agree to mixed meetings, but only an insignificant number opposed the entry of the Coloured workers into the union altogether. The members also agreed that the non-European workers were entitled to the unqualified right to manage their own affairs and finances; to elect their own officials, and to have an equal say in determining union policy and in the making of industrial agreements. Coloured workers would be entitled to take employment anywhere they chose and to perform all classes of work, but the union was urged to be on guard against the employers' taking advantage of the non-European workers at the expense of the Europeans.

We then called a meeting of the Coloured workers and put the position frankly before them, explaining that, although the leaders of the union were in favour of complete equality, the majority of the members had not yet reached a sufficiently high standard of education and tolerance to share this view and had demanded the establishment of parallel branches. The Coloured workers accepted this position and many joined the union.

We established a No. 2 Branch for Coloured workers, which elected its own officials and branch executive committee, with full powers to manage the affairs of the branch. By a unanimous decision the No. 2 Branch agreed to leave the administration of its finances in the hands of the central executive committee. In this manner what has become known as 'parallel organisation', a pattern which was later followed by other trade unions, began to develop in South Africa. The establishment of separate branches on a racial basis is against all trade union principles, which are diametrically opposed to any form of racial discrimination, and has been much criticised. In practice it worked well. Members of the No. 2 Branch were free to call at the head office of the union at any time and were always treated in the same way as the Europeans. Branch and executive meetings were held separately and the Coloured workers soon developed a true and enthusiastic spirit of trade unionism. Their meetings, at which officials from the head office were always present, were well attended and run in an orderly and businesslike fashion. The No. 2 Branch executive frequently met with the central executive to discuss union policy and these meetings were always held in a friendly spirit and were quite free from all traces of paternalism or racial superiority.

When we started enforcing the provisions of the agreement for Coloured workers we experienced great difficulties. Many of the workers were too afraid of losing their jobs to give us truthful information about the low wages they were receiving. They experienced great difficulty in finding any employment in the industry as the majority of employers engaged Europeans in the highly skilled and skilled sections, whilst the unskilled jobs were usually done by Africans.

In 1936 the union received information that, in a large factory in Pretoria, the Coloured workers were receiving only half the wages recorded in the wage register. In due course, Mr Malan, the agent of the Industrial Council, and I called at the place to make an inspection. The employer seemed extremely co-operative, handed us the wage register which appeared to be in perfect order, and put a small office at our disposal so that we could interview the workers. I realised that we would have great difficulty in getting truthful information and that everything depended on creating the right atmosphere and gaining the confidence of the intimidated workers. We called them into the office individually. The first one to come was a young Coloured girl and, after years of experience in interrogating workers, I knew at once, from her extremely worried expression, that she would not tell us the truth.

In the friendliest possible manner I told her who we were and asked her what her name was. She said at once, without any hesitation: 'Two pounds ten.' I realised at once what had happened. This poor girl, who was probably the sole supporter of her family, had been told by the employer to say that her wages were £2 10*s*.

as was laid down in the agreement. Desperately anxious not to lose her job and scared nearly out of her wits, she could think of nothing else and, as soon as she was asked a question, without even understanding what was wanted, she blurted out the reply she had been coached to give. It was absolutely essential to get the girl's whole-hearted co-operation if we were to succeed in exposing and eradicating this abominable practice of underpaying and faking wage registers. But how was I to gain the confidence and the co-operation of this very worried and frightened young woman?

I told her very quietly that I wanted some other particulars first and that we would come to the rates of pay later on. After a while, I got her name, address, age, the class of work she was doing, and the experience she had had in the industry. When I at last asked her what wages she had been getting, she repeated, with the greatest relief: 'Two pounds ten.'

This was what had been troubling her all the time and she was very happy to have got it off her chest. I then asked her for how long she had been getting this amount, but she could not remember the exact period. 'Did you get two pounds ten last week?' I asked her, and she said emphatically: 'Yes.'

'How were you paid?' I asked. 'In notes, in silver? How?'

Again the reply came promptly, as she had been taught: 'Two one-pound notes and four half-crowns.'

I looked at the register in front of me. She had not worked a full week and could not have received so much. The entry in the register showed £1 15*s.* which meant that she was not paid more than 17*s.* 6*d.* I did not ask her any more questions and she was more than glad when I let her go away.

Ninety-four Coloured and Indian workers were questioned that day, ninety-four women who knew they had been atrociously exploited and robbed of half their wages. And yet every one of them repeated the lies they had been taught for fear they might lose their jobs and the few miserable shillings they were getting. When we had finished questioning the workers, I returned the wage register to the employer, who, with a look of satisfaction on his face, said to me: 'Everything in order?'

I said: 'You are a dirty scoundrel and you know it. You may have taught your workers to lie, but you did not succeed in teaching them to tell lies without being found out. You will see. We will get you yet.'

He seemed frightened, but could not think of anything to say.

Subsequently we visited many of the workers in their homes and at last got down to the truth. We then called a meeting of all the workers and their parents and explained matters very clearly and carefully to them. They were grateful for what we were doing, but very worried, and asked what they should do if they were sacked. Most of the women, some of whom were very young, were the sole support of their families. We told them that the Industrial Conciliation Act had a provision protecting workers who gave information against possible victimisation and we pointed out that the union would give financial assistance to any worker who was victimised. We told them that any one of them who left the factory or was dismissed should come to the union office and we would take up her claim for back-pay. They were friendly and grateful but still not co-operative.

Meanwhile we instituted several prosecutions against the employer for technical breaches of the agreement, e.g. not paying council contributions in time, failing to display a copy of the agreement in the factory etc. He was convicted and fined. Some time later about six of the workers made truthful statements about their wages and again we instituted prosecutions. But by the time the case came to court the employer had managed to win over the witnesses with bribes and, in the box, they all went back on their words. We told the employer that we had infinite patience and would continue to prosecute him until he learnt to observe all the provisions of the agreement. It took us some years to reform him, but in the end we succeeded, partly through court action, but mainly through the workers' increased confidence in the union and in themselves.

The Second World War gave tremendous impetus to South African industrial development and, from 1940 onwards, the clothing industry began to expand rapidly. Thousands of garment workers left the industry to work in munition plants or volunteered for the forces. For over a decade the industry in the Transvaal had been drawing most of its workers from among the Afrikaner women, but this source was now practically exhausted for a number of reasons. Although the clothing industry paid higher wages than most other industries, garment-making is very hard work and many young women preferred to take employment at lower wages in industries where the strain was not so great. Most girls from the towns preferred office and shop jobs to factory work. With an improvement in the economic conditions, the flow of poverty-stricken Afrikaner women from the rural areas stopped. More and more manufacturers began to employ Coloured workers. The exclusively Coloured factories had no racial problems, but in the mixed factories the union had to spend much time and energy maintaining peace and harmony. The majority of European workers, when left to themselves, shed their more extreme racial animosity and many even showed friendliness towards non-European workers. But from 1936 onwards, when the Nationalist Party resolved to capture or disrupt our union, the white workers were subjected to a constant stream of propaganda against the Coloured workers. The Dutch Reformed Churches also played a very active part in encouraging race hatred. Under the pretext of holding prayer meetings, their ministers made regular visits to the factories during the lunch hour intervals, but instead of spreading the message of brotherhood and tolerance they did their best to incite the white workers against the Coloured. They said it was a shame that white Afrikaner ladies had to work in the same factories with Coloured girls and usually attacked the union for this disgraceful state of affairs. In most factories the Afrikaner workers resented these intrusions. After five hours at the machine or table they wanted to relax. But in some factories these prayer meetings caused a great deal of unrest, and the union often had to spend much time settling the racial strife that followed. The Factories Act already makes provision for apartheid. Separate cloak and rest rooms have to be provided for the different racial groups and the Act also obliges employers to set up partitions between whites and non-whites wherever they work together on the same floor. But that did not satisfy the Nationalist Party. In some factories the mischief-makers would urge the workers to demand separate time clocks and separate entrances and exits as well. The use of lifts was a great source of trouble. Many factories were situated in large buildings, on the fifth and sixth floors, and usually the lifts were marked: 'Europeans only.' The Coloured workers, not wanting to walk those numerous flights of stairs, would also use them. The Coloured workers, whilst resenting insult and abuse, generally behaved quietly and with dignity and rarely retaliated with anti-white abuse. Only in Germiston, a strong Nationalist stronghold, did the disrupters succeed in causing serious division in the ranks of the union. In Johannesburg most of the six thousand white workers remained loyal to the union and, while never completely free from race prejudice, tolerated the non-Europeans as fellow workers, even if they did not accept them as social equals.

After 1936 officials of the union had to devote more time and energy to combating race hatred, settling race conflicts, and defending the union against the pro-Nazi disrupters, than to economic problems. To lead workers who are united in a struggle for higher wages and better conditions is not difficult. But when one finds the very same workers, who are themselves suffering exploitation and poverty, hating and persecuting their fellow workers merely because they belong to a different race, and supporting the fascists, then one comes very close to despair and needs strong nerves and a cool head to keep one's faith in humanity.

I remember one occasion when I received an urgent telephone message from a leading employer informing me that a strike had started at his factory on racial grounds. We had agreed with the employers that all race conflicts would be settled by union officials and I immediately went to the factory. The employer had to execute urgent orders and, not being able to find European table hands, had engaged a woman whose name sounded German and whose father was a European. She was a Creole, a widow with two children to support. One hundred and two European workers were employed in the factory, which was modern in every respect and engaged in the making of better-class ladies' dresses. The employer was quite progressive, a ruthless capitalist, but honourable and very much respected by the workers. I saw him at once at his office and he remarked ironically: 'The members of your union, go and see what they are doing. I engaged one non-European and they all came out on strike.'

I went into the large workroom and found all the machines standing idle and two ringleaders surrounded by a crowd of girls, shouting wildly and hurling abuse at their victim. The Creole woman, attractive and neatly dressed with a pleasant, dignified appearance, was standing alone, about ten yards away from the others. She was nervous and embarrassed and completely at a loss. The workers, normally disciplined, loyal members of the union, had turned themselves into a disorderly mob ready to lynch the unfortunate woman who had done nothing to harm them. I was so taken aback by what I saw that, for a moment, I did not know what to do. Then one of the leaders, her pretty face contorted with rage, shouted in Afrikaans: 'We Christians will not allow the Bastermeide to work in this factory. Get the hell out of here.'

I was filled with horror and disgust. How loathsome and tragic the South African way of life seemed at that moment, as I watched this quiet, poor widow being abused and threatened by a vicious crowd of otherwise decent, well-behaved white girls, solely on account of her different colouring.

'If you are a Christian,' I shouted, 'then I will gladly stay a heathen all my life. What right have you to call yourselves Christians? You abuse that poor woman. You want to throw her out into the street. You want to see her and her two children starve. How dare you call yourselves Christians, when you have not a drop of compassion, of love and charity in you and all you want of Christianity is another crucifixion?'

As I went on all the workers in the factory came nearer and I could almost watch their complete change of attitude. The menacing, shouting mob, taken aback by the unexpected violence of my outburst, again became the quiet, orderly girls I had known as members of the union. I called up the shop committee and, in the presence of everyone, demanded to know who had given the workers the right to strike. If they had any complaints, why had they not brought them to the union first? We had an agreement with the employers and strikes were illegal. Some of the more intelligent workers then explained that the whole mischief had been caused by two workers who, although loyal members of the union, were supporters of the Nationalists. I told them that they had had their 'fun' and should now decide by secret ballot if they would allow the Coloured woman to work in the factory, or whether they still wanted to throw her out into the street. Sixty-one voted in favour of allowing her to remain, thirty against, and the rest abstained. They went back to their machines, the woman returned to her table, and the incident was over.

A month later, when about sixty Coloured people lost their lives in a terrible train disaster and the union organised a collection for the orphans, this factory contributed more per member than any other.

For nearly twenty years now, the Nationalist disrupters have exploited race hatred in an attempt to destroy the union. Strange as it may seem, some of the most vicious disrupters within the union were themselves Coloured, and even looked Coloured. But, if it suits the purposes of the Nationalists, then Coloured are turned into Whites and accepted within their ranks.

In 1950 the union held a national conference to adopt a constitution. Thirty-five delegates, including twelve Coloured, from all branches throughout South Africa assembled at the Trades Hall, Johannesburg, to deal with the matter and spent three days drafting a new constitution. After numerous and lengthy debates a new constitution was adopted unanimously. When the president, Anna Scheepers, was about to close the conference, a delegate from Germiston, a Nationalist agent, moved that the new constitution be circulated among all the white members of the union for their approval or otherwise. The rest of the delegates were furious and, in the debate which followed, they denounced the racialists in very outspoken terms. The proposal was completely out of order, as the original constitution provided that only branch delegates could amend the constitution. The simple fact that twenty thousand rank-and-file members could not possibly deal with a new constitution made this proposal quite impracticable. It was also irregular, since there was no colour bar in the constitution and all members were entitled to vote in any ballot.

A Coloured delegate, who spoke in the debate, summed up the tragic situation with a joke and said: 'Miss X is always harping on the Coloured workers. I should like to remind her that, if her ancestors had paid more attention to the flies in their trousers, there would be no Coloured problem today.' There was a roar of laughter and the proposal was rejected by thirty-three votes to two.

The spirit of trust and confidence between the European leaders of the union and the Coloured workers has grown stronger over the years, but among the mass of white workers prejudice and even hatred of the Coloured people are still very much in evidence and are kept alive by the Nationalists. South Africa is so poisoned by race hatred that many of the Coloured workers even consider themselves superior to Africans.

In 1944, for example, when the Supreme Court held that African women were 'employees' and could, therefore, be members of registered trade unions, there was some opposition from Coloured workers to their acceptance as members of the No. 2 Branch. The mass of Coloured workers, however, vigorously opposed every form of racial discrimination against Africans. Nationalist policy has caused a terrible division between White and non-White, but it has also had the effect of uniting the African, Coloured, Indian and Malay people. They understand that they may be rich or poor, educated or uneducated, and have great differences in their respective cultural standards, but they are all the victims of the same cruel oppression, for the same reason—because their skins are not white.

When the union was involved in serious conflicts with the employers, workers' solidarity always triumphed over racial division. White and Coloured workers co-operated whole-heartedly in times of strikes or threatened strike action. In the monster demonstration outside the City Hall steps, Johannesburg, on 24th May 1952, the White workers loudly cheered the twelve thousand Coloured workers as they marched up to the demonstration. Later, when the police charged the demonstrators and injured scores of people, White and Coloured readily rendered assistance to the victims, irrespective of their race.

CHAPTER SEVENTEEN

Afrikaner Nationalism and the Workers

FEW PEOPLE, including most English-speaking South Africans, know anything at all about the Afrikaner people, their history and their national aspirations. Yet it is impossible to grasp South African events, political conflicts and problems without an understanding of Afrikaner nationalism, which for over a century has played a major rôle in the life of the country. The Afrikaners have a remarkable history, rich in suffering and sorrow, courage and heroism, triumph and defeat, of which any nation might be justly proud. That the whole world now looks upon the Afrikaner people merely as pro-Nazi and champions of apartheid is largely the result of the infamous policy of the present leaders of the Nationalist Party.

For over a hundred years the Afrikaner people have fought with great determination for their national independence. In the South African War of 1899 to 1902 the two Boer Republics, the Transvaal and the Orange Free State, were crushed by British imperialism. This defeat brought untold misery to the Afrikaners, and for a time it seemed as if they would never recover. And yet, in less than half a century, they gained complete independence and developed into a nation, with a national culture and tradition. It is one of the tragic ironies of history that nations which have themselves suffered oppression and fought for independence often become cruel oppressors in their turn when they have at last achieved their freedom.

The Afrikaner people have a truly noble heritage from which to draw inspiration. They are the descendants of the Dutch who, for eighty years, waged a war for freedom against their Spanish oppressors, and of the French Huguenots, who came to South Africa at the end of the seventeenth century to escape religious and political persecution. They fought for independence for over a century and, in the Boer war, their heroism gained them the admiration of the whole world. Resolved to survive as a nation, inspired by a deep love for freedom, they rebuilt their shattered lives and triumphed over the tragedies of the past. Here was an opportunity for national statesmen to lead South Africa along the road of progress, tolerance and freedom. But the Nationalist Party leaders spurn noble traditions. Corrupted by Nazi doctrines, they have rejected the idea of building a great South African nation, where all groups could enjoy security and freedom, and instead are determined to create a 'volk', a master race in a slave state. Under the guise of saving 'white civilisation', they have become the champions of intolerance and tyranny and are leading the country back towards the Dark Ages.

The Nationalist Party was formed in 1912 by the late General Hertzog. Until the rise of Nazism in Europe, the party stood for 'South Africa first', but was neither violently anti-British nor fascist. Its attitude to the trade union and labour movement was not hostile and, at certain periods, it was even friendly. In the general strike on the Rand in 1922 Nationalist Afrikaner workers and British workers fought side by side against Smuts and the Chamber of Mines and, of thc hundreds of workers who were sent to gaol for treason and sedition and the eighteen who were sentenced to death, the majority were Afrikaners. In the general election of 1924 the Nationalist Party, under General Hertzog, and the Labour Party, under Colonel Cresswell, formed a pact and the Smuts Government was heavily defeated, Smuts himself losing his seat. The workers, British and Afrikaners, supported the pact, and even the group of young socialists to which I belonged enthusiastically worked for its victory. In the new Government Colonel Cresswell became Minister of Labour, and Sampson, another Labour M.P., Minister of Posts. There appeared to be an unwritten agreement between Hertzog and Cresswell that the Nationalist Party would look after the rural areas and the Labour Party would look after the towns. At no time, during the five years of the Pact Government, did the Nationalist Party try to interfere with the trade unions. To the mass of Afrikaner people, who were still on the land, trade unions were strange, alien organisations, which did not concern them. An anecdote current during the general strike in 1922 illustrates this attitude. An Afrikaner farmer, speaking to another, says: 'Man, I have fought under General de Wet, I know General Botha and also General Smuts, but who is this General Strike? I have never heard of him.'

Many of the earlier leaders of Afrikaner Nationalism are reputed to have had a leaning towards socialism in their younger days.

This applies particularly to Dr Malan. In 1920 General Hertzog praised Lenin's policy of national self-determination. In 1927 Mr Oswald Pirow, a Nationalist Minister of Justice, visited the U.S.S.R. His only comment in a press interview on his return was that he had seen no prostitution in Russia. With the rise of Hitler in Germany the character of the Nationalist Party changed. The man who was chiefly responsible was Oswald Pirow, a barrister of German descent, ambitious, vigorous and a leading Nationalist. In 1930, when as Minister of Justice he introduced the Riotous Assemblies and Criminal Law Amendment Bill, his speeches in Parliament took the form of anti-communist diatribes following the accepted Nazi pattern. The Act itself is fascist in character. Pirow was almost alone in his Nazi crusade before 1933, when Hitler came to power. Thereafter, the 'Auslands Abteilung' of the Nazi Party, recognising the fertile soil which a country, tormented by violent racial and national conflicts, presented for the spreading of the Herrenvolk philosophy, became active in South Africa. Various fascist organisations, such as the Grey Shirts, Black Shirts, Ossewa Brandwag and others, came into being, financed to a large extent by funds from Berlin. The Germans in South-West Africa openly formed Nazi organisations and German agents began to operate freely throughout the country.

The year 1933 was a milestone in South African history. A political 'fusion' took place between the Nationalist Party, led by General Hertzog, and the South African Party, led by General Smuts. The result was the formation of the United South African Party (popularly referred to as the United Party), with Hertzog as Premier and Smuts as Minister of Justice. Almost immediately afterwards, however, the most extremist Nationalist group broke away under Dr Malan to form the 'purified' Nationalist Party. Bitterly anti-British and staunchly republican, Dr Malan's Nationalists became the main opposition party.

The period during which this fusion took place (1933 to 1939) was one of prosperity and a lessening of tension between British and Afrikaners. At the same time there were definite signs of growing German influence, although they were not always recognised as such. Disclosures made public after the outbreak of war confirmed, what had long been known to many, that the Nazi Foreign and Propaganda Offices had operated on a large scale in this, as in other countries, trying to gain public sympathy for Nazi ideas and aspirations. Nazi literature in great quantities circulated freely; the German Consulates were centres of intense activity. The Zeesen Broadcasting Station directed a regular barrage of propaganda to South Africa, much of it in Afrikaans, calculated to inflame Afrikaner Nationalism and to excite racial antipathies. The Jews, in particular, were constantly under attack. South African professors and students were encouraged to visit Germany and were made very welcome there. German South-West Africa, which was administered by the Union Government under a mandate of the League of Nations, became a hotbed of Nazi intrigue. This was established in 1936 in an official report by a Commission consisting of two judges and a high civil servant which was appointed by the Union Government.

In 1937, the secretary of the Nationalist Party officially wrote to the leader of the Greyshirts:

> My Party is glad to give expression to its sincere appreciation of the useful work done by the Greyshirts in one respect, namely, that they have very pertinently drawn the attention of the people to the Jewish problem, which has indeed assumed very threatening dimensions. . . . We consider that a service has here been done to the nation, which deserves recognition and perpetuation. On the other hand, we think that the identification of this service with a Nazi or Fascist movement, as is the case with your Party, can only retard this service, and can only do harm to the objective in view.

On tactical grounds, therefore, the Nationalist Party rejected the hand of co-operation proferred by the Greyshirt movement. Nevertheless, both held similar views and election pacts were concluded later in several constituencies.

The earlier nationalism of the Afrikaners was in large measure replaced by a new and narrow Nationalism that has much in common with Nazi doctrines. Yet many of its supporters were probably unaware of the character and source of the changes which were brought about, for at heart the Afrikaners are individualists and dislike dictatorship and excessive discipline intensely.

The new 'mystical' conception of Afrikaner Nationalism has been voiced by the 'Broederbond' (League of Brothers), a secret super-organisation of Afrikanerdom, which dates back to 1918 and has achieved great power in recent years. The general secretary of the Bond wrote:

> The Afrikaner Broederbond is born from a deep conviction that the Afrikaner nation has been planted in this country by God's hand and is destined to remain as a nation with its own character and its own mission.

This sense of a divinely appointed mission, derived from the Calvinistic doctrine of predestination, explains the fanatical sincerity of the movement and its guiding force, the Broederbond.

The 'Herrenvolk' idea of Hitler had a tremendous appeal for the leaders of the Nationalists, who regard the 'true Afrikaners' as people chosen by God to constitute a master race; Afrikaners who disagree with this doctrine are considered traitors.

Between 1925 and 1935 great numbers of poverty-stricken Afrikaners trekked from the rural areas into the towns and saw there comfort and affluence enjoyed by the 'uitlanders' (foreigners), while they themselves suffered extreme poverty. The 'have nots' everywhere, especially those who feel nationally oppressed, either become revolutionaries or fall an easy prey to fascist demagogy. The Nationalists showed these dispossessed, embittered people prospects of national independence and a society in which every white-skinned man would be master.

> The Communists want your sisters to marry kaffirs. Down with Communism! We must save White, Christian, Western Civilisation from the Communists, the kaffirs and the Coolies,

the Nationalists proclaimed. The newcomers wanted jobs, decent standards and to escape from the squalor of the slums. The leaders of the Nationalist Party have always been unscrupulous politicians, not nation-builders. The suffering of the poor Afrikaners meant nothing to them. They never helped these landless, jobless and underpaid people to lift themselves out of the abyss of misery in which they lived. They only exploited the Afrikaners' national feelings and poverty for their own ends.

Our union was the first to experience the Nazi tactics of the Nationalist Party. In 1932, after the general strike in the clothing industry, Mr Oswald Pirow, the Nationalist Minister of Justice, issued a banishment order against me under the pretext of my being a 'dangerous communist'. I had been expelled from the Communist Party of South Africa in September 1931, for 'right-wing deviation' and Mr Pirow's action was purely a fascist stunt. Just before the banishment order was issued, I came to a meeting of garment workers in Germiston. There were about 120 women in the hall when, suddenly, an unruly mob invaded the meeting. Half-drunk and brandishing empty sherry bottles, they shouted: 'Ons is Nasionaliste. Waar is die Kommunis Sachs?' They were obviously a band of Nationalist Storm Troopers sent to break up the meeting. The women became indignant and threw them out of the hall.

In 1935, when our union organised protest meetings against Mr Fourie, Minister of Labour, for refusing to make the recommendation of the Wage Board for the clothing industry a determination, *Die Vaderland*, an Afrikaans daily, published a scurrilous and defamatory article headed: 'Bolsheviks incite Afrikaner girls against the State.' We had committed no act of treason. We had only protested against Mr Fourie's high-handed action. Had Fourie made the recommendation law, the garment workers would have expressed gratitude to him. What made him change his mind and leave the girls in their misery? Fourie never explained why he had denied elementary justice to these exploited workers.

On the 16th July 1936, *Die Vaderland* published a leader headed: 'Foreign exploiters amongst South African workers.' It vilified me for opposing the interference of the Afrikaans Cultural Societies in the trade unions. The article concluded:

> But people who cannot find a place among the agitators in the agitator régimes of Europe, like Mr Sachs, can freely spread their poisonous teaching among our workers, destroy our spiritual values and uproot the South African worker from his association with relation and nation, to remain inarticulate and to live only for his stomach, like himself. It is quite immaterial to him among whom he spreads his poisonous communist teachings. Today it is a White South Africa, with its men and women workers, but for Mr Sachs it will make no difference if tomorrow he does the same among natives or Chinese. The motive and the aim remain the same for him.

I was not a regular reader of *Die Vaderland*, but about nine years later, when I was involved in another action for defamation against a minister of the Dutch Reformed Churches, I came across this article and issued a summons against the paper. I was paid £100 and costs without the matter going to court.

CHAPTER EIGHTEEN

Disrupting the Trade Unions

IN *Mein Kampf*, Hitler propounded at length the need for capturing or disrupting all mass organisations in the interest of National Socialism. The leaders of the Nationalists, having absorbed Hitler's teachings, energetically began to apply these Nazi tactics.

By 1936 the Dutch Reformed Churches, the predominantly Afrikaans universities of Stellenbosch and Pretoria, the Afrikaans Cultural Societies, various sport and youth organisations, had all been brought under the tutelage of the Nationalist Party. In July of that year a furious campaign was launched by the Afrikaans Cultural Societies against the trade union movement. This campaign started in the form of a crusade: 'To save the souls of the Afrikaner workers from the corruption of the foreigners, imperialists, communists, Jews, liberals and kafferboeties (nigger lovers).' The crusade was led by Afrikaans professors, lawyers, farmers, financiers and ministers of the Dutch Reformed Churches—not by workers.

A wealthy woman landowner from Stellenbosch in the Cape Province, who was a staunch supporter of the Nationalist Party, donated the sum of £10,000 towards this campaign and a 'Reform Organisation' under the leadership of Dr Albert Hertzog, the son of the Prime Minister, was established. This body, supported by the Nationalist Party, politicians and press, launched a vicious campaign on a nation-wide scale against the existing trade union movement.

The methods of these disrupters were in every way identical with those of the Nazis in Germany, right down to the phraseology. First, there was the bogy of communism, and all trade union leaders, including many who were bitterly anti-communist, were branded as 'Communists' and 'Moscow agents'. Even the conservative former president of the South African Trades and Labour Council, Mr A. J. Downes, who on more than one occasion had publicly attacked communism, was labelled a communist. Anti-semitism, too, was exploited with great vigour. Although very few trade union leaders in South Africa were Jewish, the

Malanazis, in their papers and from platforms, accused the trade union movement of being a 'foreign' institution 'entirely controlled by Jews'. It was said to be hostile to the interests of the Afrikaners, since it wanted to divide them into employers and employees, workers and capitalists. Last, but not least, the reactionaries appealed to the colour prejudice of the Afrikaner workers—'White civilisation must be saved.' In the trade union movement European, Coloured and Native workers were all of equal importance. This, they said, constituted a danger to 'white' South Africa.

The crusade was directed mainly against those trade unions which had a predominantly Afrikaner membership, especially the Mineworkers' Union and the Garment Workers' Union. Most of the members of the Mineworkers' Union—the largest and, from an economic point of view, the most important union of European workers—are Afrikaans-speaking and violently anti-African. The union's constitution has a colour bar, only workers of European descent being eligible for membership. The leadership was in the hands of people who cared little for the true principles and functions of trade unionism.

Since South Africa had gone off the gold standard, at the end of 1932, the gold mines had known unprecedented prosperity, but the mine workers' conditions had not improved. The white miners were discontented. They expected their leaders to fight for higher wages, but the leaders failed them, and this gave the disrupters an excellent opportunity to pose as the workers' champions. They made full use of the fact that the mines were largely owned by foreign financiers, who were making enormous profits by exploiting the Afrikaner workers. They accused the leaders of the Mineworkers' Union of working hand-in-glove with the Chamber of Mines. For over a decade the struggle for control of the union was waged between the 'Reformers', who had gained influence among the rank and file miners, and the official leaders. The Reformers did not confine themselves to verbal arguments, but frequently resorted to physical violence. On one occasion a group of Reformers seized control of the Mineworkers' Union's office and the leaders of the union had to apply to the Supreme Court for an order to eject them.

In 1937 the Mineworkers' Union, together with eight other unions with membership in the mines, entered into a closed shop agreement with the Chamber of Mines. The agreement deprived the mining unions of the right of any real trade union activity and placed them, to all intents and purposes, under the control of the Chamber of Mines. The closed shop clause in the agreement, however, compelled every mine worker to be a member of his union. The Reformers denounced the closed shop principle and ministers of the Dutch Reformed Churches preached against it from their pulpits.

On the 15th June 1939 Charlie Harris, secretary of the Mineworkers' Union, was shot dead outside his office by a young Afrikaner, who had been influenced by this propaganda. Tried for murder, the assassin was found guilty and sentenced to life imprisonment.

As a result of two political strikes in the mines, engineered by the Nationalist Party and its stooge organisations, in 1948 the Mineworkers' Union came under the control of the Nationalists.

The campaign of the Nationalist Party and its stooge organisations against the free trade union movement made rapid progress within the ranks of the Mineworkers' Union and frightened several leaders in other trade unions. In the Garment Workers' Union it had the very opposite effect. The vast majority of workers, themselves Afrikaners and often Nationalists, became incensed at the vicious attacks on the union and its leaders by cultural organisations, Nationalist politicians, Dutch Reformed Church ministers and others. General meetings of the union, which were always attended by thousands of members, unanimously adopted resolutions, denouncing the insidious activities of the self-styled saviours of the Afrikaner 'volk'. Members of the union were warned that any association with these fascists, disruptive organisations would lead to disciplinary action. Meanwhile Dr Albert Hertzog toured the whole country, attacking the trade union movement in the vilest fashion. The Nationalist Members of Parliament and ministers of the Dutch Reformed Churches poured out an incessant stream of abuse and vilification against the trade union movement and made me a special target. Nevertheless, for many years the ranks of the garment workers remained unshaken.

In 1938 the disrupters, with the vast sums of money at their disposal, appointed several full-time agents to concentrate on our union. Most prominent of these was a certain D. B. H. Grobbelaar, who had never had any association with the trade union movement. He soon set about his task, using the usual Nationalist tactics.

* * *

The year 1938 marked the Voortrekker Centenary, and the occasion was exploited to the full by the Nationalist Party to revive the spirit of Afrikanerdom. Tens of thousands of Afrikaners, although opposed to the Nationalist Party, wanted to pay tribute to the Voortrekkers, and participated in the celebrations. The Garment Workers' Union decided to form a Kappie Kommando of women dressed in Voortrekker costumes to take part in the various processions and celebrations. One might have expected the Nationalists to appreciate this gesture but their unscrupulous leaders, far from being interested in furthering true nationalism and culture among the Afrikaner people, were only concerned with exploiting national sentiments for party gain.

On the 28th October 1938, I received the following letter:

> I enclose herewith a specimen copy of a pamphlet published by me, in which I point out the mockery of our national traditions your participation in the Centenary Celebrations will mean.
>
> The same applies to Johanna Cornelius and your other Communistic accomplices. The Afrikaner nation is busy uniting—to mobilise its forces against you and your sort. The thousands of Afrikaner daughters whom you have in your clutches will settle with you and, with them, the whole Boer nation, who are finding themselves in the Voortrekker year. Our people do not want anything to do with Communism and the Jews—the high priests thereof—least of all. The day when we Afrikaners begin to settle with you Jews, you will find out that Germany is a Jewish paradise compared with what South Africa will be! The garment workers will very soon be able to handle their Jewish bosses and do not need your so-called 'help'. We Afrikaners acknowledge no 'classes' as you and your satellites are trying to introduce—therefore, we do not want the garment workers as a 'class' to participate in the celebrations, but all together with us as Boers—the factory girl with the professor's wife. You and Johanna Cornelius, who all day organise and address kaffirs—will you dare to bring them also along to the celebrations? They are your fellow workers and 'Comrades'.
>
> We challenge you to come to the celebrations and this is our last warning.
>
> (*signed*) D. B. H. GROBBELAAR

Here is an extract from my reply:

> I am quite prepared to allow the thousands of 'Afrikaner Daughters' to settle with me and I extend an invitation to you to come and address a meeting of these thousands of 'Afrikaner Daughters'. Although I do not consider it an honour to be with you on the platform, I am prepared to appear with you at a mass meeting of garment workers and unreservedly to abide by their decision. Each of us will address the workers and then we will submit the following two resolutions:
>
> (1) That this mass meeting of garment workers has no confidence in the Jew Communist, E. S. Sachs, and demands his immediate resignation.
>
> (2) That this mass meeting of garment workers has no confidence in Mr D. B. H. Grobbelaar and his friends and requests him to leave the garment workers alone, and when they need his help they will send for him.

Mr Grobbelaar accepted the challenge and, on the 9th March 1939, over two thousand garment workers crowded into the Selborne Hall, Johannesburg, to decide whom to support. The indignation of the workers was so great that Anna Scheepers, who was in the chair, and the stewards had great difficulty in restraining them from dragging Grobbelaar off the platform. Each of us spoke for fifteen minutes and, when the two resolutions were put to the vote, Grobbelaar received thirteen votes and the rest voted for me. From the ovation I received and from the spirit of the workers one could easily see that the propaganda of the disrupters had not only misfired, but had greatly increased the workers' support for and loyalty to the union.

On the 31st January 1939 Grobbelaar held a private meeting in the house of a garment worker in Vrededorp, a working-class suburb of Johannesburg. Eight workers were present. Grobbelaar made a long speech in the usual slanderous manner and assured the group that, at the forthcoming meeting, 'Mr Sachs would have to hand over the keys of the office of the union to him'. The workers present were apparently not impressed with Mr Grobbelaar's diatribes and, the following day, they came to the office of the union to give a full account of what he had said. In due course I instituted an action for defamation against him in the Witwatersrand Local Division of the Supreme Court. Grobbelaar took exception to my Declaration and I to his Plea. The matter was heard on the 28th August 1939. Grobbelaar's exceptions were dismissed and mine were upheld and he was ordered to pay the costs of both. The case was set down for hearing, but in September 1939, when war broke out, Grobbelaar joined the army and disappeared from the scene.

In 1939 the Nationalist disrupters, under the leadership of the Reformers, for a time transferred their activities to Port Elizabeth. In this important industrial centre, where the union had formed a branch a year previously, nine paid agents started their activities. With the support of several local ministers of the Dutch Reformed Churches they called a meeting of garment workers and began their crusade to save the souls of the Afrikaner garment workers.

There were over eight hundred garment workers in Port Elizabeth in 1939, of whom about half were non-European. Among the Europeans, the fascist agitators managed to subvert about thirty and, on several occasions when I went there to address factory meetings, I was greeted by small groups of workers with shouts of 'Heil Hitler!' One of the leaders of the disruptors was a certain Mrs Bekker, who had been a garment worker in Potchefstroom for some time and then came to Johannesburg. There the union found her a job at more than double the pay she had earned previously. During 1934 and 1935 she co-operated wholeheartedly with the union in helping to organise the garment workers of Potchefstroom and to improve their conditions. She was even elected vice-president of the union, but later it was discovered that she was a Blackshirt agent and her membership was suspended. Mrs Bekker accompanied the 'Crusaders' to Port Elizabeth and made a speech of the usual type. *Die Oosterlig*, organ of the Nationalist Party in the Eastern Province, reported her speech at some length and I issued a summons against the paper for defamation. *Die Oosterlig* paid me £250 damages and costs and published apologies in leading newspapers throughout South Africa. I thereupon withdrew the action. Another official of the union instituted an action for defamation against Mrs Bekker and obtained judgment for over £100, but as Mrs Bekker had no means, the judgment could not be enforced.

CHAPTER NINETEEN

The Dutch Reformed Churches

BEFORE THE RISE OF NAZISM the ministers of the Dutch Reformed Churches did not interfere with the trade unions, but from 1934 onwards the three Dutch Reformed Churches in South Africa began to play a leading part in the campaign of the Nationalist Party to disrupt the trade unions. They came out openly on the side of Nazism and in support of a policy of ruthless oppression of non-Europeans. They exploited the deeply religious feelings of the Afrikaner people to spread Nazi propaganda and to make converts for the Nationalist Party. At a general meeting of the Hervormde Kerk at Pretoria ,held in June 1937, members of the Church and others were warned not to join trade unions; they were communist organisations, godless and knowing no colour bar. In May 1937 the Synod of the leading Dutch Reformed Church set up a special commission to inquire into and report on Communism in the South African Trade unions. The report was published in booklet form in 1939. Goebbels himself could not have improved on the style and presentation of the brochure. Two thousand copies of the report were published. A copy was brought to me during a strike of tobacco workers in Rustenburg in the Transvaal in 1940. Several hundred tobacco workers had been employed under appalling conditions, at a maximum wage of about 25*s*. a week, and they had asked Johanna Cornelius, then organiser of our union, to help them. During the strike that followed, the ministers of the Dutch Reformed Churches sided openly with the employers and distributed copies of the report, directing special attention to a photograph of white and non-white workers together at a meeting. I read the report and found nothing Christian in it. In content, style and vulgarity, it was a crude imitation of *Mein Kampf*—one long, foul slander against South African trade union leaders, with myself heading the list.

I issued summons against the reputed author of the report, Dr H. P. Wolmarans, and the publishers, Voortrekkerpers Beperk, a publishing house in Johannesburg, owned by leaders of the

Nationalist Party. Each of the Defendants paid £300 and costs into court. I dropped the action against Wolmarans, but decided to proceed against the Voortrekkerpers. I knew that, in deciding to proceed with the action, I took a grave risk. The publication, admittedly, was highly defamatory, but the two defendants had each paid in £300 and costs. The court might very well hold that £600 was adequate damages, in which event I would be liable for the costs of the trial, amounting perhaps to many thousands of pounds. I decided, however, that the reactionaries who were trying to turn South Africa into a Third Reich and to destroy democracy and the free trade union movement must be fought at all costs. The case, therefore, would not merely be an action between Sachs and a Nationalist publishing company. It would be a battle between democracy and fascism.

The case was heard in the Witwatersrand Local Division of the Supreme Court before Mr Justice Murray, a descendant of an old and proud Afrikaner family. It lasted about two weeks and attracted widespread public interest.

On the 3rd February 1942 Mr Justice Murray delivered his judgment. The court was packed with garment workers and ministers of the Dutch Reformed Churches. I was awarded £600, instead of the £300 paid into court by the Voortrekkerpers Beperk, and over £6,000 costs.

The garment workers were jubilant and so were true democrats. My success inspired all the members of the National Executive Committee of the South African Trades and Labour Council, numbering over twenty, to institute actions for defamation against the Voortrekkerpers. These actions were settled out of court, the defendant company paying substantial sums to every plaintiff. I had hoped that the Nationalists had by now learnt their lesson and would stop slandering trade union leaders. In fact, for several years the Nationalist speakers and press did refrain from defaming their opponents. Subsequently, however, slander continued to be a major weapon of Nationalist propagandists.

From 1934 onwards the Nationalist Party and its stooge organisations began to use not only slander, but also physical violence against individuals and organisations opposing them. Labour, trade union and even United Party meetings were regularly invaded and broken up by bands of fascist hooligans, armed with bicycle chains, knuckledusters and other weapons. As stated previously, the Reformers even went so far as to seize by force the office of the Mineworkers' Union and had to be ejected by a Court Order. The day after the assassination of Charlie Harris by a Nationalist fanatic, scores of people in the streets of Johannesburg greeted me with the macabre question: 'Are you still alive?' Indeed, the chief of the C.I.D. in Johannesburg sent for me and told me that my life was in danger and that I should carry a gun to protect myself. A licence for a revolver was duly issued to me and also to other officials of the union, whose lives were threatened. I carried on with my work as usual, but found it revolting that, in a so-called civilised community, peaceful and law-abiding citizens should be subjected to threats of violence and murder. Officials and members of the union and many of my friends worried about me constantly and, whenever I had left a meeting or a friend's home at night, would anxiously telephone to inquire whether I had reached home safely.

On 13th February 1940 I was addressing a meeting of about a hundred garment workers in Brixton, a working-class suburb of Johannesburg, on a purely trade union matter. Suddenly a band of about fifty Nationalists, armed with all sorts of weapons and led by one Simon Schoeman, a Reformer, rushed up to the meeting and, shouting: 'Where is the Jew Communist Solly Sachs?' dragged me off the platform and violently assaulted me. I was taken to hospital by ambulance and remained in bed for nearly two weeks. Later Schoeman appeared in the magistrate's court to answer a charge of assault. The Magistrate, Mr H. J. S. Johannes, described the violent assault as a 'political brawl' and fined Schoeman £1. The public of Johannesburg was somewhat shaken by this trivial sentence imposed for a brutal and unprovoked assault, and *The Star*, the leading daily paper, criticised the sentence. The union sent a strong protest to the Minister of Justice, Dr Colin Steyn, who shared our concern, but was apparently powerless to do anything. There were some peculiar features about the conduct of the trial. First, the magistrate allowed numerous irrelevancies to be introduced by the defence, secondly, despite my requests to the prosecutor to apply Section 363 (1) of Act 31 of 1917, for an order for compensation for my spectacles, which had been broken by the accused, the prosecutor refused to do so. For some reasons unknown to me, two ministers of the Dutch Reformed Churches, in clerical garb, sat in court throughout the proceedings. Subsequently, when I instituted a civil action against Schoeman, I was paid £30. The entire costs of the defence were borne by the Reformers.

CHAPTER TWENTY

Malan's Road to a New South Africa

ROUND ABOUT 1940 the propaganda committee of the Nationalist Party issued a pamphlet under the title, *The Road to New South Africa*, in which the party's attitude towards trade unions is clearly stated. This policy is identical in every respect with that expounded by Adolf Hitler in *Mein Kampf*, as Section IX of the pamphlet states:

> Labour is as indispensable as capital for the country's economic welfare. Both must serve the country; neither may be applied solely to selfish ends. The National Party is accordingly of the opinion that, taking into account the interest of the nation at large, labour is entitled to the special care and protection of the State. But, as elsewhere, State responsibility must be attended with a stated degree of State control.

The Party lays down the following chief points in its labour policy:

> (*a*) ADMINISTRATION
>
> (1) There must be a Labour Council which will devote itself exclusively to the problems and needs of labour. This Council will act on the principle of responsibility to the government and be subject to its ultimate decisions.
>
> (2) The Labour Council will be representative of both the employers and the employees in State and State-supported as well as in private undertakings.
>
> (3) The responsibilities and duties of the Labour Council will include, *inter alia*, the determination of wages and labour conditions for all employees.
>
> (*b*) ORGANISATION OF LABOUR
>
> (1) *The Party considers the organisation of the working classes, just as that of any other economic section of its own terrain, as desirable and necessary for protecting and serving their own specific interests*. Such organisation must therefore be encouraged by the State. Conversely, the State ought to guard against such organi-

sation being misused, for purposes inimical to the country and its people, or in order to disturb the proper and necessary equilibrium between the respective sectional interests in our economic structure.

(2) The Party considers the present system of wage control and the regulation of working conditions as ineffective, and proposes that the system of *collective bargaining* be supplemented by a system of *State responsibility*, exercised by means of the Central Economic Council and the Labour Council, as described above.

(3) The Labour organisations will indicate on their own the members who are to represent them on the Labour Council and its subordinate councils or committees and will have the right to make representation to the Government, to whom the Labour Council is to be responsible.

(4) The Labour Council will exercise effective control over the appointment of officials by, and the general activities of, the trade unions or workers' organisations.

Mr B. J. Schoeman who, in 1948 when the Nationalist Government came to power, was appointed Minister of Labour, said in a speech outlining future policy:

> The basic principle of trade unionism—collective bargaining—will be abolished, since the State will fix wages. What powers the union will have left will be in the hands of the Volk, for all foreigners, kaffir-boeties, communists and parasites will be removed.

On the broader issue of Nationalist policy, Dr N. Diederichs, a leading theoretician of the Nationalist Party, who had spent many years in Germany and openly proclaimed his sympathies with Nazi ideas, explained his party's policy in a speech in Parliament.

> On the one hand we have nationalism, which believes in the existence, in the necessary existence, of distinct peoples, distinct languages, nations and cultures, and which regards the fact of the existence of these peoples and these cultures as the basis of its conduct. On the other hand, we have liberalism and the basis of its political struggle is the individual with his so-called rights and liberties. Nationalism is the standpoint of members on this side of the House; and we say that this ideal

> of liberalism is unnatural and impossible and should it be achieved one day, which fortunately is not possible, the whole world would be the poorer for it. (*Hansard*, Vol. II, Col. 1620, August 1948)

The Dutch Reformed Churches enthusiastically accepted all the principles of the Nationalist Party and, from 1936 onwards, devoted much energy and attention to the trade union movement. In most countries it is usual for ministers of the Church to confine their activities to religious matters; in South Africa some manage to combine business with their spiritual work. In 1942 Dr G. E. N. Ross, a minister of the Dutch Reformed Church and for some time also a director of a clothing factory in Johannesburg, violently attacked the closed shop principle: 'The principle of the closed shop is an unholy weapon for the accomplices of the bosses to deprive Afrikaners of their bread.'

Another minister of the Dutch Reformed Church, Mr van der Walt, also a director of a clothing factory in Johannesburg, heartily supported these views and regularly attacked the trade union movement in the official Church organ *Kerkbode*, and at meetings.

When war broke out in September 1939 General Hertzog, who was then Prime Minister, made an impassioned plea in support of Hitler Germany and opposed the declaration of war on Germany by South Africa. His Government was defeated on this issue and Smuts became Prime Minister; Hertzog, grown old, subsequently retired from politics. Mr Oswald Pirow, who had been Minister of Defence and of Railways, fell out with both the United and the Nationalist parties and set up an organisation of his own, known as the 'New Order'. Confident of Hitler's ultimate victory, he was undoubtedly anxious to become the leader of South Africa. The Nationalist Party and its stooge organisations opposed the war throughout the years and did everything possible to hinder the war effort. The more extreme elements even engaged in sabotage. Bands of Nationalist ruffians frequently beat up men in uniform. Hundreds of their members were interned and several were convicted of acts of sabotage and high treason. Ministers of the Dutch Reformed Churches prayed for a Hitler victory and many refused to solemnise marriages of members of their Churches who volunteered for war service, or to baptize their children.

CHAPTER TWENTY-ONE

Civil War in the Factories

ALTHOUGH THE UNION had previously denounced the treachery of Neville Chamberlain, once war was declared, it supported the war effort, and hundreds of members, men and women, volunteered for the army. When the 'blitz' started over England a press statement announced that several thousand British children were coming to South Africa to escape the horrors of bombing.

The Central Executive Committee of the union decided to call for volunteers amongst garment workers to make clothes for these children and, within a short period, over twelve thousand members readily offered to work overtime to do so. Many employers agreed to place their factories, machinery and staff at the disposal of the volunteers and the union voted funds to buy materials. Volunteers from different factories competed to see who could produce the best and largest number of garments. Many Nationalist workers, on purely humanitarian grounds, were among the volunteers. The Nationalist press and a few agents of the Nationalist Party within the union started a furious protest against the proposal to clothe 'foreign' children. 'Why don't we clothe our own poor children?' they demanded. The union thereupon decided to ask for volunteers to clothe an equal number of South African children and to vote the necessary funds for materials. There was not a single volunteer. The Nationalists were obviously more interested in rousing anti-British feeling than in helping South African children. Ultimately, only about one hundred British children arrived, although clothing had been prepared for many more.

The union also took steps to safeguard the interests of the members who had joined the forces. With the co-operation of the employers we raised thousands of pounds to help the soldiers and their dependants. Altogether tens of thousands of pounds were collected during the war by voluntary contributions from members for various humanitarian purposes.

The overwhelming majority of the garment workers gave their whole-hearted support to the war effort. Small groups, however, had come under the influence of fascist organisations and often caused disturbances in factories. In one factory where over a hundred workers were employed, four women started repeating a rumour, which had been spread by the Ossewabrandwag, to the effect that policemen had brought to the homes of widows the blood-stained uniforms of their husbands, who had been killed in the war. The rest of the workers became incensed and, during the argument that ensued, the four started praising Hitler and expressed the fervent hope that he would soon come to South Africa. Work stopped and I was called in to restore peace. About a hundred indignant Afrikaner women demanded the immediate expulsion of the four Hitlerites from the factory. I called in these victims of Nazi propaganda and spoke to them for about half an hour. At first they tried to deny that they had spoken about the blood-stained uniforms, but eventually they admitted that they had acted foolishly and promised to behave better in future. All the workers went back to the machines, but late in the afternoon, when they stopped work, I received another message, that trouble had started again. A group of young Afrikaner women whose relatives had joined the army, had sent a note to the four trouble-makers, in Afrikaans, saying: 'We democrats want to fight the Nazis.' And fighting, in this case, meant not a verbal argument, but fisticuffs. When I arrived I explained to the angry workers the futility of physical violence. I told them that we would have to show the masses of misled Afrikaner workers the dangers of Nazi ideas and propaganda, but could do it more effectively without scissors or hatpins.

On another occasion I received an urgent phone message from another factory employing about five hundred workers. There I found that a group of patriotic workers were in the habit of coming to the factory with Union Jacks pinned to their lapels. A much smaller group of about twenty retaliated wearing the Vierkleur, emblem of the Nationalists. Offensive remarks from one group to the other had led to a state of civil war. At first it was confined to words, but a few days later, scissors and other weapons came into play. When I arrived at the factory, the place was in an uproar and the foreman was utterly helpless to cope with the situation. I asked him to switch off the motors and let me speak to the workers. I told them that they came to the factories to make garments and earn a living. Life was always difficult for the workers, and even more so now, with a terrible war raging. They should help each other and not cause more unhappiness. They had every right to display the Union Jack or the Vierkleur; people should be proud of their flags; but they must not start quarrels, make their own lives miserable, and disorganise production. The union was determined to ensure peace in the industry. All members of the union would have their livelihood protected and be allowed to do their day's work without threats or violence. Henceforth no flags must be brought to the factory until the workers had learnt to treat each other's national emblems with respect. In future anyone who was likely to cause a disturbance would be dismissed from the factory and might even become liable to disciplinary measures by the union. There was tremendous applause and both sides came up to me to express their gratitude to the union. I saw clearly the tragedy of the workers. Ordinarily they co-operated in their work in the factory and were quite friendly towards each other. But now, as a result of the war and the Nationalists' propaganda, racial bitterness filled their lives. Everyone felt irritated and extremely unhappy and life in the factory, where co-operation and amity are essential, became unbearable. On neither side would passion yield to reason until the union's policy of toleration was put to them. Then they readily agreed to put a stop to their useless feud. Hatred and bitterness had been suffocating them, but now they could breathe freely again.

In another factory a young Afrikaner woman flaunted a swastika in the face of another, who had that morning learned that her husband was missing up north. The workers got up from their machines and demanded she should be dismissed immediately. She was charged before the union committee with a breach of discipline. Asked why she had tried to cause such pain to a fellow-worker, who was already in great distress, she offered no defence and was expelled from the union.

During the war years the Nationalist Party made little headway in the trade union movement. Tens of thousands of Afrikaners from the industrial and rural areas had volunteered for war service and many found employment at reasonable standards in civilian and war industries. In the general election of 1943 Smuts, in co-operation with the Labour Party, was returned by an overwhelming majority. As more and more Afrikaners left the rural areas to come into the cities, the leaders of the Nationalist Party began to realise the importance, not only of holding the Platteland, but also of capturing the towns. Propaganda against the free trade unions was intensified, especially by the ministers of the Dutch Reformed Churches. Not only did they deliver sermons from the pulpit denouncing the trade unions, but in addition they organised regular visits to clothing factories, ostensibly to hold prayer meetings, but actually to incite the white workers against the non-Europeans. On almost every occasion when such a prayer meeting was held in a clothing factory, relations between white and non-white workers deteriorated.

Early in February 1944 a large clothing factory in Germiston employing about seven hundred Europeans engaged nine Coloured women to help execute urgently-needed war contracts. These Coloured workers were employed in a section of the factory separated from the Europeans. Indeed, for several days the European workers did not even know that Coloured workers had been engaged. On Wednesday, 9th February, two Nationalists in the factory discovered this fact and immediately started trouble among the workers. A deputation was sent to the employer demanding the instant sacking of the Coloured workers. The Nationalist trouble-makers switched off the motors, called a strike and harangued the workers, violently attacking the union and officials for allowing Coloured workers to work. The branch secretary, Hester Cornelius, arrived at the factory to deal with the matter, but was shouted down by a group of Nationalists, who also threatened those who would not take part in the strike with physical violence. For several hours there was chaos and mob rule in the factory and the employer was compelled to dismiss the nine Coloured workers. On the 18th February 1944 the Germiston branch committee of the union held a meeting, at which the two ringleaders were charged with calling a strike and causing a disturbance in breach of the union's agreement with the employers, and also with howling down the branch secretary. Of the sixteen members of the executive, only one was not an Afrikaner. By unanimous decision the branch committee found the two women guilty on both counts and resolved to expel them from membership of the union. The Nationalists and other pro-fascist organisations started a nation-wide campaign against the union and its leaders. The Nationalist newspapers came out with big headlines: 'White Civilisation in Danger.' In Parliament members of the Nationalist Party moved 'the adjournment of the House to consider a matter of grave public importance' and, during the debate on this motion, vicious attacks were made on the Garment Workers' Union and the trade union movement generally. The three Dutch Reformed Churches immediately established an Enlarged Church Committee to deal with the 'danger facing white civilisation'. This committee organised numerous public meetings throughout South Africa, at which the union leaders were vilified. The whole campaign was engineered by the Nationalist Party and was designed to weaken trade unionism and to provoke race hatred. Ministers of the Dutch Reformed Churches not only joined willingly, but took a leading part in it.

The shameless machinations of the Nationalist leaders and the extent to which the ministers of the Dutch Reformed Churches readily abandoned Christianity to serve the interests of reaction and racial domination are clearly demonstrated by a confidential report, which the union received from a thoroughly reliable source in 1st March 1944. The report read as follows:

A meeting took place last night and lasted until midnight at which a member of the Reformers organisation was one of the principal speakers. This was a private meeting and only those intimately associated with the events in the Germiston factory took part. Discussion took place as to whether the girls at the factory would strike or not, but eventually it was decided that the two girls who had been dismissed from the factory and suspended from membership of the Garment Workers' Union should force their way into the factory today (Monday). If they were then ejected, the rest of the girls would be so enraged that a general strike in the factory would ensue. This would give the impression that the strike was a spontaneous one by the workers themselves in protest against the two girls' dismissal for refusing to work under the same roof as Coloured workers.

X . . ., a Nationalist leader, sent out scouts to ascertain the position at the factory and found that the two girls had entered the factory and sat down to work. He was very pleased and believed that this would set everything going in the direction planned.

He then contacted several Afrikaner parsons and told them that the preservation of Christianity and white civilisation was in jeopardy and that they must join him at the consistory of the Rev. Boneschans at five-thirty p.m. today, when the whole matter would be discussed. In the course of other conversations, X . . . said that the whole affair must appear to be under the aegis of the Afrikaans churches and that no word of Reformers must be mentioned. The public must be made to believe that the workers were fighting the black menace and that the Churches had given this fight their blessing. In the meantime, the Reformers and X . . . would work behind the scenes, egging on the workers and endeavouring to make the flames spread to every corner of the Witwatersrand, so that all the workers of the Garment Workers' Union would be out on strike in due course and, feeling that Solly Sachs and his associates on the committee of the union were not disposed to help them fight the black menace, the workers would eventually throw Sachs and his friends out of the control of the union and good Afrikaners would be elected in their place. The nation must be roused to action as this was a golden opportunity for the Afrikaners to gain control of the industrial workers.

There must be no mention of any political intrigues. Stress must be laid on the fact that the Churches were in the forefront of the struggle to preserve Christianity and white civilisation. The Armsorg Raad (an Afrikaner welfare organisation) would be approached in Johannesburg and X . . . was to leave at nine a.m. for Johannesburg to see everyone worthy of contacting in the matter. He asked all the parsons whom he contacted to lay aside any business they might have for the next few days, as it was essential that all forces should be marshalled for a lightning strike.

The Enlarged Church Committee issued a pamphlet entitled *White South Africa, Save Yourself*. The pamphlet was not only an incitement to race hatred, but also defamatory. I thereupon made an application to the Supreme Court and was granted an order forbidding the distribution of the publication, with costs against the individual members of the committee.

The union issued a circular to all its members, exposing the tactics of the Nationalist leaders and their stooges. We could not call a public meeting in Germiston as the Nationalist hooligans would have broken it up. But on 16th March 1944 a mass meeting of garment workers was held at the City Hall, Johannesburg. Some five thousand members of the union crowded into the hall. A gang of about fifty Nationalists, some in clerical garb, armed with sticks and bicycle chains, tried to force an entry into the hall, but were barred by the stewards, nearly all of whom were women. Several of them were violently assaulted. One was hit in the face, punched over the left eye and struck with a baton on the shoulder. Another woman was so severely kicked in the stomach that she had to stay three weeks in hospital. One ruffian drew a knife, but was quickly disarmed. Many other women were attacked, but the stewards succeeded in ejecting the hooligans from the hall and the meeting proceeded peacefully. Three resolutions were unanimously adopted

(1) expressing full confidence in the leadership of the union;
(2) urging all members to stand loyally by the union;
(3) instructing the central executive committee to proceed with the negotiations for a new industrial agreement.

The campaign of slander against the union was carried on for many months, all because nine Coloured garment workers had been allowed to work in a factory and earn an honest living. For years thousands of Coloured garment workers had been employed in Johannesburg and 'white civilisation' had not collapsed, but Germiston was a Nationalist stronghold.

During the campaign, a certain minister of one of the Dutch Reformed Churches, the Rev. A. B. du Preez, issued a 'congregational letter', which contained defamatory material about me. I issued a summons against du Preez and, on the 12th March 1945, the case started in the Witwatersrand Local Division of the Supreme Court before Mr Justice Neser. It lasted twenty-one days and much interest was added to the proceedings by the defendant engaging Mr Oswald Pirow, K.C., to appear on his behalf. Once more, the forces of democracy and reaction engaged in a great battle within the precincts of the court, where lawlessness cannot be tolerated. For three weeks, the newspapers gave prominence to the proceedings and this *cause célèbre* became the talk of South Africa.

Judgment was reserved and both sides waited anxiously for the verdict.

On the 24th October 1935 Mr Justice Neser delivered his judgment. The court was crowded and over fifty Dutch Reformed Ministers assembled to hear the result. I was awarded £300 and costs amounting to over £11,000.

The learned judge held that the occasion was privileged, but that the defendant was actuated by an indirect and improper motive and stated of me what he did not know to be true, or was reckless whether it was true or false.

This defeat had a disastrous effect upon the disrupters whilst it raised the prestige of our union enormously and inspired the trade union movement and other democratic forces to carry on the struggle for freedom.

CHAPTER TWENTY-TWO

A Slight Case of Blackmail

THE YEAR 1944 was one of the busiest for the union. In the midst of the trouble, which started in February, we became involved in a series of court actions, which wasted a great deal of our time and energy.

In November 1943 I was called into a small dress factory to settle a dispute caused by the employer, quite unjustly, accusing a worker of stealing a garment. It took only a few minutes to settle the matter, but as I was leaving one of the workers came to me and whispered: 'Mr Sachs, there are some funny things going on in this factory. You ask Inez Mentos.' I sent for her and, when she came to my office, she was trembling with fear. I managed to get her to calm down and then she told me her story:

> I worked for a clothing factory in Cape Town for seven years and had to support a family of six. Because of domestic troubles I left Cape Town for Johannesburg. In the train, my bag, with 11*s.*—all the money I had—was stolen and I arrived in Johannesburg penniless. I lodged with my sister, whose husband is a waiter, earning £15 a month, and I had to share their only room. I was desperately anxious to get work and applied for a job. The employer's son took me to the Industrial Council office to get a certificate of service and, when the council agent asked how long I had worked in the industry, I was going to say seven years, but Mr X junior replied instead: 'Eighteen months.' A certificate of service was issued to me on the basis of eighteen months' experience. I was afraid to contradict my boss, as I was urgently in need of work.

I duly checked the wage register and found that she had been underpaid the sum of £24 5*s.* 7*d.* I called on Mr X, asked him to refund this amount, and warned him that he would get into trouble if he persisted in these malpractices. Mr X refused to pay and said: 'Prove it. It is my word against hers.'

I then submitted the matter to the Council and both the employer and the worker were invited to attend a meeting, called for the 17th December 1943. Mr X did not attend. Inez Mentos, obviously very nervous, told her story to the nine employers and nine union representatives in a perfectly straightforward manner. The employers believed her, but instead of condemning X, they began to cross-examine her with such viciousness that the girl broke down. It was abundantly clear that she knew nothing about the agreement for the industry, about certificates of service, or even the rate of pay to which she was entitled. As she was penniless, her one and only concern was to get a job.

Disgusted with the attitude of the employers, I told them that, if their wives and daughters had found themselves in similar distressing circumstances, they too, might not have dared to contradict their employer. I moved that the employer be requested to refund the back-pay and be warned against contravening the agreement in future. The employers voted against my motion and asked that the matter should go to court. No doubt, they had in mind that, in court, with the employer's word against the worker's, it would be difficult, if not impossible, to obtain a conviction.

The case was heard early in February. X, who had at first pleaded not guilty, changed his plea to guilty, was cautioned and discharged. The magistrate ordered that the amount underpaid should be paid into the Consolidated Revenue Fund and not given to Inez, as she had been guilty of collusion.

Sections 53, 54 and 55 of the Industrial Conciliation Act give the court power to order an employer, convicted for underpayment of wages or other remuneration, to pay the amount to an officer of the court and, where there has been collusion between the employer and the worker, to order that the whole, or a portion of the amount, be paid into the Consolidated Revenue Fund. Before an order is made, however, the court must inquire: (i) whether the employee agreed to work for less, (ii) whether, if he did so agree, he knew of his rights under the agreement, and (iii) the circumstances under which the worker so agreed; and the inquiry must form part of the record. In this case, the worker's legal rights were completely ignored. Inez had not agreed to work for less wages, she had not known her legal rights and she was destitute. Indeed, her money was now being confiscated without any inquiry being held.

The committee of the union was indignant when it heard this news and decided to invite the ten women workers at the factory concerned to a committee meeting. This took place on the 9th February and in the course of it I explained that what was involved was not merely a simple underpayment, but an insidious attempt to reintroduce the reprehensible methods of faking wage registers and certificates of service, which the union had eradicated only after many years of bitter struggle. The women also mentioned numerous other complaints and transgressions of the agreement in the factory. It was left to the workers themselves to decide what action to take and they unanimously decided not to report for work the following day and to terminate their employment. Anxious to avoid trouble, I phoned the employer at his home and told him of this decision. I asked him to refund Miss Mentos the amount he had underpaid her, or he would have no workers the following day. He became argumentative and I put down the receiver. Next morning the women stayed away from work.

The laws are enforced promptly and rigorously against workers and, a week later, the ten absentees received a summons to answer a charge of striking unlawfully. On 6th May 1944 they were all found guilty and were each sentenced to a fine of £15 and to three months' imprisonment with hard labour. The latter part of the sentence was suspended for two years on condition of good behaviour.

On the 16th May 1944 I received a summons to answer a charge of extortion:

> That the accused is guilty of attempting to commit the Crime of Extortion.
>
> In that, whereas on the 2nd day of February 1944 a certain X and another had been convicted of failing to pay to a certain employee, Miss Inez Mentos, who was a member of the Garment Workers' Union, the minimum wages prescribed by certain Industrial Agreements relating to the Clothing Industry, Transvaal;
>
> And whereas the Court had determined the amount underpaid to be £24 5*s.* 7*d.*
>
> And whereas the Court had on the aforesaid date ordered the said X and another to pay to the Divisional Inspector of Labour, Johannesburg, the said amount of £24 5*s.* 7*d.* for payment to the Consolidated Revenue Fund.
>
> Thereafter, to wit upon or about the 9th day of February 1944

and at Johannesburg, in the district of Johannesburg, the said accused, being the General Secretary of the said Garment Workers' Union, did wrongfully, unlawfully and extorsively demand from the said Mr X that the said Mr X pay to him forthwith at the office of the said Garment Workers' Union, Johannesburg, the sum of £24 5*s*. 7*d*.

And did then and there threaten the said X that unless he paid the said sum of money forthwith he, the said X, would have no girls working in his factory the following day.

And did by means of such threat wrongfully and unlawfully attempt to extort and obtain from the said X the sum of £24 5*s*. 7*d*.

We consulted Mr N. E. Rosenberg, K.C., and, when he read the charge he said: 'Mr Sachs, there is no case against you.' I said to Mr Rosenberg: 'I have the utmost respect for your forensic knowledge, but I am going to be convicted.' He looked at me with the disdain of the eminent lawyer for the layman, but when in due course I appeared in the magistrate's court, he soon saw the significance of my remark. The prosecutor, Mr Vermoeten, apart from subjecting the president of the union, Miss Scheepers, to uncalled for indignities, furiously attacked the closed shop, which was quite irrelevant to the case.

On 28th July 1944 I was found guilty and sentenced to a fine of £40, or one month's imprisonment with hard labour. I also had to listen to a lecture from the magistrate.

Our enemies were overjoyed. For years, they had tried unsuccessfully to get me convicted. Now, at last, they had succeeded, and on an infamous charge of blackmail. In all, ten members of the union had received vicious sentences, a destitute working girl had been deprived of money due to her, and the general secretary of the union had been convicted of attempted extortion. But their rejoicing was premature.

We lodged an appeal in respect of all three matters, and this was heard in the Transvaal Provincial Division of the Supreme Court, Pretoria, before Mr Justice Solomon and Mr Justice Brebner on the 15th October 1944.

The application for review in the matter of Inez Mentos was heard first. While Mr Retief, who appeared for the Minister of Finance, was arguing, Judge Solomon interrupted him with the question: 'Mr Retief, is the Minister of Finance so hard up that he needs the £24 of a poor working girl who had been unlawfully deprived of it?'

Within two hours, the court gave judgment, granting the application, with costs, against the Minister of Finance. Inez Mentos got her £24 5*s*. 7*d*. and the Minister had to pay many hundreds of pounds in costs.

As I sat in court, listening to the argument, I naturally felt elated with our just and speedy success. But our real victory was still to come. Before the court adjourned for lunch, Judge Solomon said: 'Mr Rosenberg, the court will not require to hear you. After lunch, we shall hear Dr Yutar (who appeared for the Crown) as to whether there was any conscious impropriety present in the appellant when his motive and object was clearly to protect a worker who had been defrauded.'

In the morning, before the court started, I was introduced to Dr Yutar, the very able and determined assistant to the Attorney-General. He greeted me affably: 'Mr Sachs, I have heard a lot about you. I don't think you have much chance in the appeal.' I replied jocularly: 'I have also heard a great deal about you, Dr Yutar. As for the appeal, my case is in the hands of a very competent craftsman. Let him take care of it.'

The court resumed at two-thirty p.m. and, as soon as Dr Yutar commenced his argument for the Crown, Judge Solomon very angrily remarked: 'Dr Yutar, do you suggest that a trade union official, who takes steps to protect a member of his union, who had been defrauded of her wages, is guilty of extortion? Rubbish, rubbish!' Dr Yutar battled manfully, but the judge became increasingly annoyed and continued interrupting him, observing on one occasion: 'How could the Attorney-General bring a case of this nature to court?'

I have spent many a day in the Supreme Court and have never seen a judge so indignant. Everybody knew that I had been dragged into court, not because I had committed a crime, but for entirely different reasons. Almost before Dr Yutar could finish his argument, Judge Solomon delivered the judgment of the court, not only upholding my appeal and setting aside the conviction and sentence, but also telling the magistrate who had convicted me a few most uncomplimentary truths. The following are quotations from the judgment:

> The magistrate, in preparing his reasons for judgment, realised the necessity of finding that the appellant, in making his demand and threat, was seeking to gain an advantage for himself. Being unable to find any facts to support what a Court of Justice would normally deem to be an advantage, he had recourse to a flight of fancy. . . . On the evidence produced at the trial, it would be lamentable if a conviction for such a mean and cowardly crime as extortion were attached to the appellant for life. Fortunately, we are able to rectify the injustice. The appeal is allowed and the conviction and sentence are set aside.

Once more, justice triumphed over lawlessness. Congratulations poured in to the union from all over South Africa and the mass of garment workers were jubilant.

On the advice of counsel we did not proceed with the appeal in the case of the ten girls who had been convicted for unlawful striking. Instead, we sent a memorandum to the Minister of Justice, Dr Colin Steyn, and asked him to give the matter his consideration. By order of the Governor-General, the sentences were changed to a caution and discharge.

Before the appeals were heard the union decided to teach Mr X a lesson which he and other employers, who might be tempted to copy him, would remember. We went through all the cumbersome provisions of the Industrial Conciliation Act and called a lawful strike.

Section 79 of the Act reads:

> No proceedings shall be brought in any court of law against any trade union or employers' organisation, or against any member, office-bearer or official of any such union or organisation, in respect of any wrongful act committed by that union or organisation, or by that member, office-bearer or official on behalf of that union or organisation, in furtherance of a strike or lock-out; . . .

Taking full advantage of the protection afforded us by this section, we called a mass demonstration outside the factory, which was attended by several thousand workers, and issued instructions to all members of the union not to take employment there. In due course Mr X was forced to sell his factory.

CHAPTER TWENTY-THREE

Meeting with Smuts—
How the United party Betrayed South Africa

THE NATIONALIST PARTY, though always claiming to have no association with Nazism, had staked everything on a Nazi victory. Hitler's defeat, therefore, weakened the party considerably. Towards the end of 1945 it seemed as if South Africa was at last entering a new era. Twelve thousand South Africans had given their lives in the great struggle of democracy against fascism. Tens of thousands who had volunteered for service had seen the world outside their own country and had everywhere met people who strongly opposed the South African race hatred. The men and women who came back from the war, and the tens of thousands who had helped the war effort at home, began to show a new spirit of racial tolerance and of true democracy.

In the immediate post-war years South Africa seemed to be entering an epoch of great progressive development. During the war years the country had passed through an industrial revolution. Manufacturing industries had expanded and prospered. Great masses of workers, European and non-European, had come into industry and had begun to play an important part in raising the national economy. The Poor White problem, which had once been so serious, had been largely solved by their absorption into industry. Capital was coming into the country in great volume.

Great numbers of non-Europeans had found employment in industry with opportunities to improve their skill and raise their standards, in spite of the many obstacles in their way, and there was a much greater understanding between the English-speaking and the Afrikaans-speaking sections of the community than ever before. South Africa had excellent opportunities to build an industrial civilisation and help raise the whole of Africa, at any rate south of the equator, to a higher level of progress.

The one thing needed to guide South Africa away from its sordid past and on to the road of true democracy was courageous leadership. There was one man who could have led the country to a new and better way of life. That man was Field-Marshal Smuts, who had played a leading military and political rôle in the fight against Hitler.

For nearly fifty years until his death in 1949 General Smuts was the dominant figure in South African politics and the only South African politician to attain international fame. In 1902 he became a great friend of Britain, where he was held in high esteem and earned the reputation of being not only a great statesman but also a great liberal. In South Africa opinions about him were sharply divided.

I first met Smuts in 1936, when he was Minister of Justice in the Hertzog government. I was a member of a deputation from the South African Trades and Labour Council, which had called upon him to discuss matters which came under his department. Smuts had fought with great courage against the British during the Boer War and had written *A Century of Wrong*, which included the following magnificent passage:

> In this awful turning point in the history of South Africa, on the eve of the conflict which threatens to exterminate our people, it behoves us to speak the truth in what may be, perchance, our last message to the world. . . .
>
> Our people have been represented by influential statesmen and on hundreds of platforms in England as incompetent, uncivilised, dishonourable, untrustworthy etc. etc., so that not only the British public, but nearly the whole world, began to believe that we stood on the same level as the wild beasts. In the face of these taunts and this provocation our people still remained silent. . . .
>
> Our people remained silent partly out of stupidity, partly out of a feeling of despairing helplessness, and partly because, being a pastoral people, they read no newspapers and were thus unaware of the way in which the feeling of the whole world was being prejudiced against them by the efforts of malignant hate. . . .
>
> As the wounded antelope awaits the coming of the lion, the jackal and the vulture, so do our poor people all over South Africa contemplate the approach of the foe. . . .

And:

> It is ordained that we, insignificant as we are, should be the first among the people to begin the struggle against the new world tyranny of Capitalism.

Smuts was known to me not only as the Boer patriot and renowned statesman, but also as the man of 'grey steel', of utter ruthlessness; the man who was responsible for many shootings. There were the shootings on the Rand in July 1913; at Bulhoek in May 1921, where 163 Africans were killed and over one hundred wounded; in South West Africa, where masses of Bondels (Hottentots) were massacred in May 1922, and there were many others. I hated Smuts for sending Taffy Long, that brave Welsh miner, to the gallows after the strike in 1922.

From the moment I was introduced I found Smuts charming, friendly and alert. I had been told beforehand that his word was his bond and that he always fulfilled any promise he made. We chatted informally over tea, touching a variety of subjects ranging from philosophy to botany.

After this long, pleasant interlude Smuts said to us: 'Well, boys, what's the trouble?'

We had two matters to discuss with him: first, the wholesale contraventions by clothing manufacturers of the wage determination and agreement for the clothing industry in Cape Town; second, the conviction and sentence to four months' imprisonment of Dr E. R. Roux for 'insulting the King', whose appeal was then pending before the Appellate Division of the Supreme Court. Smuts listened to our case attentively and assured us that the trouble in Cape Town would receive his attention and agreed that attacks on Royalty should not constitute a criminal offence in South Africa.

Two months later a clothing manufacturer in Cape Town was convicted and fined £75 and his manager £20 for underpaying workers. For about six months prosecutions against clothing manufacturers in the Cape were dealt with regularly by the courts. Smuts kept his word. Roux's appeal was upheld and his conviction and sentence set aside.

My next meeting with Smuts was in 1940, when he invited a deputation from our union to his office in Union Buildings, Pretoria. The war was on and he was anxious to establish cordial relations with the trade unions. Anna Scheepers, the president of the Union, Johanna Cornelius, Dulcie Hartwell, Hester Cornelius and myself formed the delegation. We were introduced by Mr Morris Kentridge, M.P., and within a few minutes of meeting the 'Oubaas' (old master), I could see that my colleagues, who were all militant trade unionists and hated Smuts the ruthless politician, were enchanted with Smuts the man. Greeting me cordially, he expressed disagreement with my politics but paid tribute to the services I had rendered to the poor Afrikaner working women. There was nothing of the awe-inspiring, great statesman about him: he was the simple, genial, unaffected Boer receiving visitors over a cup of coffee. He chatted to Anna about her uncle, whom he knew well. They had fought together in the Boer War, and later had farms near each other. There was no agenda and he invited us to discuss with him any subject we liked. Dulcie, a bitter anti-Nazi, whose three brothers were at the front, raised the matter of the pro-Nazi activities of the Ossewabrandwag and other fascist organisations. Since the celebration of the Voortrekker centenary in 1938 many O.B.'s were sporting beards in imitation of the Voortrekkers and in her denunciation of the pro-Nazi elements Dulcie said: 'These young fools strut about in the streets with their goatees and consider themselves very clever.' To illustrate her point she put one hand up to her chin, and then suddenly we all looked at Smuts, very conscious that he, too, wore a goatee. For a moment Dulcie was quite embarrassed and then we all burst out laughing: 'Of course, Dulcie' (Smuts called all the women by their Christian names), 'not all people who wear beards are O.B.'s,' Smuts remarked.

As Prime Minister and Commander-in-Chief, Smuts was a very busy man; but the interview, which had been arranged to last half-an-hour, went on for over an hour. By the time we left the women were fascinated by Smuts' simplicity of manner and charm. Outside his office we met a galaxy of high ranking officers, whom he had kept waiting while he enjoyed a friendly chat with a group of militant trade unionists.

In 1942 I was elected to a committee of the Trades and Labour Council which used to meet Smuts regularly to discuss war problems. He was always amiable and attentive, hated obsequiousness and wanted speakers to come straight to the point. On one occasion I submitted a lengthy memorandum to a committee in Johannesburg, appointed by Smuts to deal with war production problems, exposing the scandalous manner in which the 'cost plus' system was operating. Government war contracts were paid on a basis of cost plus 10 per cent. Some of the employer pocket-patriots plundered the national treasury by inflating costs and thereby enlarging the ten per cent profit. I collected a great deal of information from works managers, shop stewards and ordinary workers about deliberate wastage and inefficiency. The chairman of the Committee, the late Dr Van der Bijl, was a pompous little man and sneered at my memorandum. I wrote to Smuts, and he returned my letter with a marginal note in his own handwriting 'matter under consideration'. A week later a special meeting of the committee was called, at which I was asked to read my memorandum. There was a new member present, who kept on asking questions with the obvious intention of checking the information. At the end of the meeting he introduced himself as Edward Jackson, formerly general manager of the National Bank of South Africa and now a director of ISCOR (Iron and Steel Corporation of South Africa). He was adviser to Smuts on economic matters and certainly knew his business. We had a long discussion at his office and it became clear to me that the Government knew of the cheating that was going on but was helpless—the whole system was too corrupt to make it possible to stop abuses.

In 1943 the T.L.C. Committee met Smuts to discuss a number of important matters. I was deputed to present the case for an all-round increase in the wages of African workers. The cost of living was rising, but the wages of Africans which had always been low remained unaltered. I stressed three points: the terribly low level of wages for African workers; that many employers were willing to increase wages and that the Africans were considering taking strike action. Smuts listened and for a moment I thought that I had convinced him and that he would instruct the Wage Board to raise African wages. Much to my surprise and disgust, Smuts, after thinking for a few moments, said quite calmly: 'Sachs, don't you think they are a lot of savages?' The next day I resigned from the committee.

It was the tragedy of South Africa and of Smuts himself that he failed his country at its most decisive period.

At the end of 1946 two important questions concerning South Africa were placed on the agenda of the United Nations. The first was a complaint brought by the Government of India against the Union Government, arising from the treatment of Indians in South Africa and, more especially, the passing of the Asiatic Land Tenure and Indian Representation Act by the Union Parliament at the beginning of 1946. The second arose from the Union

Government's formal request for the incorporation within the Union of the Territory of South-West Africa, which it held under a mandate from the now defunct League of Nations.

During the debates which followed at Lake Success the entire policy of the Union Government came under critical examination and representatives from various countries condemned in no uncertain terms South African policy towards its non-European peoples.

Smuts, who attended the U.N. meeting in person, returned to South Africa a bitterly disappointed man, who seemed to feel personally insulted at what had been said against South Africa at the United Nations. Instead of appealing to the people of South Africa to renounce their policy of racial intolerance, he delivered endless diatribes against the 'Kaffir', 'Coolie' and 'Communist' dangers. The spirit of democracy, which had begun to sweep South Africa after the defeat of Hitler, soon evaporated and the shrewd Dr Malan exploited the situation with the utmost cunning.

'We told you that it was a terrible blunder to fight Hitler and to ally yourselves with Soviet Communism. We warned you of the danger of the Indians and Africans demanding equality and full citizen rights. You would not listen to us, now you are in trouble,' the leaders of the Nationalist Party cried. Smuts, who all his life remained the champion of white domination beneath a veneer of liberalism, retreated to his backveld world and paved the way for Malan's victory in May 1948. Had Smuts fought for a great democratic South Africa with the same resoluteness with which he had fought against Hitler, the Nationalist Party would have been doomed. Before his death in 1949 he tried to save the situation but it was too late. The Nationalists were in the saddle and, in a short space of time, turned South Africa into a fascist police State.

The verdict of history on this extraordinary man will be given not on the basis of the speeches he made abroad, but on his actions at home. South Africa needed and still needs today an Abraham Lincoln to free it from traditional backwardness and bigotry and Smuts, although a great admirer of Walt Whitman, was no Lincoln. He was a product and a victim of historical circumstances, not an architect of history, and all his life remained a faithful servant of British imperial interests and of the backward farmers of South Africa. He was a man of great physical and moral courage.

He first fought the British and then became their best friend. His personal charm and simplicity did not stop him from being ruthless to others and unsparing of himself. He was big enough to admire Western European civilisation, but too deeply rooted in South African backwardness to introduce that civilisation into his own country. He was human, with a contempt for humanity—and especially for the little men by whom he was surrounded at home. He was a man of many parts, a brave soldier, a Boer, a statesman of international repute. He was certainly a great man but not a good one. His policy of Christian Trusteeship towards the African people differed from apartheid only in degree not in substance. He left to posterity a country, of which he was the chief designer, tormented by hatred and fear; yet he was the only person who could have led South Africa towards real progress.

During 1946-7 the influence of Malan continuously declined. Had the truly democratic forces, and those which professed to uphold democracy, taken advantage of this trend, the Nationalist Party could never have recovered and might even have disintegrated. The main support for Malan had come from the rural areas, but economic factors drove great numbers of Whites to find employment in the towns. By 1946 about 70 per cent of the Europeans had become urbanised. The towns, in the main, had been violently opposed to the Nationalist Party and, in the general election of 1943, the Nationalists had obtained only a few seats in all the urban areas. It was clear that whoever won the allegiance of the tens of thousands of Afrikaner workers would rule the country. These workers had brought with them the backward traditions of the land and, at first, were overwhelmingly Nationalist. The union had proved, however, that, given a correct lead, the Afrikaner workers could be won over from Nationalism. A new political home had to be found for these workers, and that home should have been the Labour Party.

Whilst the United Party was in power, from 1946-7, it did everything possible to antagonise the workers, so playing straight into the hands of the Nationalists. In the Mineworkers' Union, the United Party leaders supported men in whom the workers had no confidence. The cost of living was rising catastrophically, but no steps were taken to check inflation. The United Party should also have concentrated on weakening the power of the Nationalists by helping the Labour Party to gain influence among the Afrikaner workers, the majority of whom distrusted the United Party because they identified it with capitalism and imperialism. Instead, everything was done to discredit the Labour Party and to denigrate its more militant leaders who were, of course, the only ones with any influence amongst the Afrikaners. In this the United Party was warmly supported by the muddle-headed 'Lefts' and confused liberals, who took great pleasure in sniping at the Labour Party. For twenty years our union pleaded with all anti-Malan elements to do everything possible to wean the Afrikaner workers from Nationalism. Our plea was unheeded.

The decline in Nationalist Party influence among Afrikaner workers in 1947 is shown by the following. On the 22nd February 1947 our union held its annual general meeting, which was attended by several thousand members. The first item on the agenda was the election of general secretary. I was nominated. A Nationalist stooge nominated a certain Mr Vosloo, a Reformer. This nomination was not even seconded.

On the 22nd July 1947 at another general meeting of the union, attended by about four thousand workers, a resolution that the union affiliate to the Labour Party was carried enthusiastically, with only two votes against.

In previous years the South African Labour Party had supported an economic colour bar, but by 1947 it had moved far to the left of its original policy. At all events, the Labour Party, with all its faults, was always more progressive in its attitude towards non-Europeans than the United Party, and certainly more so than the Nationalist Party. Obviously, no party which claims to be democratic or Labour can have any association with racial discrimination. In South Africa, however, the major problem was, and is, how to save the country from a Nationalist fascist dictatorship. This can be done if all the anti-fascist forces concentrate on educating the Afrikaner workers in democracy.

Many trade union leaders of the right also made their contribution towards Malan's ultimate victory. Leaders of the mining unions, of the engineers, electricians, boilermakers and iron-moulders, and others, began to demand the exclusion of Africans from the South African Trades and Labour Council, and engaged in violent attacks upon the more progressive trade union leaders. Failing in their efforts to introduce a colour bar into the S.A.T.L.C. they disaffiliated and thus caused division in the workers' ranks.

The utter stupidity of the United Party was shown in the following glaring examples:

On 1st August 1947 some ten thousand building workers in the Transvaal came out on strike for increased wages, a forty-hour week and improved holiday leave. The building industry was enjoying great prosperity and, had the matter been left to the employers and workers, the strike could have been amicably settled within a few days. But the United Party Government set up a special 'Cabinet sub-committee', which exerted all its power in order to bring defeat upon the workers. In addition, the United Party press persistently attacked the strikers.

Our union donated £10,000 towards the building workers' strike fund and our leaders, with their vast experience in conducting strikes, offered their services. An amicable settlement was reached and the strikers returned to work, more incensed against the United Party than against their employers.

CHAPTER TWENTY-FOUR

Sack all Non-Europeans

IN MAY 1948, when the Nationalist Government came to power, the union was engaged in a struggle with the clothing manufacturers. The agreement for the industry was about to terminate in July and, in March, the union submitted the following demands for a new agreement:

(1) An increase of 5 per cent in the basic wage of all workers and, in addition, 5 per cent on the cost of living allowance.

(2) That the weekly hours of work be reduced from forty-two and a half to forty.

(3) That a provident fund on a contributory basis be established for the industry.

There were also several minor demands. The Employers' Association not only rejected all the union's demands but, stressing the low wages that were being paid in the coastal areas, demanded a reduction in wages. The union was faced with the choice of either taking strike action or agreeing to submit to arbitration. On the 15th July 1948 a special general meeting of the union was held at the City Hall, Johannesburg, so that the members could decide which course of action we should take. Over four thousand men and women, full of enthusiasm and determination, crowded into the hall and many more stood in the foyer. I spoke for about forty-five minutes and gave a detailed report of the negotiations with the employers which, after almost four months, had reached a deadlock. The central executive committee of the union had unanimously decided to recommend arbitration, if the employers would agree to it, and strike action, should they refuse. The final decision was to be taken by the meeting. The workers listened very attentively and, when I had finished, we invited members from the floor to come up and express their views. Immediately, a small woman, accompanied by three others, mounted the platform, took a piece of paper from her handbag and started to read from it. Afrikaners are born orators and have no need to read their speeches. I at once guessed that this speech had been prepared elsewhere.

Instead of discussing the very important vital matter before the meeting, this Nationalist stooge surprised us all by saying: 'Mr Sachs has promised that, after the war, he would demand from the employers the dismissal of all the "Kaffirs" (a very insulting term for Africans) and the "Bastermeide" (an equally offensive word meaning the Coloured girls).' Altogether there were about five thousand Africans and over seven thousand Coloured workers in the industry in the Transvaal, constituting between them an overall majority. All the Coloured workers and over two thousand African women were members of the union. To ask for their wholesale dismissal would have been not only absolutely contrary to union principles and the union's constitution, but sheer lunacy. Those who had prepared the speech knew perfectly well that I had neither the authority to make such a promise, nor would I ever, under any circumstances, have stood for the exclusion of workers from the industry because of their race and colour. The Nationalist disrupters, however, have never concerned themselves with facts and truths, or with helping to improve the workers' conditions. Their only aim was to sow suspicion and discord among the workers and to try to break up the union.

After four months of negotiations with the employers, working practically day and night to prepare the union's case, I felt utterly exhausted. But this deliberate attempt to disrupt the union filled me with such rage and disgust that it acted like a tonic and gave me new energy. When Anna Scheepers, who presided, asked me to reply, the little woman and her supporters refused to leave the microphone, but I pushed them aside. Burning with anger, I told the workers that, whilst we were fighting desperately for better conditions, the Nationalist agents were plotting to destroy our organisation. I demanded that, before the meeting proceeded any further with the vital questions under discussion, a vote of confidence, or no confidence, in the central executive committee and the officials must be taken. And I told the meeting, in the crudest and plainest words, that I was sick and tired of the Nazi scum and their filthy, underhand tricks. I was prepared to serve the workers as a trade unionist to the best of my ability, but if they wanted a 'Kaffir-Coolie' politician, they must look for someone else.

A storm of indignation swept through the hall and hundreds of workers stood up in their seats, demanding the expulsion of the four disrupters. But order was quickly restored and thousands of hands were raised in a vote of confidence in the leaders of the union. Only three hands were raised against.

For another thirty minutes I lashed out against the enemies of the workers and of the trade union movement. Of those present, well over four thousand were Afrikaners and many were Nationalists. Very few were completely free from racial prejudices, but all clearly showed their hatred of the Nationalist Party's tricks.

The meeting unanimously decided to accept the recommendations of the committee and to seek arbitration. At first the employers rejected arbitration, but later changed their minds.

In the existing dispute, the main concern of the union was the forty-hour week. This demand, if granted, would have meant not only fewer working hours, but also another important advantage for the thousands of workers who, by leaving work half an hour earlier, would have avoided the rush-hour traffic. The passenger transport system in Johannesburg has always been one of the worst in the world, and workers are compelled to waste much time waiting in bus or tram queues. The introduction of a forty-hour week would have saved the workers much discomfort and delay.

Since the union was the 'plaintiff', it was mutually agreed that it should present its case first. The officials and staff, for many weeks, had worked until two and three in the morning to prepare the union's case, and a bulky memorandum, which covered over a hundred pages, was presented to the arbitration tribunal. We felt that we had a good case, but our greatest difficulty was to make the three learned barristers who had been chosen as arbitrators and who had no previous association with industry, understand our arguments. Two days after the proceedings started, we decided on a complete change of tactics. Discarding our lengthy memoranda, we put into the witness box twenty women workers with long experience in the industry. We asked them to describe to the tribunal the working day of a woman garment worker. In simple language the witnesses told of their unceasing toil both in the home and the factory and of their efforts to live cleanly and decently on the low wages they were paid. Their obvious honesty and the conviction with which they related their stories made a far greater impression on the arbitrators than all the facts and figures which the union had prepared. We then suggested to the arbitrators that they visit a number of factories to see for themselves. When these three gentlemen, who had spent all their professional lives in the quiet precincts of their chambers and the courts, saw the mad rush, the tremendous speed, and the deadly monotony of the work, they were even more impressed.

On the 14th September 1948 the arbitrators gave their award, granting the forty-hour week and several other minor demands of the union. In spite of their strenuous opposition to the reduction in hours, the employers accepted the award and several of them thanked me because, now, they would have time to play golf in the afternoons.

There was no decrease in production. Indeed, in some factories, output increased.

CHAPTER TWENTY-FIVE

A Reichstag Fire Trial complete with a Van der Lubbe

IN THE GENERAL ELECTION of May 1948 the Nationalist Party polled 400,453 votes and its ally, the Afrikaner Party, 41,885, a total of 442,338 votes. On the other hand, the United Party polled 515,373 votes, the Labour Party 32,164 votes and the Independents, who were almost exclusively anti-Nationalist, 76,279 votes. In nineteen constituencies, where the workers had the decisive vote, the Nationalists won by a combined vote of only 9,400. They obtained a majority of seven in the new Parliament, but once in power, pursued a ruthless and fraudulent policy to increase their numbers.

The new Minister of Labour, Mr B. J. Schoeman, repeatedly assured the trade union movement, during the election campaign, that there would be no interference with their internal affairs, but these assurances had the same value as Hitler's declarations that he had no more territorial ambitions. Most of the trade unions felt grave concern, but only a few, with our union at the head, were determined to fight. Some trade union leaders decided to come to terms with the new Government. Others showed a preference for discretion, rather than valour.

Inspired by the Nationalist victory, a handful of disrupters, mainly from Germiston, soon intensified their intrigues against the union. Some of them started a new terror technique. They would telephone my house late at night and shout threats and abuse. I frequently had to work late at the office, to prepare the union's case for the pending arbitration, which meant my wife, Dulcie Hartwell, who was pregnant at the time, was on her own at home. The Nationalist hooligans apparently watched my movements and invariably telephoned when I was away. Dulcie would answer, expecting a call from me, only to be told in Afrikaans that her Jew Communist husband would share the fate of Charlie Harris. They also threatened and abused Dulcie herself, who, as a former garment worker, had taken a leading part in the fight against the Nationalist policy of race hatred and oppression. Although she is a resolute and courageous woman, the constant telephone calls proved unnerving, especially as the baby was due quite soon. Andrew, our son, was born on the 4th July 1948, but the nightly telephone calls continued. Finally, we had to change our telephone number and keep the new one secret.

The Nationalists had resolved to settle accounts with the Garment Workers' Union and all other progressive unions, but, at first, they were not sure how to go about it. They were determined to remove me from my position, but their great difficulty was always to find someone to take my place. In the past, they had chosen workers who had never been in the clothing industry in their lives and these had proved hopeless failures.

Their chance came in 1948.

Early in 1947 Gert Hendrik van der Walt, a young, pleasant-looking Afrikaner, who had recently come into the industry, began to take an active interest in union work. He made militant speeches, vigorously attacked the Nationalist Party, and became an active member of the Labour Party. All the leaders of the union, except myself, were women and we were always on the look out for a promising Afrikaner man to play a leading rôle. In due course van der Walt was elected to the central executive committee, and later became vice-president of the union; he was given every opportunity of becoming a leader and by the middle of 1948 he had been recommended for a position as union organiser. The committee instructed me to interview three candidates, including van der Walt, to find out their technical qualifications. I had always been very friendly with him and liked to help people from the ranks to take leading parts in union affairs. At the interview van der Walt showed keen interest in becoming a full-time official of the union, but I felt that there was something strange about him, which I could not define. But, before I could decide whether or not to recommend him, an old and very loyal member of the executive informed us that van der Walt was a secret agent of the Blankewerkers Beskermingsbond (White Workers' Protection League) and was being paid £11 2*s.* 0*d.* a week by them. Van der Walt was charged before the executive with being an agent of a disruptive organisation and expelled from the union. The Nationalist press immediately built him up into a hero and martyr, who was being victimised by the 'Sachs clique'. His photograph, accompanied by long stories of how he and his family had been deprived of a living, was splashed across the pages of *Die Transvaler*, organ of the Nationalist Party in the Transvaal. With the help of other members of the White Workers' Protection League, he went about addressing meetings, denouncing the union, emphasising his poverty (neglecting to mention that he was still being paid by the League), and urging the workers to oust me and elect him as secretary in my place.

On the 16th September 1948 the union held a general meeting at the City Hall, Johannesburg, to receive a full report on the arbitrators' award, granting us the forty-hour week. The meeting started at about five p.m. and, half an hour later, while I was reporting on the result of the arbitration to an attentive audience, a mob of several hundred, armed with all sorts of weapons, and led by van der Walt with a revolver in his hand, smashed the doors and burst into the hall. Shouting in Afrikaans: 'Today blood must flow. Solly Sachs and Anna Scheepers will be taken to hospital in an ambulance,' they began to assault people left and right. Fifteen policemen and a police commandant stood outside the hall—the police had been warned by the union that a mob was coming to break up the meeting—but they took no action. The rioters consisted of Nationalist hoodlums from all over the Rand, with some garment workers from Germiston, who had joined them. We subsequently learned that the Railway Administration had put a special train at their disposal to bring them into Johannesburg. The president, Anna Scheepers, closed the meeting and, anxious to avoid bloodshed, appealed to members to disperse. Hundreds of women, worried and excited, ran up to the platform and begged me to leave the hall, shouting that some of the hooligans were armed and threatening to kill me. Passers-by, who saw these scenes, exclaimed: 'This is like Nazi Germany!' After breaking up the meeting, the mob threatened to march on the union headquarters but, for some unknown reason, abandoned the idea. Johannesburg was stunned by this display of mob violence and disgusted at the failure of the police to do anything about it. At a meeting in Germiston, some time later, one of the mob leaders openly boasted that several of them had obtained revolvers and had come to the meeting meaning to shoot me and then pretend that it had happened in the excitement of the moment or by accident.

The following morning, the president of the union sent a telegram to the Minister of Justice:

> General meeting garment workers Johannesburg branch held City Hall Johannesburg and attended by 2,500 women and several hundred men attacked by organised mob and broken up by force. Many people seriously assaulted. Much damage caused to property. Several people openly incited to violence and murder. Mob consisted mainly of non-garment workers. Officials and union property still being threatened by force. Respectfully request you to take steps immediately against lawless mob, also to institute public inquiry.

No reply was received to the telegram.

The Minister of Justice took no action, but a few days later, his colleague, the Minister of Labour, acting under the Commissions Act of 1947, appointed a commission with the following terms of reference:

'To inquire and report upon:

(*a*) The disturbance which occurred at a meeting of the Garment Workers' Union, held at Johannesburg on the 16th day of September 1948, and the circumstances which gave rise to such disturbance.

(*b*) The affairs and administration of the Garment Workers' Union and in particular:

(i) The extent to which, and the circumstances in which, the union has, by suspending or terminating the membership of members of the union, caused such members to lose their employment in the clothing industry in the Transvaal by reason of provisions in industrial agreements negotiated by the union in terms of which employment in the said industry with employers who were parties to such agreements was limited to persons who were members of the union,

(ii) the procedure followed in suspending or terminating the membership of any such members,

(iii) the justification or otherwise of such suspensions or termination, and

(iv) the administration of the funds of the Garment Workers' Union

and to submit such recommendations as it may deem necessary in the light of its findings.'

Instead of bringing the criminals to trial, the Nationalist Government had appointed a 'smear' commission, with the object of maligning the union and its leaders and reinstating van der Walt to membership so that he might become secretary of the union.

The Chairman of the commission, Mr H. J. Graham-Wolfaardt, was a second-grade magistrate from a small town in the Orange Free State, who knew nothing about trade unions or industrial affairs. Mr J. F. Malherbe, a very old, retired magistrate, was the other member of the commission. The Nationalists were rubbing their hands with glee. Their chief witness was to be van der Walt, who had been vice-president of the union, and he would 'expose' to the world the 'sinister' activities of the Garment Workers' Union. The commission had power to subpoena witnesses and documents and thus the private affairs of the union would be made public property.

The Nationalists did not know what was in store for them.

Before the 14th August 1948, when van der Walt had been expelled from union membership for 'association with and actively participating in the work of certain disrupters who are aiming at dividing and disrupting the Garment Workers' Union', a member had told us that van der Walt had been convicted for a serious crime and had served time in gaol. In due course, we obtained copies of van der Walt's criminal record, which indeed was impressive.

The commission began its public sittings on the 22nd November 1948. The first witness to be called was Gert Hendrik van der Walt. In the many hours he spent in the witness box he meandered in his evidence and showed no particular viciousness towards me or any other official of the union. There was nothing remotely sensational in his testimony which proved a damp squib to the reporters of the Nationalist press. The chairman of the commission seemed unmoved when the star witness finished. We had advised the anti-Nationalist papers that our side would produce a 'sensation' at the inquiry and the press was well represented.

The court was crowded when counsel for the union, Mr I. A. Maisels, K.C., stood up to cross-examine van der Walt. The following is taken verbatim from the record of proceedings of the commission of inquiry into the Garment Workers' Union:

MAISELS. Well, Mr van der Walt, we will just examine you on your work in the garment workers' industry and your ability to speak as a worker. I understand from your evidence this morning that you entered the garment industry in February 1946?

V. D. WALT. Yes.

Q. What previous experience had you in the garment workers' industry?

A. I had never been a member of the Garment Workers' Union before. At a trade school I learnt the trade as a tailor and on that experience I worked.

Q. Mr van der Walt, you started with the African Clothing in February 1946?

A. That is right.

Q. And previous to that, where had you worked?

A. I had worked in Ladybrand in a tailor shop and I had been in the industrial school. I was there for four years.

Q. You worked in Ladybrand, was that for three and a half years?

A. Yes.

Q. Oh, I see. When did you work in Ladybrand for three and a half years?

A. It was between the years '38 and '40.

Q. I think you had better be a little careful, Mr van der Walt. With whom did you work in Ladybrand in those years?

A. A Mr Thompson.

Q. What is his business?

A. He is a tailor.

Q. And you worked for him for three and a half years during what period?

A. Between '38 and '42 or '41, between that time.

Q. When?

A. '38 and '42.

Q. Was that all you did between 1939 and 1942?

A. We had a farm there, too, and there were periods when I was on the farm.

Q. Were there periods when you were elsewhere?

A. No, I don't think so.

Q. You don't think so?

A. No.

Q. Or would you try thinking a little bit harder, Mr van der

Walt. I want to know between the period of 1938 and 1942 where you were.

A. Mr Chairman, I do not wish to answer that question because it is irrelevant to the case, on the evidence I am giving in regard to the garment industry today.

Q. Now, I am not surprised that you gave that answer, Mr van der Walt, but I think Mr Commissioner will pull me up when I ask you questions which I am not entitled to ask you. Mr van der Walt, I want to know from you where you were in this period when you say you were working for a tailor. I am going to tell you what you said then was just a deliberate untruth. Now, come along, Mr van der Walt. Where were you during this period?

A. I refuse to answer this question.

Q. You refuse to answer this question. Well, then, shall I tell you where you were?

A. If you wish. You may please yourself.

MAISELS. Mr Chairman, would you mind asking the witness to answer the questions?

CHAIRMAN. Is this on a question of credibility, or what is it?

MAISELS. This is a most important question.

CHAIRMAN. In which respect?

MAISELS. Mr van der Walt has made a most serious accusation with regard to the manner in which certain disturbances arose, and made most serious accusations against persons holding positions in the trade union movement, and I think it is necessary for this commission to know who this person is, and what his qualifications are for making such statements.

CHAIRMAN. You mean that you wish to test his credibility by exposing his character, Mr Maisels?

MAISELS. Briefly, I am going to show you, Sir, if you will allow me, that this person is a convict, convicted not merely of theft, but crimes of violence, and also a person who has spent a considerable period of his life in a lunatic asylum, and that is the person who has set himself up as the liberator of the garment workers. Now, Mr van der Walt, will you answer my question?

The cross examination which followed established that at the age of twenty-six, the 'hero' and 'martyr', who was built up as a great leader by the Nationalist Party and press and as the man who was to succeed me as general secretary of the union, had the following criminal record:

DATE	PLACE	OFFENCE	SENTENCE
19.1.39	East London	Housebreaking and theft	Handed over to principal, industrial school, Kingwilliamstown
18.3.39	Durban	do.	Declared insane, to be detained in mental hospital
18.3.39	Pietermaritzburg	do. and escaping	Charges withdrawn. Accused declared insane.
5.12.39	Circuit Court, Springs	Assault with intent	8 cuts with a cane, 18 months hard labour, suspended for 3 years on conditions of good behaviour
17.12.40	Ladysmith	Theft of money	2 months hard labour, suspended for 2 years on condition accused repays £25 10*s*. 3*d*. at the rate of £2 a month
14.5.43	Supreme Court, Johannesburg	Theft of money and revolver	Two years reformatory
	Supreme Court, Cape Town	Theft (two counts), housebreaking with intent to steal	Three years imprisonment, one year suspended

The next morning, the *Rand Daily Mail* came out with a poster: 'Sensation at Garment Union Inquiry.' The enemies of the union dropped their hero like a hot brick.

The appearance of the first witness against the union had been tragic. The second proved a complete farce.

Miss Anna Knoetze had been a loyal member of the union from 1928 until 1940, when she came under the influence of a minister of a Dutch Reformed Church. During the war she had left the clothing industry to take a more lucrative job in a munition factory. When she resumed work in a clothing factory she became an active agent of the White Workers' Protection League, but conducted her activities quite openly. There was something queer about her and the workers treated her persistent attacks on the union as a joke and a nuisance, but did not take her seriously.

As soon as the Nationalist Party came to power, she became very active and was expelled from the union at the same time as van der Walt. At the riotous City Hall meeting Miss Knoetze had been second in command.

The chairman of the commission was most friendly to her and she spent three days in the witness box, giving full vent to her feelings against the union, denouncing it as a 'Kaffir', 'communist' organisation.

Under cross-examination, she was pressed by Mr Phillips, counsel for the union, to produce some concrete evidence of the communist activities of the union. She replied that she had run through the pages of the union magazine, the *Garment Worker/ Klerewerker* and found it full of 'communism'.

The following is taken from the record (page 496):

MR PHILLIPS. What sort of communist methods? Please give us one or two examples, Miss Knoetze.

MISS KNOETZE. When you read it, you can see that it is not a paper for a Christian.

Q. But that is not what you said. You say it is full of communist methods. Give me examples, please.

CHAIRMAN. That is her idea of an example.

Mr Phillips, however, was not satisfied and, before the tea adjournment, he handed Miss Knoetze all the *Garment Workers* for 1947 and 1948 and asked her to look through them during the interval. When the commission resumed, Miss Knoetze produced the *Garment Worker* for September-October 1947, and said: 'Here it deals with Abraham Lincoln.' She pointed to a picture of Lincoln and two short passages, referring to him and quoting his famous speech on liberties.

MR PHILLIPS. Is that communist propaganda, Miss Knoetze?

MISS KNOETZE. That is how I feel, because I feel that this man (again pointing to Abraham Lincoln) is one of the great living communists.

Q. Abraham Lincoln?

A. Yes, that is how I feel, I speak as I feel. I can't act otherwise.

The South African press featured Miss Knoetze's evidence with headlines reading: 'Abraham Lincoln is the greatest living communist', and it became a standing joke. Only the chairman of the commission did not laugh. He had probably never heard of Abraham Lincoln either.

The commission dragged on for about twelve months, but after the exposure of van der Walt, people lost interest in the proceedings. This 'Reichstag Fire' trial, complete with a van der Lubbe, staged by the Nationalists, not only misfired, but brought much discredit to them. In the first round with the Nationalist Government, the union emerged victorious. Van der Walt disappeared from the scene and was not heard of again. The Government spent over £20,000 on the commission, but when its report was published eighteen months later, no one took any notice of it.

CHAPTER TWENTY-SIX

Further Attacks – Passport Case

NATIONALIST GOVERNMENT ATTACKS on the union continued. Schoeman refused to gazette the agreement for the clothing industry, which contained the award of the arbitrators, on the grounds that it had a 'closed shop' provision. The agreement was a matter solely for the union and the employers, but Schoeman had hoped that the elimination of the closed shop would break the union's power over its members and that, if the agreement were not gazetted, the workers would rise in revolt against their leaders. We advised the employers' association that we had no objection to the deletion of the closed shop clause from the agreement. We went further. We issued a leaflet to all members, stating that those who wished to resign could do so and no action would be taken against them under the closed shop provision. Not one member resigned. Strange as it may seem, the employers, who in former years had vigorously opposed the closed shop, now insisted on its retention. They preferred to deal with a well-organised body, rather than with individuals. We let the workers know that, by refusing to gazette the agreement, Schoeman was attempting to ruin their hard-won standards. At the same time, we informed the employers that, whether or not the agreement was gazetted, its provisions must be observed and the union would take direct action against anyone who transgressed it. Every employer honoured the agreement and, eighteen months later, when Schoeman saw that his efforts had failed, he gazetted it.

On 6th May 1949 I applied for a passport to go overseas to attend an international conference of textile and clothing workers at Lyons, France. I paid the usual fee of £1 and received the passport. Fourteen days later the Chief Immigration Officer and one of his assistants called at my office and told me that they had instructions from the Minister of the Interior to demand the surrender of my passport. I refused and, on the 1st June, Donges, the Minister of the Interior, applied to the Supreme Court and obtained an order compelling me to surrender the passport. I lodged an appeal to the Appellate Division of the Supreme Court.

Six eminent counsel, including a well-known constitutional lawyer in England, advised me that my appeal would fail and, in a moment of weakness, I felt inclined to abandon it. But tyranny must be fought at all costs and I decided to proceed with the appeal. This arbitrary act of the Minister caused great public indignation. The *Rand Daily Mail*, a leading paper in Johannesburg, wrote on the 25th May 1949:

> A dangerous principle is involved when the Government starts to take passports from citizens whom it does not like. This procedure bears the stamp of dictatorship and one wonders where it will end.

The *Star*, another leading daily, wrote on the 27th May 1949:

> By the Minister's administrative action, the Government stands condemned of using administrative powers to curtail the freedom of people who disagree with it or are critical of its actions and attitudes. Once the principle is established that passports are available only for people whose opinions are agreeable to the Government, the Union, in effect, will become a vast prison camp.

The *Sunday Express* of the 29th May 1949, stated:

> But is the Minister really so afraid of what Mr Sachs might say, that he is ready to make this disgraceful inroad on the liberty of movement of a fellow South African?

In court the Minister relied mainly on the power of the Crown prerogative, to which Mr Justice Malan, in another appeal before the Transvaal Provincial Division of the Supreme Court, in the case of Dr Dadoo, whose passport had been seized, had remarked:

> 'The contention on the first point is based solely upon the so-called prerogative of the Crown or State—that undefined, nebulous relic of autocratic power of kings of the dim past, which is alleged still to exist and which is in modern times usually invoked by those who have arrogated to themselves autocratic power and who, upon this power being challenged, are driven to seek refuge in its very questionable existence.'

The appeal was heard in the Appellate Division before a full bench of five judges and, on the 14th March 1950 the court, by a majority of three to two, upheld my appeal, with costs.

Donges avenged himself by introducing new regulations, assigning to himself full discretionary powers concerning the issue and cancellation of passports. No citizen who held truly progressive views was issued with a passport, but many travelled abroad without them until 1955, when the Nationalist Government introduced the Passport Act, making it a criminal offence to leave the country without one.

CHAPTER TWENTY-SEVEN

The Police State in Action

THE TRIUMPHS of the anti-communist crusaders have been made possible only by the tacit support, cowardice and confusion of large sections of people who, at heart, may have had a profound love for liberty, but lacked the courage and vision to resist reaction.

In 1950, when C. R. Swart, Nationalist Minister of Justice, introduced the Suppression of Communism Act (Act 44 of 1950), South Africa was enjoying a tranquillity which was disturbed only by the Nationalists. Economically, the country was passing through a period of prosperity. The relationship between employers and workers was good and there were few strikes. The ten million oppressed non-Europeans were demanding their rights, but they were doing so peacefully, without signs of violence or revolution. The only Communist M.P., Mr Sam Kahn, who had been elected with an overwhelming majority by the Africans of the Western Cape, behaved with such dignity and brilliance that even the Nationalists developed a sneaking regard for him and packed the House whenever he spoke.

To secure public support for his monstrous Bill, Swart concocted a fantastic story of communist plots to poison the wells of South Africa.

The Act gave Swart and his police dictatorial power, not only over communists, but over all citizens. The Communist Party was outlawed and the teaching of communism was made a criminal offence, punishable by ten years' imprisonment with hard labour. The definition of 'communism' in the Act was so wide and so vague that to demand any change in the social structure of the country whatsoever became a criminal offence. Indeed, several well-known anti-communists were subsequently convicted of spreading communism, due to the all-embracing nature of the definition.

The Minister assigned to himself autocratic powers to ban meetings and prohibit anyone from attending any gathering whatsoever. 'Gathering' was defined as 'any number of people'. Hence, any person who was served with this order, prohibiting him from attending gatherings, was liable to three years' imprisonment with hard labour if he so much as stood in a queue or sat down to dinner with his family.

The Minister could also suppress newspapers and banish citizens from any area in South Africa. Victims had no protection whatever and could be condemned without trial or hearing. The courts could not intervene. Facts, or truth and evidence were to be completely ignored. The Minister's opinion was final, and so was his judgment.

The attitude of the United Party, the major opposition in Parliament, to this and nearly all other tyrannical laws passed by the Nationalist Government, was foolish and contemptible. Instead of rallying the people of South Africa in a struggle against fascist dictatorship, the leaders of the United Party have invariably contented themselves with moving piffling amendments. They readily supported Swart's concentration camp policy, but wanted hot and cold water installed and, when Swart refused to provide these amenities, the United Party accepted concentration camps all the same.

The main purpose of the Suppression of Communism Act, a typical Nazi measure, was to intimidate opponents of the Nationalist Party. It came into operation on the 26th June 1950. On the 20th September 1950, I received this letter:

Sir,

Having been directed by the Honourable the Minister of Justice in terms of Section 4 (10) of Act 44 of 1950, you are hereby afforded a reasonable opportunity in terms of the proviso of the above-mentioned section, to show why your name should not be included in a list of persons who are or have been office-bearers, officers, members or active supporters of the Communist Party of South Africa, which has been declared an unlawful organisation by Section 2 (1) of Act 44 of 1950.

Should you desire such reasonable opportunity you are requested to submit in writing such representations as you desire to make to reach me at the above address on or before the 3rd October 1950.

Evidence has been placed before me to show that you were

a member and active supporter of the Communist Party of South Africa.

I have the honour to be,
Sir,
Your obedient servant,
(*signed*) J. DE V. LOUW,
Liquidator: Act 44 of 1950.

Once a person is listed, the Minister may prescribe a standard of conduct for him, remove him from his position and prohibit him from holding any public office or becoming a Member of Parliament or of the Provincial Council.

I sent a lengthy reply, from which I quote the following extracts:

Your Minister of Justice treats liberty and justice with contempt and the people of South Africa today are denied even those rights which the people of Europe exacted from their tyrant kings in the Middle Ages.

Obviously your magnanimous offer of a reasonable opportunity to show why my name should not be included in your list is either a mockery or you do not know the meaning of the term 'reasonable opportunity'. I have not the faintest idea of what crime I am supposed to have committed, nor of the evidence which has been placed before you in support of any allegation against me. Yes, I was a member of the Communist Party until the 3rd September 1931, when I was expelled from that party, and I have never rejoined it. I quote below the Resolution of my expulsion published in *Umsebenzi*, the official organ of the one-time Communist Party of South Africa dated 4th September 1931:

The Fight Against the Right Danger—Expulsions from the Party—Resolutions of Political Bureau of C.P.S.A.—Comrade E. S. Sachs

Comrade E. S. Sachs has during recent months shown a steady drift away from all Party activities and a growing sabotage of all revolutionary work in the trade unions, whilst increasing opportunism has characterised his actions. The failure to popularise the platform of the African May Day Committee by holding back the letters and further by a recommendation to the members of the Garment Workers' Union not to associate with the African May Day Committee, nor the United May Day Committee, but to go on a picnic instead of demonstrating on the streets; the failure to participate with the members of the Union, who in spite of such recommendation demonstrated under the leadership of the Party whilst Comrade Sachs went to Germiston; the failure to attend any Party demonstrations during recent months, all these actions are manifestations of deviation from the Party line. The general work of Comrade Sachs revealed by the complete failure to conduct any activity against the reformist line of the Garment Workers' Union, the failure to organise any resistance to the class-collaboration legislation, the failure to lead action against the white chauvinism of members of the Garment Workers' Union, and recently the opportunistic action whereby Comrade Sachs threatened to resign his Union position (without reference to the Party) unless his wages were substantially increased, all of these activities reveal a steady and persistent drift away from the line of the Party which have led to the compromising of the Party amongst the workers. These activities demand that the Party take drastic disciplinary action against Comrade Sachs.

The Suppression of Communism Act is presented by Mr Swart ostensibly as a measure to combat Communism, but it is in fact designed to wipe out all human liberties, to destroy the free trade unions, to intimidate and terrorise all opponents of the Nationalist Party, and to inflict arbitrary punishment upon those who stand for a truly democratic South Africa. On the basis of all the facts and information at my disposal, I must come to the conclusion that the ultimate object of listing me is not to combat Communism, but to remove me, and no doubt others, from the leadership of the Garment Workers' Union, so that this proud, militant organisation may become a political football of the Nationalist Party, repeating the tragic story of the Mine Workers' Union.

I submit that in law you are not entitled to include my name in the list referred to in your letter. If you intend to include my name in the list referred to in your letter, please advise me immediately so that I can institute legal proceedings to declare the inclusion of my name in the list as being unlawful and beyond your powers.

Swart, in his great hurry to rush the Act through Parliament, had not spread his net wide enough. Possibly he found it expedient to destroy individual liberty in stages. Whatever the reason, the definition of 'communist' in the Act did not include ex-communists, to which category I belonged. The following year, however, Swart introduced the Suppression of Communism Amendment Act, Act 50 of 1951, which stated:

'Communist' means a person who professes or has at any time before or after the commencement of this Act professed to be a communist or who, after having been given a reasonable opportunity of making such representations as he may consider necessary, is deemed by the Governor-General or, in the case of an inhabitant of the territory of South-West Africa, by the Administrator of the said territory, to be a communist on the ground that he is advocating, advising, defending or encouraging or has at any time before or after the commencement of this Act, whether within or outside the Union, advocated, advised, defended or encouraged the achievement of any of the objects of communism or any act or omission which is calculated to further the achievement of any such object, or that he has at any time before or after the commencement of this Act been a member or active supporter of any organisation outside the Union which professed, by its name or otherwise, to be an organisation for propagating the principles or promoting the spread of communism, or whose purpose or one of whose purposes was to propagate the principles or promote the spread of communism, or which engaged in activities which were calculated to further the achievement of any of the objects of communism.

By giving himself power to punish people for acts which had been perfectly lawful at the time they were done, Swart not only committed an outrage upon the Rule of Law, but had also proved conclusively the dishonesty of his party and its aims. Under the pretext of suppressing communism, the Nationalist Party was out to remove the last trace of individual liberty.

Early in 1950 Dr Albert Hertzog, a Nationalist Member of Parliament and leader of the Reformers, announced in a press statement the formation of The Workers' Press and Publishing Company Limited, with himself as chairman. The company intended to publish three workers' weekly newspapers, the *Mine Worker*, the *Garment Worker* and the *Building Worker*. The object of the publications would be to combat racial equality and communism in the trade unions and to capture the trade unions for Afrikanerdom.

The first numbers appeared on the 10th February 1950, and in subsequent issues, Piet Huyser, the very progressive national organiser of the Building Workers' Union, Anna Scheepers, president of the Garment Workers' Union, and myself, were slandered and vilified with a fury and recklessness surpassing anything we had previously experienced. After some six issues had appeared the three of us instituted actions for defamation against the company and the printers, the Voortrekkerpers. The printers settled out of court and paid each of us £300 and costs. The company paid £500 to Anna Scheepers, but decided to defend the action by Huyser and myself. Even after we issued summonses they still continued to publish defamatory articles.

My case was heard before Mr Justice Clayden, who gave judgment on the 30th May 1951, awarding me £3,200 damages, less the £300 which I had already received, and costs. Huyser was awarded £1,850 damages and costs by Mr Justice Ramsbottom.

The company had been registered with a nominal capital of £7, but received many thousands of pounds from the Mineworkers' Union and from advertising. It did not honour the judgment and I applied to the Supreme Court for a liquidation order. My application was granted, the company was put out of business, and Albert Hertzog's venture came to an end.

In July 1951 I issued a further summons against the printers for continuing to print defamatory matter after they had paid me £300. When the case opened in the Supreme Court on the 25th March 1952 my counsel announced that a settlement had been reached.

The defendants agreed to pay me the sum of £1,000 through their attorneys, as well as the taxed costs of the action up to the date of trial, including counsel's fees on trial.

By now the Nationalists had to acknowledge that I could not be removed from the secretaryship of the Garment Workers' Union by slander, vilification, physical violence or terror tactics. They had to find other methods.

On Monday, the 19th May 1952, at five p.m. I returned from an important meeting of the national executive committee of the South African Trades and Labour Council to attend the usual weekly meeting of the central executive committee of the union at the union's head office. I found two detectives waiting for me. They handed me the two following orders, signed by C. R. Swart, Minister of Justice:

I

UNION OF SOUTH AFRICA
Office of the Minister of Justice,
Palace of Justice,
Pretoria.

To Mr Emil Solomon Sachs,
50 Donegall Avenue,
Greenside,
Johannesburg.

THE SUPPRESSION OF COMMUNISM ACT No. 44 OF 1950
AS AMENDED

WHEREAS YOUR NAME APPEARS ON THE LIST IN THE CUSTODY OF THE OFFICE REFERRED TO IN SECTION EIGHT,

PLEASE TAKE NOTICE THAT:

UNDER THE POWERS VESTED IN ME BY SECTION 5 OF THE SUPPRESSION OF COMMUNISM ACT (ACT NO. 44 OF 1950 AS AMENDED), YOU ARE HEREBY REQUIRED:

(*a*) To resign within a period of 30 days from date hereof as an office-bearer, officer or member of the following organisation and not again to become an office-bearer, officer or member thereof and not to take part in its activities:

THE GARMENT WORKERS' UNION

(*b*) not to become an office-bearer, officer or member and not to take any part in the activities of the organisations called

CIVIL RIGHTS LEAGUE
SOUTH AFRICAN PEACE MOVEMENT
FREEDOM OF THE PRESS COMMITTEE

Given under my hand at Capetown this 8th day of May 1952

(*signed*) C. R. SWART
Minister of Justice

II

THE SUPPRESSION OF COMMUNISM ACT No. 44 OF 1950 AS AMENDED

PLEASE TAKE NOTICE THAT:

1. Under the powers vested in me by Section 9 of the Suppression of Communism Act (Act No. 44 of 1950 as amended), you are hereby prohibited from attending any gathering whatever within the Union of South Africa and the Territory of South-West Africa for a period of two years from date hereof other than gatherings of a bona fide religious, recreational or social nature.
2. Under the powers vested in me by section ten of the Act and after thirty days from date hereof you are hereby prohibited for a period of two years from being within any province in the Union of South Africa or the Territory of South-West Africa other than the province of the Transvaal.

Given under my hand at Capetown this 8th day of May 1952

(*signed*) C. R. SWART
Minister of Justice

This action on the part of Mr Swart was not unexpected, yet coming face to face with the police State gave me a shock.

Without any hearing or trial, I was ordered to leave my job and abandon the work to which I had devoted my entire adult life. The clause which forbade me to attend any gatherings other than social ones created considerable difficulties. What is a 'social gathering'? The vagueness of this part of the order was most embarrassing. I might attend a gathering which I considered 'social' but the law did not and, by so doing, become liable to three years' imprisonment.

CHAPTER TWENTY-EIGHT

I Fight Back

SERVING THE ORDERS UPON ME at the union office was the first of a series of blunders on Swart's part. For many months the committee had been discussing what action the union should take in the event of Swart making an attack upon me or any other official and opinions were divided. Some members felt that a call from the union to take militant action might meet with resistance from the rank and file workers. (How utterly wrong subsequent events proved them!) But the show of the ugly hand of tyranny in the union office removed all differences and, when I returned from my private office, where I had invited the detectives, I immediately sensed the change. I explained to the committee the significance of the orders. For a while there was an uncanny silence, then sobbing. And it took some time for the members to recover from the shock. I made it quite clear that I had never been intimidated before and had no intention of running away from the struggle now. Division and hesitancy disappeared and gave way to a spirit of unity and determination such as I had never seen. Even those who had hesitated before were ready to do everything possible to fight back. Grief was turned into indignation, and indignation into action. For myself, I had no difficulty in deciding what course to follow. Fascist tyranny must always be fought. If we fight, we have a chance of winning and, if we go down, at least we leave a tradition of struggle behind us to inspire others.

I was in Berlin in 1933, when Hitler became Chancellor. The German workers then had the chance to fight, but did not take it and later paid dearly for not resisting tyranny. I decided to defy the Minister and take the consequences. As I did not want to involve the union, I chose the order prohibiting me from attending gatherings for a show-down.

The central executive committee adopted unanimously a resolution expressing indignation at the action of the Minister and decided to mobilise all the members of the union and call upon the rest of the trade union movement to fight Mr Swart's action. A shop stewards' meeting was to be convened the following evening to explain the position and to call for immediate strike and other action.

As soon as the meeting was over I called at the home of the counsel who often appeared for the union and had a long consultation with him. He advised that application be made to the Supreme Court to have the two orders set aside. I then issued a press statement, denouncing Nationalist tyranny, stating that I would resist the orders with every means at my disposal.

On Tuesday, the 20th May 1952, the daily press published the action taken by Mr Swart against me in banner headlines. This soon became the talk of the town and the workers in the factories sent messengers to the union office to find out what had happened. At five-thirty p.m. about seven hundred shop stewards of the No. 1 Branch of the union (European) assembled at the Trades Hall and at seven-thirty p.m. an equal number of shop stewards from the No. 2 Branch (Coloured) came to a meeting.

The following brief report of the two meetings appeared in the *Garment Worker* of May/June 1952:

> The shop stewards unanimously adopted resolutions protesting against the high-handed and tyrannical actions of the Minister and expressing the fullest confidence in Mr Sachs and deepest gratitude for his services to garment and other workers in the past twenty-four years. They called on all members and branches of the union to stage a one-day protest strike and to fight with the utmost determination for the cancellation of the orders against Mr Sachs.
>
> The No. 2 Branch meeting deleted the words 'one day' from the resolution, as they felt that the strike should last at least a week. Many workers took up the cry: 'Thirty days, thirty days.'
>
> The meetings protested against similar orders to other trade union leaders and called upon trade unionists and their leaders to defend the trade union movement and workers' standards, which the Nationalist Government were threatening to destroy.

After the shop stewards' meetings, the central executive committee decided to call a public protest meeting on the City Hall steps, Johannesburg, for Saturday morning, the 24th May.

The workers in the factories showed not the slightest sign of hesitation or cowardice, but, on the contrary, only a firm determination to resist to the bitter end. Numerous factories and individual workers sent telegrams to the Minister. I quote one sent by a factory employing over eight hundred workers, which was typical.

> *To the Ministers of Justice and Labour:*
>
> We, the workers of United Dress, want Mr Sachs as our secretary and no one else. He fought our battle loyally and we will stand by him. We will choose our leaders. Your persecution of Sachs makes us more determined to stand by him. Long live Solly Sachs, the workers' courageous leader. Hands off our union.

On Saturday, the 24th May, shop stewards assembled at the Trades Hall at nine a.m. and, when I arrived, I was greeted with loud cheers. I was touched by the loyalty of the workers. All the years I had been secretary, I had felt that the workers trusted and respected me. I was their servant and leader and they were members whose interests I had to serve. From the moment I received the orders, I became a person in their eyes. I had had no reason to doubt their loyalty, but had not known what their attitude would be in times of trouble. Their complete devotion and magnificent courage were a great inspiration to me.

At nine-thirty a.m., preceded by banners and with Johanna Cornelius and myself at the head, the shop stewards marched to the City Hall steps. Meanwhile, workers from all suburbs, many marching in formation and carrying banners, began to assemble. When we arrived there were about fifteen thousand people present, including many who were not garment workers. Within a few minutes twelve thousand Coloured garment workers, marching eight abreast, reached the meeting place. I was anxious to know the attitude of the mass of Europeans towards them. I did not have to wait long. Loud cheers greeted the Coloured workers. In the face of the common enemy, racial barriers were forgotten. The meeting, one of the largest South Africa had seen for many years, was most impressive. Anna Scheepers, president of the union, opened it promptly at ten a.m. and speakers from various organisations, including the United Party and the Labour Party, addressed the assembled crowd.

At eleven a.m. I came forward to speak. Scarcely ten minutes later some fifty police rushed from an entrance in the City Hall behind the platform. They seized me by the shoulders and tried to drag me away. There was a tremendous commotion. Some of my supporters held on to my legs and would not let the police take me. For a minute, I was in danger of being torn in halves by the tug of war between the police and the workers. Then they let go, and two detectives, accompanied by a dozen policemen in uniform, rushed me through the City Hall, pushed me into a prison van and drove me to Marshall Square. There I was searched and made to take off my collar and tie. A stupid police sergeant even demanded that I should take off my spectacles. After a while, I heard, for the third time in my life, the grating sound of the warder's keys turning the rusty lock of the prison cell. I found my new lodgings extremely unattractive. The cell was about fifteen feet square, with no window. Light was supplied by an electric bulb in the ceiling. Some dirty, rough, woollen blankets were lying on the cement floor. There was nothing else—only the bare walls, which previous lodgers had covered, almost from floor to ceiling, with poems and witticisms.

The prison warder was a pleasant young Afrikaner and, after I had been locked up for a few minutes, he opened the door, looked in and said: 'Oh, you must have a bed.' He shouted in Afrikaans to Kitchen, an African long-term prisoner, who was helping to run the 'King's Hotel': 'Kitchen, bring a bed for the master.' Even in prison, the superiority of the white man is not overlooked. The warder and the African took the blankets out of the cell and dusted them and I then lay down on the iron bedstead to sum up the events of the day and to plan for the future.

Half an hour later I heard loud cheers outside. Thousands of garment workers had marched to Marshall Square and were demanding my release. The police became frightened and armed themselves with rifles and sten guns. To prevent bloodshed, I offered to address the crowd. My offer was declined, but I was allowed to send out a message to the demonstrators, thanking them for their loyalty and urging them to remain calm.

At first I was not permitted to see anyone, but later my lawyer visited me. My four-year-old son, Andrew, also came, with his mother. He took me by the hand and said: 'Daddy, must come home.' When he saw the warder jingling his keys, he understood that Daddy could not just walk out.

I was released at seven p.m. I then learned that Dulcie Hartwell had read my speech to the crowd after I had been carried off and that the police had charged the crowd several times and assaulted over a hundred people, many of whom had been taken to hospital.

Johannesburg was agog. The brutality of the police caused bitter indignation, even among Nationalists. From press reports it was clear that public resentment against the Government was widespread. In twenty-four hours I had become the symbol of resistance against Nationalist tyranny. The Sunday papers gave these events the greatest publicity.

I now hoped to see the struggle against fascist dictatorship raised to a higher level. Here was a unique opportunity to convert the people's anger into large-scale action against the Government. I urged my colleagues in the trade union movement to call a general strike.

The mass of non-European workers would have joined in gladly. Probably several hundred thousand European workers, who loathed Nationalist tyranny, would have stopped work. The general public, incensed by Swart's Gestapo methods, would have co-operated, and so would a large number of industrialists, who hated Nationalist policy.

Had the South African Trades and Labour Council called a general strike, it might have led to unity among all the anti-Malan forces, who potentially were far stronger. The mass of white and non-white workers were prepared to fight, but the trade union leadership did not measure up to the task.

On the morning of Monday, the 26th June, eighteen thousand garment workers on the Rand and several thousand members of the union in other centres came out on strike. At nine-thirty a.m. I appeared in court. My case was remanded. As I left the court, I was told that many thousands of workers had assembled outside the City Hall. I decided to address them, but as soon as I started speaking, Major Prinsloo, chief of the Security Police, tapped me on the shoulder and told me I was under arrest. I said that there was no need for the police to break any more heads and that I would accompany him quietly. When I was brought to Marshall Square, the same young warder greeted me like an old friend. Again he and Kitchen saw to my comfort, and I must admit that the rest, after a long period of nervous strain, was most welcome. I made an urgent application for bail, but this was refused and I spent the night in prison—the first restful night in many months. The next morning I appeared in court. The case was remanded and I was released on £250 bail. I was subsequently charged on two counts, for attending two gatherings in contravention of the Minister's orders.

Judgment was delivered on the 15th July 1952. I knew that I would be convicted and had prepared a written statement for submission to the magistrate, after verdict, but before sentence. Through some confusion, my solicitor handed my statement to the court, even before the magistrate started reading his lengthy judgment. My statement read:

I am deeply grateful to Mr N. E. Rosenberg, K.C., who appeared for me, for the very able and clear manner in which he presented the legal grounds for my acquittal and the mitigating circumstances in the case, and I merely desire to add the following:

It has been suggested by the prosecutor that I have defied the law. With respect, I must refute that charge. I have always been law-abiding and have never been convicted of any offence in a court of law. I am a fervent supporter of the rule of law and a bitter opponent of lawlessness and disorder. It is not I who defiled the law. It is the Minister of Justice, Mr C. R. Swart, and his Nationalist Government, who have defied it and have made a mockery of the fundamental principles upon which the law is based. They have substituted the law of the jungle for the law of civilised communities. Civilised people find punishment without due process of law revolting. Without a hearing, without the semblance of a trial, without a single fact, without any evidence, in the secrecy of Mr Swart's ministerial offices, I was judged by him, condemned and sentenced to lose my livelihood, my work and my liberty.

The fascist tyrants who rule South Africa today have gone even further and have turned Parliamentary sovereignty, which our executive-minded lawyers treat with the sanctity of the Ten Commandments, into a farce, into an instrument of the Broederbond. They have destroyed the very foundation of representative government and constitutional liberties.

When I refer to the law, I do not mean the out-moded legal doctrines which our executive-minded lawyers are so fond of propounding and which have no relation to factual realities and existing circumstances. The law to me 'is a fiery sword of freedom', as the late Mr Justice Brandeis of the United States Supreme

Court described it. It will be a sorry day for all the people of South Africa when the law becomes an instrument in the hands of tyrants, instead of a shield to protect the liberty of the individual.

Yes, I am defiant, but not of the law—only of the wicked, lawless acts of the band of tyrants who, to maintain themselves in power, have wiped out every trace of liberty.

The Act under which I have been charged and found guilty is named 'suppression of Communism'. The 'Suppression of Liberty' would be a more correct title.

Why has Mr Swart ordered me to resign as secretary of the Garment Workers' Union, which I have served loyally for nearly twenty-five years? Why has he deprived me of the right of attending any gatherings? Mr Swart says that he took action against me to give effect to the objects of the Act, namely, to combat communism. Mr Swart knows that he is telling an untruth, just as he told an untruth when he introduced the Act in Parliament, by proclaiming that the communists were planning to poison the wells of the country and were preparing for a coup d'état, a statement which he later admitted to be totally untrue.

The whole world knows the truth. Mr Swart has taken action against me, not to combat communism—he knows that, since my expulsion from the Communist Party of South Africa in September 1931 I have not engaged in any communist activities, that for at least five years I have been a loyal member and an active supporter of the South African Labour Party, of which body I am national treasurer. Mr Swart has taken action against me and other trade union officials only to give effect to the policy of the Nationalist Party, inspired by Adolf Hitler, which aims at the capture, disruption or destruction of the free trade union movement.

Seventeen years of slander, vilification and violence having failed to remove me from my position, Mr Swart now employs the Suppression of Communism Act to effect the purpose of the Nationalist Party. He should realise by now that he made a grave blunder and his tyrannical action has only served to turn thousands of garment workers and others into bitter opponents of Nationalist Government tyranny. My crime is not that I am likely to engage in any communist activities, but that I have taught thousands of Afrikaner workers to love democracy, value human decencies, fight for a better living and loathe fascist tyranny and oppression.

I am a criminal in the eyes of the Nationalist Government

because I oppose racial hatred and intolerance and want to see South Africa a great democratic nation instead of a slave, fascist, police State.

Mr C. R. Swart is so frightened of facts that he had to withdraw the further order he issued against me under Section 10 of the Act, prohibiting me from leaving the Transvaal Province. Section 17 of the Act provides for the appointment of a fact-finding commission before action is taken under Section 10. Where is Mr Swart's fact-finding commission? Why did he not appoint such a commission?

All civilised people, whose vision has not been obscured by casuistry and legal technicalities, will know the true facts, and will also know who the real criminals are, and will not include me among them.

I have no regret whatever at the action I have taken and, no matter what penalty the court imposes upon me, I shall never give up the struggle for liberty and for a great, truly democratic South Africa.

I know that my sentence will be received with joy by the Broederbond, the *Transvaler* and the leaders of the Nationalist Party. My only regret is that I shall not be able to carry on as I should like the fight against the fascist tyrants, who are ruling and ruining South Africa, but I shall find consolation in the fact that many people will begin to see the revolting nature of brutal tyranny. At all events, my sentence will be a small contribution towards the great struggle for human liberty, for which twelve thousand noble South Africans and millions of others only recently gave their lives. I have already tasted the humiliation of imprisonment, but I shall not be intimidated.

Having been denied by Mr Swart even those rights which are accorded to the worst criminal—trial by a competent court—and having been condemned and punished by him in a manner which all decent people in South Africa and abroad will find disgusting, from now on my indignation will crystallise into courage, energy and determination to carry on the struggle until South Africa is rid of oppression and tyranny.

I have no desire to be a hero or a martyr, but I shall never submit to the dictates of fascist tyrants, nor 'bow and sue for grace with suppliant knee'. Proudly, and with a free conscience, I am ready to receive the sentence of the court.

The magistrate accepted this statement without any comment.

As expected, I was found guilty and sentenced to six months' imprisonment with hard labour on each of the two counts, the sentences to run concurrently. I lodged an appeal, which was dismissed by Mr Justice de Villiers in the Transvaal Provincial Division of the Supreme Court. I then lodged a further appeal to the Appellate Division of the Supreme Court and decided to argue my appeal in person.

On the 24th November I appeared before the five judges of the Appeal Court in Bloemfontein. I submitted several grounds of appeal, the most important being that the order of the Minister was vague. Since I was liable to three years' imprisonment for disobeying it, I was in law entitled to be told in plain words, free from ambiguity, what I could do and what I was prohibited from doing. What is a 'social gathering'? Is a function given by a political party a social gathering or not? The term 'social' is very wide and vague. Is standing in a bus queue, or in a queue in a bank or shop a 'gathering' or not?

Judgment was delivered on the 12th December 1952.

The Chief Justice complimented me on the manner in which I had argued the case, but the five judges confirmed the conviction.

By a majority of three to two, the court suspended the sentence for a period of three years.

The suspension of my sentence was a relief to my numerous friends, who were happy that I was not to go to gaol. To me, it was a bitter blow and the worst possible outcome. For a time I had been the symbol of resistance to Nationalist tyranny. My open defiance of Swart's order, the splendid spirit shown by the garment workers and, more especially, the brutal and unprovoked assault of the police upon citizens at the City Hall steps meeting had roused all opponents of Malan.

Had the court set aside Swart's order, I should have resumed the fight with new energy. On the other hand, if I had been sent to prison, there would have been widespread indignation. The garment workers would have come out on strike again and might have been joined by other sections of workers. The suspended sentence allayed public feeling and tied my hands. I had escaped gaol but, in fact, the whole of South Africa had now become one vast prison for me.

In the Act, 'gathering' is defined as: 'Any gathering, concourse or procession in, through or along any place, of any number of persons having a common purpose, whether such a purpose is lawful or unlawful.'

Unless I lived in complete isolation, it was impossible for me to avoid gatherings. If I stood in a queue, travelled in a vehicle with others, or sat down on a bench with two other people, I was liable to three years' imprisonment, in addition to the sentence that was already hanging over my head.

In an application against the Minister's order, which I had made earlier to the Transvaal Provincial Division of the Supreme Court, Mr Justice Ramsbottom, in a question to Mr Pirow, K.C., who appeared for the Minister, observed: 'Surely a man must know what he can do or cannot do. He must know what he is contravening, if he is liable to be sent to prison for three years.

In argument in the Appeal Court, I asked that the Minister's notice should be set aside on the ground of vagueness. The Minister prohibited me from attending 'any gathering whatever, other than gatherings of a bona fide religious, recreational or social nature.' It may be easy to define a gathering of a *religious* or *recreational* nature, but what is a bona fide gathering of a *social* nature?

The Oxford dictionary defines the word 'social' as 'living in companies, gregarious, interdependent, co-operative, concerned with the mutual relations of men or classes of men'. Almost every human activity in relation to or in association with others may be termed 'social'. On the other hand, the term 'social' might mean 'festive'. The Appeal Court judgment, far from clarifying my position, made it more nebulous. The Chief Justice, in his judgment, said:

> It may be conceded that cases may arise when it may be difficult to determine whether a particular meeting falls within the exempted category of gatherings. But the mere fact that there may be such a difficulty does not justify the contention that the notice is void on the ground of vagueness. Each case must be determined on its own facts.

It is necessary to examine what the effect of this judgment meant to me in practice.

I lived in a flat in a big building. At seven-thirty a.m. two Africans would come to clean the flat, and this constituted a 'gathering'. A few minutes later, I would go down in the lift. Other passengers might travel in it—another gathering. Buying a morning paper and a bottle of milk, a loaf of bread, perhaps some groceries, meant standing in queues—four more gatherings. To get to town, I would have to stand in a bus queue and then enter the vehicle—two more gatherings. Walking along the streets, I might be stopped by some people who would inquire how I was getting on, or find myself in the company of persons waiting on the corner for the traffic light to change. I might want to enter a bank, a post office or a public convenience. Mere attendance, without uttering a word, was enough to constitute a crime. Within a few hours, I might have attended twenty gatherings and made myself liable to sixty years' imprisonment.

Possibly all these gatherings were of a 'social nature', but what if the courts held that they were not? Swart's Gestapo are in the habit of keeping a close watch on their victims and, under the judgment of the court, the only way I could obtain guidance was by risking a prosecution.

The court may have been perfectly justified in holding that Parliament had given the Minister dictatorial powers, with which it could not interfere. But, neither in the statute, nor by legal precedent, was the Minister given power to issue a notice which was grossly vague and embarrassing to his victim.

Indeed, my attendance at court to answer the charges that had been preferred against me was a crime on my part. There were many people in court and the proceedings were certainly not of a religious or recreational character. They might have been 'social'. Who knows?

My position in South Africa had become untenable. I decided to leave the country and, on the 30th January 1953, I sailed for England. The farewell message of Coriolanus to his fellow citizens came to my mind. 'For you, the city, thus I turn my back. There is a world elsewhere.'

I was determined, however, to carry on the fight for a free, democratic South Africa and, for the last three years, I have worked hard to convert the world-wide sympathy for the cause of African freedom into practical support.

After my removal from office the Nationalist Party continued with its campaign to take over the leadership of the union. They made a desperate attempt to get one of their nominees, a certain

Mr Hartman van Niekerk, elected as general secretary of the union. In a secret ballot, however, Johanna Cornelius secured ten thousand votes against van Niekerk's three thousand. Similarly in the election for president, Anna Scheepers defeated the Nationalist nominee, Carel Meyer, by about the same majority.

In the past three years Anna and Johanna have led the union in many struggles for better conditions and have proved themselves thoroughly capable leaders. In spite of the activities of the Nationalists within the union and constant attacks by the Government, the Garment Workers' Union, under extremely difficult circumstances, is still maintaining its proud fighting tradition.

New clouds, however, are looming on the horizon. Jan de Klerk, brother-in-law of Mr J. G. Strijdom, Nationalist Prime Minister, one-time leader of the White Workers' Protection League and now Minister of Labour, has introduced a new Industrial Conciliation Bill which is designed to split the entire trade union movement on racial lines. The Bill will, in due course, become law and the Garment Workers' Union will have to separate into three legal entities. This fascist measure will, no doubt, cause grave division within the ranks of the trade union movement, but if the White, Coloured and African workers remain united in their determination to protect their standards and their liberties the efforts of Jan de Klerk will be defeated.

In November 1953 the Appeal Court, in the case of *Johnson Ngwevela* v. *Rex*, delivered a judgment which, in effect, set aside all Swart's notices under the Suppression of Communism Act. The court held that persons upon whom notices were served were entitled to a hearing and, since none had been given a hearing, the notices were invalid.

Early in 1954 Swart introduced an amendment to the Act to close all loopholes.

CHAPTER TWENTY-NINE

Policy and Tactics of the Union

THE TREMENDOUS ACHIEVEMENTS of the union in all spheres since 1928 were made possible largely by the rapid development of South African industry generally and more particularly by the extraordinary growth and extension of the clothing industry. The policy and activities of the union, however, played a major rôle, not only in effecting a complete change in the standards of the workers, but also in raising the industry from its original primitive level to a position which is modern, not only by South African, but even by world, standards.

Until 1928 the South African trade union movement had been largely 'British' in spirit and organisation and its structure and methods were not suited to the changing conditions. What had been perfectly adequate for the workers of London, Glasgow and Birmingham, and for artisans with a long trade union tradition, had little to offer to the daughters of Senekal and Lichtenburg. An entirely different technique was needed to make union members of these young Afrikaner women, who had brought with them the traditions of the rural areas and to whom even the terms 'trade unionism', 'labour', 'socialism', were completely alien. We had to look to the world trade union movement, its history, methods, tactics and struggles, for guidance in our own work. The newcomers, however, knew little or nothing of the workers' struggles abroad and only later did they learn of the international character of trade unionism.

We did not apply the accumulated experiences of the international trade union movement indiscriminately and always considered carefully the problems peculiar to our own country. From Britain we learnt the basic principles of trade unionism; from America modern technique; and from Central and Eastern Europe how to tackle problems of workers in a country which was troubled by grave national and racial issues, in which the economy was unevenly developed, and which was only in the first stage of its industrial revolution.

The Witwatersrand Tailors' Association, the predecessor of the

Garment Workers' Union, was an entirely different organisation from the present body. The men tailors, who controlled the union's affairs, had been brought up to follow the old-fashioned methods and, although proudly boasting a militant past and anxious to help the Afrikaner women, they knew little or nothing about their problems. Master craftsmen, deeply rooted in the British craft tradition, dominated the union. The women, who made up about 75 per cent of the membership, were engaged in mass production. They paid the same dues and had, theoretically, the same rights as the men, but in practice they had little or no say in the policy and management of the union. They were treated as 'children' by the older men, who were the 'fathers' and who, like fathers, thought they knew best. At general meetings, which hundreds of them attended, they remained silent. Even in many advanced countries women workers have had to fight hard for equality with the men. How much more so in a backward country like South Africa.

The meetings and the affairs of the union were conducted in English, while the majority of the workers were Afrikaans-speaking, although they understood English. These farm girls had to listen to speeches and read documents in a language which was foreign to them. There was not, at that time, one single book or pamphlet explaining in Afrikaans the aims and functions of trade unionism.

We had to fight hard to overcome the stubbornness of the men in order to bring the masses of Afrikaner women into active trade union work, and it was not until the middle of 1934, when the tailoring workers seceded from the union and formed an independent organisation, that the women began to play a leading rôle.

Many trade union leaders complain that their members take no interest in union affairs and blame the workers for apathy and poor attendance at meetings. Once these conservative, old-fashioned leaders learn to adopt modern methods, forget about their own importance and pay more attention to the needs and wishes of their members, they will soon get an enthusiastic response from them.

We realised that it was not enough to enrol the newcomers, collect their contributions and invite them occasionally to meetings. Very much more was needed if we were to build a strong union which could successfully fight exploitation and poverty. We had to start right at the beginning; to give these workers a faith and an ideal and develop a spirit of unity and sacrifice among them. Above all, we had to make them trade union conscious, and get them to feel that the union was their own organisation and not just an alien body. A trade union which really wants to serve its members and achieve something must not only have efficient administrators and expert negotiators, it must also create a feeling of solidarity and inspire hope and confidence in its members. We always remembered this throughout the years, even when conditions had improved and we had become somewhat more respectable and well-behaved. To create and maintain a spirit of militancy, speeches and pamphlets are not enough. The entire work of the union has to be planned and carried out in a manner which keeps that spirit alive. We encouraged the workers to strike when conditions were intolerable and, when they came out on strike without first consulting the union, we did not inquire whether the action was official or not. If it helped our struggle, it was accepted and we gave it our full support, for we knew that workers would not strike without a real grievance. We recognised that officials of the union were not impartial persons whose task it was only to maintain peace in the industry. They were elected and paid by the workers to further and to protect the workers' interests. Their duty is similar to that of the barrister briefed by a client—to serve his client and not worry about anything else.

For many years the value of strikes has been debated. Our union can claim some experience for, between 1928 and 1932, we led over a hundred strikes, two of which brought the entire industry to a standstill. From this long experience, followed by twenty years of highly efficient and successful conciliation, we contend that, as long as there are employers and workers, the strike weapon must be maintained. It must not be allowed to become blunt or rusty, for it is the only effective instrument the workers have in the struggle against the employers. Labour laws have helped in some instances, but only to an insignificant extent. We built up our conditions from the lowest possible level to one of the highest in the world only through strikes and threats of strikes. Strikes must never be called indiscriminately, merely to cause trouble. But this is certain: those who criticise, denounce or decry the strike weapon as obsolete are fighting on the employers' side, consciously or unconsciously, and are rendering a great disservice to the workers. For, in every country in the world where workers have secured better standards and conditions, these gains have been due almost entirely to strike action.

Individually our employers are probably more generous and humane than most and yet rarely did we get concessions from them through reasoned arguments.

We also know from our own experience that the workers learn far more from taking part in one strike than from years of propaganda. To us a strike did not mean only a stoppage of work by a number of workers. It was class war, and wars have to be organised to attain victory. Morale is always a determining factor in wars and in strikes, and we evolved a technique which proved very effective. Whenever a small or large group of workers came out on strike, we immediately mobilised the maximum support for them from our own members, the other trade unions and the general public. To give an example: on one occasion a very wealthy merchant tailor, who had been convicted of a breach of the agreement, dismissed two workers who had been the reluctant complainants in the case. We not only called the five other workers in the workshop out on strike, but promptly held a series of factory meetings to explain to our members the principle involved. Within forty-eight hours a thousand workers with banners demonstrated outside the shop. We used this opportunity to denounce the guilty employer and also to expose sweating conditions generally. Demonstrations of this nature invariably taught a lesson to the employer directly concerned and to all other would-be transgressors. They also had tremendous educational value for our members and the workers in general, and stimulated class consciousness and a spirit of militancy and confidence.

In 1943 the employers declared a lock-out without any valid reason. Before the trouble started I warned the chairman of the employers' association that we intended to organise public demonstrations to expose their high-handed action. The chairman, a personal friend of mine, who had come into the industry long after the period of successive strikes, said to me: 'Solly, if you are going to have street demonstrations, please come to my factory first.'

I warned him that he would regret this invitation, but he insisted. On the day of the lock-out we marched six thousand workers to his factory in the middle of the Johannesburg commercial centre. A platform was improvised outside and I addressed the large audience, which was soon increased by thousands more passers-by. I explained that we had been 'invited' and went on to denounce the unwarranted action of the employers.

In times of strike the workers often showed a rough spirit of poetry which found a quick expression in improvised composition. On this occasion they soon made up some songs poking fun at the owner.

The press gave our activities great publicity. The lock-out was duly called off and the workers received pay for time lost. My rash friend, who became the talk of Johannesburg, felt very sorry for himself. Never again did he invite us to stage demonstrations outside his premises.

The appearance of police at meetings, which is a regular feature of South African life and often led to the beating-up and arrest of workers, did not intimidate our members. On the contrary, it roused them to greater activity and gave us much valuable publicity. We missed no opportunity of denouncing the evil doings of the employers and the so-called protectors of law and order.

A thorough understanding of national and racial problems and their solution is indispensable when dealing with major social questions in South Africa. The Afrikaner workers who flocked into the industry had brought with them an intense nationalism and hatred of the English, who had fought their fathers in the Boer War and had put their mothers into concentration camps. National oppression makes peoples extremely suspicious and often over-sensitive. Further, the poverty-stricken Afrikaner workers felt embittered by the wealth and splendour surrounding them while they had to endure poverty and misery in the land of their birth. They saw the palatial homes of Johannesburg and had themselves to live in wretched slums. Not even their language was left to them. Many knew English, but it was not their mother tongue.

One of the union's first moves was to introduce absolute equality of the two languages, Afrikaans and English. At general meetings, in committees and at the union office, Afrikaans-speaking workers were invited and urged to express themselves in their mother tongue. Formerly Government letter-heads had English wording at the top of the page with Afrikaans underneath. Since the Nationalists have come into power this process has been reversed. Our union was the first public body in South Africa to print English and Afrikaans letter-heads side by side, without any favouritism. Speeches by members were recorded in the language in which they were delivered. Our magazine *The Garment Worker/ Klerewerker*, was published in English and Afrikaans with such perfect equality that a British Labour paper commented: 'It was the only magazine in the world with two fronts and no back.'

When we dealt with the tragic memories of the Boer War we never made the all-too-common mistake of thinking that the past can be wiped out merely by appealing to people to forget it. I know from experience how greatly such an approach angers the Afrikaners. We would tell the workers, both Afrikaners and English, that the Boer War had been a crime which could never be forgotten. But we always added that the British labour movement and the best among the British people had also fought against Rhodes, Chamberlain and the other imperialists, who alone had been responsible for the war. And we explained that the English-speaking workers in the South Africa of today were not 'empire builders', but bricklayers, artisans, miners and clerks and, like themselves, were fighting for a better life. We also stressed the great service which the British workers, who had built the South African trade union movement, had rendered the South African workers, and we missed no opportunity for telling the Afrikaners that those who had deprived the two Boer Republics of their independence had been responsible for the exploitation of millions of workers in Britain as well. The Afrikaner workers listened eagerly to accounts of the long and bitter struggles of their British comrades against economic slavery and the tyranny of the Conspiracy Laws.

We did not confine our appeals and activities to narrow trade unionism, pure and simple. The workers urgently needed a faith, something worth living for, fighting for and, if necessary, dying for, and to these thousands who suffered national oppression and economic misery we held out the prospects of a new and changed world, a world where men and women would be free and equal, where national and racial oppression would be unknown, a world free from want and poverty, where the workers and their children would at last enjoy happiness, security and prosperity. This vision of a fuller, richer and better life held a tremendous appeal for them, but we taught them always to combine the dreams of a brighter future with present-day realities. The new world could not be achieved by wishes alone. It had to be fought for. Hard struggles and great sacrifices would be necessary, but every fight in which we engaged today, every sacrifice we made, every victory we scored, would be a step forward towards the future happiness of all working people. As long as we fought with courage and determination, even our defeats would be a source of inspiration to others. Throughout the years we told the workers that we were fighting not only for higher wages and shorter hours, but also for a happier life. They should not be considered merely as factory hands, suffering poverty and hardship from the cradle to the grave. We were fighting for their right to live as free citizens in their own land, assured of decent living conditions, security and social justice.

The farm girls responded magnificently. They were militant, courageous rebels, unshackled by middle-class traditions and upbringing. Generous, friendly and still full of youthful exuberance, they had not yet become corrupted by highly-paid jobs, bureaucracy and respectability. They truly had nothing to lose but the chains of their poverty and the whole world to gain. They had not yet any clear idea of what this new world would be, or how it could be achieved. They had never heard of socialism and, even today, few are acquainted with socialist theory and principles. In 1934 when Johanna Cornelius, the most illustrious of the Voortrekkers' daughters, was sent as a workers' delegate to the Soviet Union, she did not know who Lenin was. But they soon learnt. The world they lived in was cruel and unbearable. A better world could be won and it was up to them to fight for it and to win it.

In 1935 Johanna Cornelius was elected president of the union and nearly all the members of the new central executive committee were Afrikaner women. Seven years of struggle had transformed scores of simple farm girls into organisers and leaders. Johanna was succeeded by a man, Peter Scheepers, but he lasted only one year and was succeeded in turn by Anna Elizabeth Scheepers (no relative), who has been repeatedly re-elected by the members and still holds the position of president.

A trade union must have the greatest measure of efficiency and democracy to attain maximum success in its work. How to combine the two, how to act effectively and with promptness and, at the same time, carry out the wishes of the members, is a problem which even many old-established trade unions have failed to solve. Some unions have a most efficient machine and a very high standard of business administration, but the mass of membership is not consulted on important matters and, in the course of time, such unions inevitably become bureaucratic and soulless and lose the confidence of their members. On the other hand there are trade unions with very democratic constitutions, where every question of importance has to be decided by a cumbersome process of ballots and conferences. In many trade unions leading officials become entrenched in their positions and exercise dictatorial powers. These officials and the coteries which they build up around them argue that trade union leaders need greater security, as they will find it extremely difficult to obtain employment with private employers once they have to give up their positions. There is some logic in that argument, but experience has shown that workers and trade unions may, in their turn, require protection against their own officials, when the latter become too dictatorial. In framing the constitution of the Garment Workers' Union, the leaders, in consultation with the rank and file, succeeded in combining democracy with efficiency. The central executive committee had full control over the affairs of the union, but the general membership had the power, not only to control and direct the work of the committee, but to remove any member, or even the entire committee, as well as the general secretary, from office.

In terms of the constitution the general secretary was merely a glorified clerk. In practice he played a very important part. His duties, as defined in the constitution, were frequently carried out by a competent technical staff of secretaries and book-keepers under his supervision. Many trade union secretaries spend far too much time on purely administrative matters, which can be done more quickly and more efficiently by others who are specially trained for these tasks. A trade union secretary must be a leader and a teacher. He must help to make policy, but never try to become the master of the members. He must remain their servant. And that was what I always tried to be. We rarely, if ever, deliberately transgressed any provision of the constitution, but we paid little or no attention to it in our daily work. We insisted that agreements entered into with employers must be scrupulously honoured by the members. They had every right to refuse to make agreements, but once they were made there must be no transgression on our part. We demanded that the employers observed all the provisions of agreements and the employers had the right to expect the same from us.

Real trade union democracy means more than merely inserting a provision in the constitution that members shall decide questions by majority vote. The closest and most effective contact must be maintained between the officials and the members to ascertain the real wishes of the workers. And it is necessary to inform members fully of the issues on which they have to make decisions and to arouse their interest. Printed circulars, however attractively drafted and designed, are inadequate.

It was easy to establish personal contact between officials and members of our union. Everybody could call at the head office at any time and interview the general secretary, the president, or any organiser. Hundreds of individual members, and often entire factories, would call at the union office and invariably receive prompt attention. Most people hate waiting in queues and we always took great care to make the workers feel at home. If tea was served to the staff the callers were invited to have a cup as well. We never missed an opportunity of telling our members that the offices were theirs and that the officials were paid by them to look after their interests. This informality and friendliness was deeply appreciated by the workers and helped to stimulate their faith in the union and their respect for the officials.

The central executive committee, the supreme body of the union, consisted of thirty-two members and we always tried to make it representative of all sections, co-opting members if any section failed to secure representation at elections. The committee met weekly and business was conducted efficiently. Meetings seldom lasted longer than two hours and special all-day meetings were called to deal with problems which required lengthy discussion.

The central executive committee was too small to speak for all the workers and general meetings, which were often attended by three to four thousand members, were too large for a full exchange of views. Shop stewards were elected in all factories by secret ballot and their meetings, which were generally held on Saturday mornings, had attendances ranging from three hundred to six hundred. Agendas were sent out in advance and, at these meetings, the true feelings of the mass of workers were clearly and correctly expressed by their elected representatives. The meetings usually lasted about three hours and as many as fifty speakers could take part in discussions.

Our general meetings were the envy of the trade union movement. Weeks in advance union officials would visit factories, hold meetings and discuss items on the agenda with members and distribute leaflets in which the business of the meeting was explained. The industrial agreements for the industry contained a provision compelling employers to admit union officials to their factories on union business. Often open-air meetings in factory areas would be held, which the workers readily attended.

We had learnt from experience that our members never showed the slightest interest in administrative matters. The constitution provided that audited balance sheets had to be submitted to general meetings half-yearly and, later, yearly. I have read and explained balance sheets at more than forty general meetings; invariably the workers sat there bored stiff, never once asking a question about the finances of the union but waiting impatiently for the economic and political discussion to begin. Once the balance sheet and profit and loss account were disposed of the meeting would really come to life. Many trade unions kill their meetings by spending too much time on these routine matters. We also learnt that general meetings had to finish within an hour and a half or the members would start walking out, so we kept our agendas as short as possible.

In spite of the modern technique we applied in calling meetings and the huge attendances we attracted, there were large numbers who failed to turn up and a little prodding became necessary. The members who came regularly were annoyed with those who did not and passed resolutions that fines be imposed on those who failed to attend unless they had a reasonable excuse which they had sent in in writing before the meeting began. We were amazed to find that there was little resentment at this drastic measure and hundreds of workers brought their fines of half-crowns or five shillings to the office for not attending without an excuse. We got hundreds—often as many as fifteen hundred—written excuses. The reasons given were sometimes very funny. We had members who attended their aunt's or grandmother's funerals as often as six times. But most excuses were genuine and often the writers expressed deep loyalty to the union and a pledge to abide by any decision taken. Every letter was answered.

Until the Nationalists started their disruptive activities we were one large, happy family, with the most cordial relations between the members and officials. The workers, especially the women, were very easy to get along with. They were pleasant, extremely well-behaved and always anxious to avoid trouble. They came to us with their problems and appreciated civility and a sympathetic hearing far more than practical service. Once they got their troubles off their chests, they were quite happy and did not worry any more whether we took action or not. It was a common practice for working mothers to bring their children to shop stewards' meetings. The youngsters were fascinated. They watched the proceedings with rapt interest and frequently joined in applauding the speakers. I often told the mothers that it was our duty to build a happy South Africa, free from poverty and hatred, if not for ourselves, at least for the coming generations, and the presence of the young ones gave added weight to my appeal.

Two of the most popular organisers of the union were Margaret Malan and Sannie van Wyk. Both were women of the motherly type, who had themselves experienced years of hardship. The workers came to them with all their troubles, even personal ones. Both women would chat, laugh, scold, advise, and the members loved them. Their written reports were 'strange', but what they lacked in secretarial efficiency was more than balanced by their human qualities.

Members could also bring their personal problems to the head office of the union and, over the years, I listened to thousands of tales of woe from hard-working, decent women, whose lives were full of troubles. Members were entitled to free legal advice from the solicitors engaged by the union and this service proved of great benefit to workers, many of whom are constantly involved with the law.

The training of leaders from the ranks of the workers presented great difficulties. Many had fairly good schooling in Afrikaans, but the business side of the union, such as preparing memoranda, negotiating with employers, drafting press statements, had to be conducted in English. There were no books in Afrikaans dealing with the problems of workers. The working day was long and tiring and, when it ended, the workers were too worn out to study in the little time they had left after their household work was done. In 1934 Johanna Cornelius showed the most promise among the rank-and-file workers of becoming a leader, but when I suggested that she should be taken out of the factory and engaged as a full-time official of the union there was little enthusiasm among the committee for my suggestion. Johanna herself was not keen and felt that her place was in the factory, or on the picket line. She was a first-rate speaker and not afraid to go to prison in the cause of her fellow-workers, but she was not interested in office routine, and even afraid of it. Finally I persuaded her to try but before she would agree she laid down her own conditions: firstly, her salary must not exceed the £2 10*s*. a week which she earned in the factory, and secondly, she wanted to be free to give up her job as union organiser and return to the factory at any time she chose.

Johanna and the other rank-and-file women who were later appointed or elected to full-time positions in the union had to prepare memoranda, write letters, issue press statements, study the clumsily-drafted labour laws of South Africa, take minutes, issue reports—in short, do all the union work. Their devotion to the cause of labour and their integrity helped them to overcome all obstacles and made them understand that only by learning and hard work could they become real leaders. Today women like Johanna Cornelius, Anna Scheepers, Katie Viljoen and Dulcie Hartwell are amongst the best known and most respected Trade Union leaders in South Africa.

The admiration, and even affection, which some employers have for the leaders of the union is shown by this incident. When I was in New York in 1946 I called on the managing director of one of the largest shipping companies with offices in South Africa, who had substantial interests in the South African clothing industry. His first question to me, in Afrikaans—he was born in the Free State and spoke English with a marked Afrikaans accent—was: 'How goes it with my old friend, Johanna Cornelius? She led many strikes in my factory and gave me many headaches, but she is a real fine woman of character and courage.' He then took out a box of nylon stockings from his desk and asked me to give them to her on my return 'as a token of esteem'.

In many countries trade unions are divided between 'left' and 'right' and much time and energy is spent on witch hunts. Many trade union leaders, some of international repute, are more interested in denouncing militants than in fighting for their members. By and large, our union was spared the strife arising from this division. Before 1928, the union, like many others, had been affiliated to the South African Labour Party. Between 1928 and

1947 our attitude to the Labour Party, while in the main sympathetic, yet varied according to the policy pursued by the leaders. We usually supported the party financially and organisationally during elections, but when the leaders pursued an anti-working class policy, we did not hesitate to fight openly and vigorously against them. Thus, in 1941, when Walter Madeley, then leader of the party and Minister of Labour in Smuts's Government, introduced a new Factories Bill which gave the workers no protection, our union led a national campaign against him and his new measure and received widespread support.

At a general meeting of the union held at the City Hall, Johannesburg, on Tuesday, 22nd July 1947, it was resolved to affiliate to the South African Labour Party. Only two out of about four thousand voted against. I disagreed with the Labour Party on many fundamental issues, but I whole-heartedly supported affiliation. A political home had to be found for the thousands of Afrikaner workers who, although Nationalists at heart, became increasingly convinced that the leaders of the Nationalist Party were their enemies. Today South African workers are paying a terrible price for the stupid and cowardly attitude of many trade union leaders who have failed to educate the workers, especially the Afrikaner workers, politically. Over the years the majority of the trade union leaders obstinately pursued a policy of 'no politics in the trade union movement'. This would be wrong in any country but in South Africa it was disastrous and played right into the hands of the Nationalist Party which, for the last twenty years, has been plotting the destruction of the trade union movement. Hundreds of thousands of Afrikaner workers, loyal trade unionists and potential supporters of the Labour Party, receive their political education almost exclusively from the Nationalists. Every attempt we of the Garment Workers' Union made to bring the Afrikaner workers into the Labour Party was bitterly opposed by the Nationalists and the conservative trade union leaders. It will probably take many years to free the white workers of South Africa from their racial intolerance, but the majority of them, whose votes are decisive in any general election, could be weaned away from the Nationalist Party. The rest of the South African trade unions should follow the example of the Garment Workers' Union, educate the workers politically and, like the trade unions of Britain, build a strong Labour Party, which large numbers of

Afrikaner workers could be persuaded to join. Such a policy will not solve all of South Africa's problems, but could play a decisive part in ousting the reactionary, fascist Nationalist Government.

Although officials of the union actively worked for the Labour Party, and Johanna Cornelius and Anna Scheepers and I fought elections as party candidates, we never attempted to interfere with members whose political views differed from ours. In twenty-five years we took disciplinary measures against few members and expelled only eight for disruptive activities, but we never discriminated against those who supported the Nationalist Party, the Communist Party (which was proscribed in 1950), or the United Party. On the other hand, except when prompted by outsiders, our members did not raise any objections to our affiliation to the Labour Party or to the support we gave that party.

In our relations with trade union and labour organisations abroad, we pursued a similar policy of 'friendship with all'. We gladly accepted invitations from the Soviet trade unions and about six of our workers visited the U.S.S.R. We later reciprocated the kindness and hospitality of the Russian workers by raising over £6,000 towards medical aid for Russia during the Second World War. We would have been happy to accept invitations from the trade unions of other countries, with whom we always maintained cordial relations. I personally was shown much kindness by the International Ladies' Garment Workers of the United States, the Amalgamated Clothing Workers of America, the garment workers of France, Italy, Switzerland and Canada. The garment workers of Holland received some of our leaders with great hospitality.

It is with regret that I must record that the leaders of the National Union of Tailors and Garment Workers of Britain proved the exception and showed no friendliness either towards me or any other officials of our union. Hundreds of British tailors and garment workers came to South Africa after the war. We not only welcomed them with open arms but also found them jobs, helped them to get accommodation and looked after them in every way. I spent many long hours advising those whose contracts of employment were not properly drawn up and I can assure British workers who intend emigrating to South Africa that our union officials and staff will always be glad to be of help to them.

During the past three years I have visited almost every industrial centre in Britain to lecture on South African problems.

Everywhere I was received with the utmost friendliness and hospitality. I shall never forget the warmth and comradeship of the miners of South Wales and Scotland, of the textile workers of Yorkshire, of the leaders of the Union of Shop and Distributive Workers, of the Association of Engineers and Draughtsmen, the engineers of Sheffield and of scores of other trade union, Labour Party and Fabian and women's organisations, and of students and church bodies. I shall always remember with gratitude the sympathy shown to me by British Labour Members of Parliament and the friendliness of the British press.

I have seen a good deal of the activities and methods of work of the British trade union movement and of the trade union movement in other countries and, without arrogance, I can say that I feel proud of the Garment Workers' Union of South Africa. I sincerely hope that the union will always remain faithful to its great tradition of militancy and common sense, will continue to combine efficiency with warm-heartedness and will never lose its spirit of international solidarity.

Conclusion

THE STORY of the Garment Workers' Union of South Africa concerns only a comparatively small group of people directly, not more than 150,000 in all. In the little world of the garment workers, however, we see clearly reflected most of the major problems facing the people of South Africa and a possible solution of these problems.

Over two hundred million people on the African continent are on the march and nothing can stop them. Fifty million Arabic-speaking people in the north are in a state of revolt. Indeed, a national revolution is sweeping that part of the continent. In the west, independent African nation states are emerging. In the south, millions of Africans have awakened and are slowly organising their forces in the struggle for freedom. We live in one world today and events in Africa must be examined in the light of world events.

For generations, Europe and, more recently, the United States have played a dominant rôle in world affairs, but new developments are taking place at breakneck speed and revolutionary changes have made their effects felt in many spheres. Within the last generation, over a thousand million Asian people have ceased to be 'coolies'. They have secured national independence and are building a new social, economic, political and cultural life. Twenty-five years ago Pandit Nehru was in prison and Chou En-Lai in exile. Today India and China are two major world powers, playing a decisive rôle in international affairs. And this is only the beginning of a new epoch of world history.

In the past, many people spoke of a 'yellow peril' and foretold a coming clash between the people of Asia, on the one hand, and the white people of Europe and America on the other. These prophets have proved false. The people of Asia, having won their emancipation, show no inclinations to overrun Europe or conquer America. They are not racialists and do not seek revenge for past wrongs.

But the relationship between the seven hundred million white people and the sixteen hundred millions who do not qualify for membership of the white master race has reached a critical stage. The two-thirds of non-white humanity are determined to put an end to colonial oppression and racial discrimination. They bitterly, and quite justifiably, resent being treated as 'inferior', as 'coolies' or 'kaffirs', anywhere and their resentment is shared by all civilised Europeans and Americans. One of the major tasks facing the whole of humanity in the second half of the twentieth century is how to bring about amity and co-operation between east and west, between the white and non-white people of the world. Much progress has been made to remove the barriers which divide mankind, but a comparatively small number of white people on the African Continent, in the Union of South Africa, the Rhodesias, Kenya and in other African territories, are determined to perpetuate colonialism and racial oppression and are dreaming of building permanent slave States, where whites will be the masters and the 'inferior' non-whites the slaves. Whether they label their policy 'apartheid', 'Christian trusteeship' or 'partnership', their aim is identical—the African shall not be free. The methods of repression vary, not fundamentally, but only in degree and according to circumstances. The Nationalist Government of South Africa has been responsible for the killing by police action of only about three hundred Africans since they came to power in May 1948, not much to boast of compared with the proud record of the Kenya settlers, warmly supported by the British Government, who, in the course of five years, have killed some ten thousand Africans, and put about a hundred thousand in concentration camps. There is less open violence in the Rhodesias, but there, too, the gun has often been used against Africans and all the hypocritical talk of 'partnership' has proved of little real value.

The three million white settlers in Southern Africa have not learnt any history. In an age of the jet engine, their ideas still move at the pace of an ox-wagon. They want to isolate themselves and resent outside interference in their 'domestic' affairs. They would like to become insulated against world events and are obstinately resisting the tide of history.

But more than two-thirds of humanity proclaims very emphatically that racial discrimination and oppression are not the private affairs of the white settler, but direct outrages against coloured peoples everywhere. For the present they confine themselves to resolutions, protests and denunciations. Tomorrow they may employ more effective methods. History is full of startling developments and the shades of Asia are beginning to make their appearances on the African continent. The outrageous policy of the whites in Africa and their supporters in London and Paris is uniting Asia and Africa and the spirit of Bandung is growing stronger. Not so long ago Egypt was a colony. Today it makes one deal and the military strategy of the western powers is thrown into confusion. Within ten or twenty years, over a hundred million African people will be living in independent national States and each one will be in a position to engage freely in arms deals. The whites in Africa are fond of prating about saving European civilisation, western civilisation, Christian civilisation etc. etc. Nobody abroad is impressed by these noble professions and not even its exponents in South Africa believe in the myth. They have no moral basis on which to stand, for their present policy is the very negation of morality, civilisation and human decency. They rely on the superiority of their arms and, since the Africans are unarmed, they are able to maintain their power and domination. Deep in their hearts, even the most rabid Nationalists know that they will ultimately fail, that their aim to build exclusive, permanent, stable, white nation-States on the African continent is a fantasy which is rapidly becoming a nightmare. They must, therefore, realise that their attitude of 'after us the deluge, we shall keep the "kaffir" in his place, let coming generations worry about the future', is sheer criminal folly. Historical development cannot be measured in terms of years or decades. Have the whites in Southern Africa thought of what their position will be in fifty, a hundred or two hundred years' time?

In their blind ignorance, they are even incapable of viewing matters clearly as they are at present.

Economically, Southern Africa has made great progress in the last thirty years and hundreds of thousands of whites have had their incomes raised from £50 a year and less to £500 a year and more. The sixfold increase in the cash national income of the Union and the improvement in the standards of the people has been achieved, not through apartheid, but in spite of it. A healthy national economy cannot be built on racial theories, but only on work, production, organisation and the application of modern technique. Indeed, the economic development of South Africa has made nonsense of apartheid and more African workers have become integrated into the economy of the country than ever before.

In spite of all-round economic development and prosperity, fear stalks the whole of Southern Africa. In Kenya white settlers take guns with them when they go to their bathrooms and sleep with guns under their pillows. As children we used to play at night in the slums of Johannesburg without any fear. Today even the brilliantly illuminated shopping centres of the town are practically deserted after dark.

People abroad, and many Europeans in South Africa, feel pessimistic about the future and believe that, inevitably, disaster will overtake the country. Even the most fervent supporters of apartheid are not sure of the future. The question all South African patriots, all who want to see the country a great, prosperous, democratic nation, must ask themselves is, whether there is a way out of the present crisis.

The story of the Garment Workers' Union of South Africa supplies the answer to this important question and, indeed, to many other problems confronting the people of Africa.

I have come to these conclusions, which anyone is entitled to challenge:

(1) The immediate hope for the people of Southern Africa is extensive and intensive industrial development and the application of modern methods of production to every branch of economy. Mining is highly profitable for a few mine-owners, but can provide employment only to a small number of whites. In the not too distant future, the most important minerals will be exhausted and the country will be left with only mine dumps and large holes. For the hundreds of thousands of Africans, who work in the mines, there is only a £40-a-year standard, coupled with life in a compound, without family and bereft of any social and cultural amenities. Under the existing colour bar laws, there is no hope for the African miner of ever attaining a civilised standard of living. The land in most parts of Africa does not, and cannot, yield enough to solve the problem of Africa's poverty. At present a small number of European farmers are prosperous; the one million African farm labourers live on a £20-a-year standard under semi-slave conditions, without immediate prospects of improvement. If the methods of production in agriculture were modernised, there would be

greater benefits all round, but the problem of poverty would still not be solved. A prosperous white landed aristocracy, as in Kenya, can only exist as long as the white population is small. Within three or four generations the whites will become impoverished unless other spheres of economic activity are developed. Industrial development, on the other hand, has untold and practically limitless possibilities, without any of the major drawbacks of mining and agriculture. In the course of twenty-five years, industry alone has: (*a*) raised the national income at least sixfold; (*b*) given employment to over seven hundred thousand people directly and to many more indirectly; (*c*) raised the average annual income of over half a million Africans from about £20 to £200 and of a quarter of a million whites from under £50 to about £500; (*d*) largely solved the poor white problem and, to some extent, the poor black problem.

(2) The beliefs held by Europeans that the influx of Africans into industry and their acquiring of skill will lead to a lowering of standards and unemployment for Europeans are quite fallacious. The facts prove that the very opposite is the case. Indeed, it may be stated with absolute certainty that the tremendous advance in the standards of European workers and the corresponding increase in employment opportunities for them have been largely due to the progress of the non-European workers. Equally, the exclusion of Africans from industry and the efforts to prevent them from becoming efficient producers will retard the progress of Europeans and may ultimately bring back poor whiteism. Over a hundred thousand workers of all races and colours have co-operated to build the clothing industry and everyone, as well as the country as a whole, has benefited enormously from that co-operation. Not a single white has suffered from it.

(3) The Afrikaner workers, who must play a decisive rôle in South African affairs, can still be won over to the cause of progress. Ridding these workers of race hatred and backwardness is no easy task, but with tact, hard work, clear and courageous leadership, it can be accomplished. In the light of South African conditions, it is the duty of every South African who believes in freedom to help to build a powerful trade union movement and a strong Labour Party. The message of progress must be taken to the Afrikaner miners, railway workers and factory workers, without pandering to backwardness and without revolutionary phrase-

mongering. We must help progressive Afrikaners to become leaders amongst their people. Against the sinister attempts of the Nationalist leaders to build a master race State, which is really a slave State, must be placed the ideal of a great, democratic South Africa, with all sections of the people living in peace, prosperity and security, free from fear and confident of a brighter future.

(4) There does not seem any possibility of the Nationalist Party abandoning its policy of oppression, ruthlessness and tyranny, and it becomes, therefore, the bounden duty of every true South African patriot to render maximum support to the effort to rid the country of the present Government. First things first, and the most urgent and immediate task is to remove from office those who are determined to bring ruin to South Africa. The defeat of reaction in South Africa will have not only a beneficial effect upon the country itself, but upon the whole of Africa. The present leaders of the United Party are incapable of solving the country's problems, but, with the removal of the Nationalists from power, it will be possible for clear-thinking South Africans to express their views and to advocate a truly progressive policy, without fear of persecution.

(5) The new generation of garment workers and all other workers can learn from the past activities of the Garment Workers' Union how the union was built, how improved conditions were obtained, and how to fight against poverty, exploitation and tyranny. They can learn from the experience of workers abroad, but must revive and make known the great deeds of their own heroes and heroines, who have given their lives so that we may enjoy higher standards. The garment workers of South Africa have written a glorious chapter in the history of their country. Their achievements and the method they employed, the principles they stood for and fought for, must be kept alive to help the new generation of workers to continue no less nobly than their parents. Courage, determination, a spirit of sacrifice, a deep love for humanity, have secured for the garment workers of South Africa vastly improved conditions and a place of honour in the labour movement of the country. In the same spirit, the people of South Africa—all the people, Afrikaner, English, African, Coloured and Indian—can lay the foundations for a true civilisation and thus bring lasting happiness and prosperity where fear and poverty rule today.

(6) Under-developed countries everywhere can learn from our story how to build prosperous industries, how to turn backward workers into highly efficient producers, how to raise standards of living from the lowest level to the highest, and how to create a stable national economy. If a backward country like South Africa, with its policy of race hatred, colour bars and bigotry could, within one generation, turn over a million primitive Africans, accustomed to live under tribal conditions, into efficient workers, it should surely be possible for countries with progressive national policies to show better and speedier results. Modern methods of production and efficiency are not the monopoly of white-skinned people. People of all races and colours, when afforded the opportunities, can learn to handle modern machinery and thus extricate themselves from the age-long abyss of poverty.

The policy of the Nationalist Government has inflicted upon the people fear, hatred and despair of the future.

The story of the Garment Workers' Union of South Africa inspires hope and confidence in the future and proves conclusively that all racial groups can and must co-operate to promote the interests of all the people and of the country as a whole.

APPENDIX ONE

	Under £50	£50 *to* £99	£100 *to* £149	£150 *to* £199	*Over* £200
Owners	6,705	9,434	7,264	5,666	25,929
Tenants	6,161	6,316	3,651	2,102	4,954
'Bywoners'	8,744	5,184	1,669	668	781
Employees	1,684	2,214	1,071	458	794
All Farmers	23,342	23,212	13,699	8,933	32,658

APPENDIX TWO

THE FOLLOWING RESULTS were obtained in a poll conducted by the Army Education Service during the Second World War. A representative sample of about 7,000 European soldiers was asked to indicate its attitude towards African advancement.

	per cent
(1) Natives ought to have the same chances as white men in competing for any kind of job; a man ought not to be kept out of a job just because of his colour . .	5
(2) Natives ought to be given more chances of getting better jobs and earning more money, but this ought only to develop slowly	47
(3) As things are now, Natives get a fair chance to do whatever work they are fit for	24
(4) This is a white man's country; Natives should not be allowed to do any job except unskilled jobs . .	20
(5) Don't know or no answer	4
	100

The analysis of the answers (disregarding (5)) in terms of education is very striking:

Education Standard Attained	*Percentage answering* (1) & (2)	(3) & (4)
University	84%	16%
Matriculation	73%	27%
Junior Certificate . . .	49%	51%
Std. VI and under . . .	30%	70%

(Social and Economic Planning Council Report No. 13 U.G. 53/1948 par, 164)

A poll among workers would I think give a similar result, except that the least progressive would be found among miners, unskilled workers and railwaymen and the most liberal among women workers, artisans and workers in the manufacturing industries.

APPENDIX THREE

A List of the more important Court Cases

in which the Garment Workers' Union, officials and members have been involved since 1929

1929 *R.* v. *Scapszak and others* T.P.D. p. 980
Appeal against conviction and sentence of three members of the Union. Appeal upheld, conviction and sentence set aside.

1931 *Sachs* v. *Johannesburg City Council* T.P.D. p. 443
Appeal against conviction and sentence—obstruction—holding a meeting in the street. Appeal upheld. Conviction and sentence set aside.

1931 *R.* v. *Blignaut and Malan* T.P.D.
The two accused editors of a weekly publication were convicted and sentenced for criminal libel, Sachs being the complainant. Appeal dismissed.

1932 *Sachs* v. *Kalmek* (Not reported)
Action for defamation. Sachs awarded £75 and costs.

1932 *R.* v. *Sachs* T.P.D. p. 201
Appeal against conviction and sentence for contempt of court. Appeal upheld. Conviction and sentence set aside.

1933 *Sachs* v. *Pirow* N.O. A.D. p. 11
Appeal against banishment order issued by the Minister of Justice. Application to the T.P.D. was dismissed with costs, portion of the costs awarded to Sachs. Appeal dismissed with costs. Smuts became Minister of Justice and withdrew order.

1933 *Tiger Trading Company* v. *Garment Workers' Union, E. S. Sachs and G. Malan* W.L.D. p. 131
Application by clothing manufacturers for interdict. Temporary interdict granted. Company withdrew application before trial action and paid all costs.

1936 *R.* v. *De Freitas and 21 Others* C.P.D. p. 413
Rose De Freitas and 21 other garment workers convicted of inciting employees of Back & Company, Cape Town, to take part in an illegal strike. Appeal dismissed, but some of the sentences reduced.

1936 *Garment Workers' Union* v. *Minister of Labour*. N.O. T.P.D. p. 113
Application of G.W.U. for an order on the Minister, compelling him to make a determination under the Wage Act for the clothing industry, Union of South Africa. Application dismissed with costs.

1938 *Sachs* v. *Moore and Others* W.L.D. p. 69
Application by Sachs against order of expulsion from the National Executive Committee of the South African Trades and Labour Council. Application granted with costs.

1939 *Sachs* v. *D. B. H. Grobbelaar* W.L.D. p. 383
Action for defamation. Preliminary points taken by Plaintiff and Defendant. Judgment in favour of Plaintiff on all points, with costs.

1939 *Sachs* v. *Die Oosterlig*
Action for defamation. Defendant paid £250 and costs, also published apologies in leading newspapers. Matter settled out of court.

1940 *R.* v. *Cornelius* T.P.D. Not reported.
During a tobacco workers' strike Johanna Cornelius was convicted in the Magistrate's Court, Rustenburg, of assaulting a policeman and fined £10. On appeal conviction confirmed, but fine reduced to £3.

1941 *Sachs* v. *Dr H. P. Wolmaraans*
Action for defamation. Matter settled out of court by Defendant paying into court £300 and costs.

1942 *Sachs* v. *Voortrekkerpers* W.L.D. p. 99
Action for defamation. Plaintiff awarded £600 and costs.

1944 *R.* v. *Sachs* T.P.D. (Not reported).
Attempted extortion. Appeal by Sachs against conviction and sentence of £40 fine or six weeks' imprisonment with hard labour. Appeal upheld. Conviction and sentence set aside.

1944 *Inez Mentos* v. *Minister of Finance* T.P.D. (Not reported).
Application by Inez Mentos, a member of the Union, for refund of £24 which a Johannesburg magistrate ordered to be paid into the Consolidated Revenue Fund. Application granted with costs.

1944 *William Baloyi and Christina Okolo* v. *The Industrial Council for the Clothing Industry, Transvaal* T.P.D. (Not reported).
Application for declaration of rights. First applicant, who was exempted from the obligation of carrying a pass, applied for a declaration that he was not excluded from the definition of 'employee' in the Industrial Conciliation Act. Court held he comes within the exclusion; application refused. In the case of the second applicant court held that she does not come within the exclusion. Costs of the proceedings were paid by consent by respondent.

1945 *Sachs* v. *Pisanie and Another* W.L.D. p. 262
Application by Sachs to be supplied with names of all members of the Enlarged Church Committee. Application granted with costs.

1945 *Sachs* v. *A. B. Du Preez* W.L.D. p. 94
Action for defamation. Sachs awarded £300 and costs, which came to over £10,000.

1946 *Sachs* v. *Stuart*
Action for defamation. Stuart paid £300 and costs. Matter settled out of court.

1946 *Sachs* v. *Die O.B.*
Action for defamation. Die O.B. paid £250 and costs. Matter settled out of court.

1946 *Sachs* v. *Die Vaderland*
Action for defamation. Die Vaderland paid £100 and costs. Matter settled out of court.

1946 *Sachs* v. *Stuart* W.L.D. p. 433
Application by Sachs for postponement of an action for defamation instituted by Stuart which had been set down, on the ground that he (Sachs) had to attend an I.L.O. conference at Montreal. Application granted, costs to be decided at trial.

1946 *Stuart* v. *Sachs*
Action for defamation. Stuart withdrew action after one day of the trial action.

1946 *Garment Workers' Union of the Cape* v. *Garment Workers' Union* A.D. p. 370
Application by Cape Union to bar G.W.U. from proceeding with appeal under Section 77 of the Industrial Conciliation Act. Application granted in W.L.D. On appeal to the T.P.D. by the G.W.U. appeal upheld with costs. On a further appeal to the A.D. by the Cape Union appeal dismissed with costs.

1947 *Garment Workers' Union* v. *Minister of Labour and Another* W.L.D. p. 361
Appeal by Union under Section 77 of the Industrial Conciliation Act (Extension of Union's constitution to include Cape millinery workers). Appeal dismissed with costs.

1949 *Garment Workers' Union* v. *Minister of Labour and Others* A.D. p. 455 (S.A.L.R.)
Application by Union to declare the notice appointing the Garment Workers' Union Commission of Inquiry null and void. Application refused with costs.

1950 *Sachs* v. *Donges* (N.O.) A.D. p. 265 (S.A.L.R.)
Passport case. Appeal of Sachs upheld with costs against the Minister.

1950 *Garment Workers' Union* v. *Botha and Others* (T.P.D. 235) (S.A.L.R.)
Application by Union for costs arising out of an application against the Industrial Legislation Commission. Union's application granted with costs.

1951 *Garment Workers' Union* v. *Scholeman* N.O. 1951 4 (S.A.L.R. p. 9)
Appeal under Section 77 of the Industrial Conciliation Act. Appeal upheld with costs.

1951 *Sachs* v. *Simon Roy*
Action for defamation. Roy paid £200 and costs. Matter settled out of court.

1952 *Sachs* v. *Werkerspers Beperk* 2. S.A.L.R. p. 261
Action for defamation. Sachs awarded £3,200, less £300 paid into court. Defendant not being able to meet judgment, Sachs applied for order of liquidation. Order granted. Company liquidated.

1952 *Sachs* v. *Voortrekkerpers Beperk*
Action for defamation. Defendant paid £1,000 and costs. Matter settled out of court. Anna Scheepers, President of the Union, and Johanna Cornelius, then National Organizer, and all the members of the Central Executive Committee were also paid damages for defamation.

1952 *Garment Workers' Union and Sachs* v. *Minister of Justice* T.P.D. 3 S.A.L.R. p. 528
Application to set aside Minister's order removing Sachs from Secretaryship of the Union. Application refused with costs.

1952 *Sachs* v. *Minister of Justice* N.O. 4 S.A.L.R. p. 416
Application by Sachs to set aside Minister's Order prohibiting him from attending any gathering. Application dismissed with costs. An appeal to the A.D. was dismissed with costs.

1952 *Sachs* v. *Ellis and Albert Hertzog*. 4 S.A.L.R. p. 419 T.P.D.
Application by Sachs for an order directing a magistrate to open a preparatory examination for criminal defamation against Ellis and Hertzog, directors of the Werkerspers. Application refused with costs.

1953 *Sachs* v. *Ellis and Hertzog* 2 S.A.L.R. p. 452
Application for review of taxed bill of costs. Court ordered substantial reduction.

1953 *R.* v. *Sachs* 1 S.A.L.R. p. 392 A.D.
Appeal against conviction and sentence of six months' imprisonment on each of two counts for defying Minister's order. Appeal dismissed, but sentence suspended for three years.

1954 *Sachs* v. *Voortrekkerpers*
Action for defamation. Defendant paid £250 and costs without the matter going to court.

1954 *Johanna Cornelius* (*Fellner*) v. *Minister for the Interior* N.O.
4 S.A.L.R. p. 523
Passport case. Application for renewal. Application refused in the first instance and appeal dismissed with costs.

* * *

The Supreme Court of South Africa has the following divisions:

(*a*) Appellate Division (A.D.)
(*b*) Four Provincial Divisions: Cape, Transvaal, Natal and Orange Free State. (C.P.D., T.P.D., N.P.D. and O.P.D.).
(*c*) Local Divisions, e.g. Witwatersrand Local Division, W.L.D.

Until 1947 separate Reports were published in respect of each Division. Since then all cases are published in the South African Law Reports, S.A.L.R., Quarterly.